ORIGINS OF THE COMMON LAW

ARTHUR REED HOGUE (1906–86) was born in Pittsburgh, the son of the distinguished Presbyterian minister, Walter Jenkins Hogue. He received his A.B. magna cum laude from Oberlin College in 1928. At Harvard, he studied under the medievalist, Charles Homer Haskins, and the historian of political thought, Charles H. McIlwain, receiving his M.A. in 1929 and his Ph.D. in 1937. At Hanover College from 1935 until 1948, he rose from Assistant Professor to Professor of History, Chairman of the Department, and Academic Dean. After two years at the University of Illinois, he moved in 1950 to Indiana University, where he remained until his retirement in 1974, as Professor Emeritus of History. His publications and his service to the American Society for Legal History attest to his professional interest in the study of legal history. His books, articles, and papers have illuminated two primary components of the American tradition of freedom: the development of the English Common Law and the influence of continental Liberalism in the person of Carl Schurz. *Origins of the Common Law* was first published in 1966 by Indiana University Press.

A R T H U R   R .   H O G U E

ORIGINS OF THE COMMON LAW

Liberty Fund

INDIANAPOLIS

1986

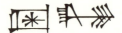
Copyright © 1966 by Indiana University Press. Reprinted 1974 as an Archon Book by The Shoe String Press, Inc., Hamden, CT. Copyright transferred by Indiana University Press to Arthur R. Hogue, 1984. Reprinted by Liberty Fund, Inc. 1986. All rights reserved. All inquiries should be addressed to Liberty Fund, Inc., 8335 Allison Pointe Trail, Suite 300, Indianapolis, IN 46250-1687. This book was manufactured in the United States of America.

Plan of Medieval Village used in cover design from The Bettmann Archive, New York, N. Y.

Library of Congress Cataloging-in-Publication Data

Hogue, Arthur R. (Arthur Reed), 1906-1986
    Origins of the common law.

    Reprint. Originally published: Bloomington: Indiana
University Press, 1966.
    Bibliography: p.
    Includes index.
    1. Common law.   2. Law–Great Britian–History and criticism.
I.   Title
KD671.H63   1985   349.42   85-15949
ISBN 0-86597-053-X   344.2
ISBN 0-86597-054-8 (pbk.)

94 93 92 91 90 C 8 7 6 5 4
01 00 99 98 97 P 10 9 8 7 6

for E. S. H. *and* D. B. H.

Contents

Preface

The common law of England may confront students and scholars in many fields. Information about this legal system and its history can be found in court cases, treatises old and new, monographs, law journals, law encyclopedias, and law dictionaries. The investigator untrained in law finds materials which easily carry him beyond his depth into technicalities set forth in an unfamiliar terminology. Literature about the common law is usually written by trained lawyers for trained lawyers. There is a place, I believe, for a book which does not assume professional legal training. There is a place for a book which anticipates the difficulties one encounters when approaching the common law—possibly for the first time. To accomplish this object I have chosen the early period of the common law between 1154, when Henry II became king, and 1307, when Edward I died, when it was a relatively simple body of rules enforced in the English royal courts. An understanding of the formation of the common law during these years provides excellent grounding for the history of later developments.

The English monarchy encouraged the spectacular growth of the legal system by enforcing with formidable authority the decisions of royal courts. But royal policies occasionally met serious resistance on the part of English subjects. These controversies between Crown and subject led to important declarations of English law, most notably at the time of Magna Carta. So I have briefly traced the events of English history during several reigns which are linked inseparably with the precocious development of early common law.

I have attempted to show the relation between early rules of common law and the social order which they served, because I am certain that laws should not be treated as though they float in air, timeless and apart from circumstance. Laws bear directly on the incidents of daily life. The medieval society in which early rules of common law took form was feudal and agricultural and rapidly changing. I have described it in some detail for the modern reader, who is usually better acquainted with industrial, urban communities than with agricultural, village communities dominated by a landed aristocracy.

To remove all doubt of the relevance of earlier common law to the modern Anglo-American legal system, I call attention throughout the book, but particularly in the last two chapters, to legal and political institutions destined to flourish in later centuries.

This book, then, does not hurl the narrative at the reader. By means of definitions, examples, and illustrations, I have tried to give clarity to each of its parts. But one short book cannot be expected to encompass a legal system which has evolved over a period of eight centuries; to understand the common law requires more than the leisure of a summer day. In the notes I have pointed occasionally to literature amplifying many of the main outlines of the common law. No serious investigator should ignore the important works of the British historians, Frederic W. Maitland and W. S. Holdsworth, nor should he fail to consult the stately series of volumes published since 1887 by the Selden Society, which has steadily provided sources useful for the study of English legal history.

There are excellent bibliographies of the subject of English legal history. The most valuable and comprehensive is the annotated *Legal Bibliography of the British Commonwealth of*

Nations, compiled by W. Harold Maxwell and Leslie F. Maxwell; the second edition, in seven volumes, was published in London by Sweet and Maxwell, Ltd., in 1955. Volume 1 lists materials on English law to 1800, including books dealing with the period from 1480 to 1954; Volume 2 continues from 1801 to 1954. There are also many excellent law dictionaries and glossaries listed by the Maxwells in Volume 1 (pp. 6–14). For most purposes *Bouvier's Law Dictionary*, edited by William E. Baldwin, is quite adequate, and so is W. J. Byrne, *Dictionary of English Law*. These can be used to supplement the glossary of terms which I have appended.

Here I wish to acknowledge gratefully the help many people have given me with this book. By their questions and comments over the years students have called attention to numerous points, which I have tried to present clearly for the layman. Several lawyers have been kind enough to talk with me about legal matters and, in the course of pleasant conversations, have improved my understanding of materials touched on in the text. Among these I am particularly obligated to Austin V. Clifford, F. Reed Dickerson, W. Howard Mann, and Leon H. Wallace. If I have failed at places to grasp their instruction, the fault is, of course, entirely my own. Also I wish to thank Robert H. Ferrell for his expert assistance in improving the arrangement of three chapters. I am indebted to the editorial staff of the Indiana University Press, particularly to Miriam S. Farley and Susan D. Fernandez, for their patience and care in preparing the book for the printer. Nancy E. MacClintock made the index. Again, I am grateful to my wife for her assistance and encouragement at every stage in the writing.

A.R.H.

The following abbreviations for frequently cited sources have been used throughout the notes:

P & M   Frederick Pollock and Frederic W. Maitland, *The History of English Law Before the Time of Edward I*, 2nd ed., 2 vols. (Cambridge Univ. Press, 1898).

S & M   *Sources of English Constitutional History*. Carl Stephenson and Frederick George Marcham, eds. and trans. (New York: Harper, 1937).

S.C.   *Select Charters and Other Illustrations of English Constitutional History*, edited by William Stubbs, 9th ed., revised by H.W.C. Davis (Oxford, 1921).

Y.B.   *Year Books*

ORIGINS OF THE COMMON LAW

Chapter 1

Introduction: Social Change and the Growth of the Common Law

LAW AS THE BOND OF CIVIL SOCIETY

Throughout its long history the English common law has borne directly on the raw facts of daily life in English society. The rules of common law are social rules; never remote from life, they serve the needs of a society once feudal and agricultural but now industrial and urban. Gradually, as social changes have occurred, the law has been adapted by judicial interpretation to meet new conditions. It continues as always to reflect the character of the social order.

Englishmen in the Middle Ages accepted, as they do now, the need for rules governing such recurring relations as those between buyer and seller, landlord and tenant, guardian and ward, creditor and debtor. Rules of common law touch a farmer's property rights in a crop of wheat planted in a rented field or the right to use a public roadway. Nor is the common law a stranger in the market place; the fishmonger as well as the banker may invoke its protection. The bond, then, between law and society is close and intimate; the history of the common law is matter-of-fact and rests ultimately on the relationships of people who have taken their differences before a court for

3

settlement. And it will be assumed in all of the discussion which follows that the common law has grown, now rapidly, now reluctantly, to keep pace with changes in the social order, from which, again, it is inseparable.

Social change and legal change are more easily discerned than accounted for, and the process by which legal changes are made is often far from clear. The mystery surrounding many legal changes may be particularly baffling when we deal with a system of judge-made law. For who can determine with precision the thought of medieval royal judges as they built up a body of principles in case after case, decision after decision? It is difficult enough to grasp the nature of the judicial process in the present, when we have full reports of trials and the opinions as well as the decisions of judges. Even so, there is value in an account of the common law during its foundation years, when its principles were not overlaid by a vast burden of statutory legislation designed for the complexity of modern life.

An account of the common law in medieval England will bring us close to many, if not all, of the elements which must be considered in dealing with the law in any period. Here we shall touch on substantive rules and rules of procedure as well as on courts of justice and agencies of enforcement. Moreover, in the medieval period we shall find excellent examples of legal change accompanying social change. Men of the twelfth century and the thirteenth knew both the vigor and the decline of feudalism. In these centuries population increased rapidly, and agriculture flourished in an epoch of good markets and rising prices. English merchants traded with Lombards from Italy, Hansards from Germany, and wool merchants who supplied the looms of Flanders. Oxford and Cambridge universities trace their histories back to the thirteenth century, when builders were at work on such English Gothic cathedrals as those at Salisbury and Wells. England in the thirteenth century was a society of rapid change.

A DEFINITION OF COMMON LAW IN THE MIDDLE AGES

The greater a man's knowledge of the law, the more hesitant he will be in answering the question: What is common law? But we need a working definition here, and perhaps we can distinguish the common law in the twelfth and thirteenth centuries from other legal systems by calling it simply the body of rules prescribing social conduct and justiciable in the royal courts of England. Although this definition is admittedly general, it is difficult to be more precise.[1] We should remember that the law enforced in royal courts, and common to all the realm of England, was in competition with concurrent rules enforced in other courts. Save when a matter of freehold was at issue, Englishmen were not compelled to present their causes before the king's courts. Men were free to take their cases into the local courts of the counties, which administered local, customary law; men might seek justice from the church courts administering rules of canon law, which touched many matters, especially those related to wills and testaments, marriage and divorce, and contracts involving a pledge of faith; feudal barons might accept jurisdiction of a baronial overlord whose court applied rules of feudal custom; townsmen might bring their causes before the court of a borough, which would judge them by rules of the law merchant. All these courts and systems of law deserve mention in an account of growth of the common law, for by the end of the thirteenth century the common law had absorbed much, if not all, of the judicial business of its competitors and may have borrowed heavily from them in the process of aggrandizement.

The medieval common law, then, was not local or particular. We should distinguish it from whatever smacks of a specialty. It

---

[1] Hermann Kantorowicz, *The Definition of Law*, ed. A. H. Campbell (Cambridge Univ. Press, 1958), p. 79; see also Sir William Blackstone, *Commentaries on the Laws of England*, 9th ed. (1783), I, 68–71; and P & M, I, 156, where the authors contrast common law with "whatever is particular, extraordinary, special. ..."

is not to be identified with rules of law administered by local, baronial, or manorial courts, or by ecclesiastical courts, or by borough courts. Some of the difficulties confronting the uninitiated in understanding medieval common law undoubtedly stem from insistence on applying modern definitions to medieval materials. For example, modern usage tends to distinguish common law from "written law," or statutory legislation. Again, the modern lawyer, as well as the layman, may think of the common law as a body of principles embodied in or derived from precedents—the decisions of certain courts in England and other common-law countries. To add to the misunderstanding of medieval common law there is the occasional modern effort at defining the common law as a body of rules based upon custom alone.

Walter Ullmann has recently provided a statement clarifying the medieval concept of the common law; while discussing *lex terrae*, a much debated phrase appearing in Chapter 39 of Magna Carta, he observes:

> We may justifiably call the *lex terrae* the early thirteenth century expression for the common law. Taken in this sense the concept loses a good deal of its vagueness and refers to ordinances, rules, decisions of the courts, in short to that body of legal rules which had its roots deep in the soil of native feudalism, notably the land law—hence the land law and the law of succession, personal property and tenure were the earliest developed laws—and which derived its binding character from the (explicit or implicit) consent of the feudal tenants-in-chief. . . . Precisely because no distinction was as yet possible between legislation . . . and judicial actions, any rule, which was considered binding, derived its force—in the contemporary feudal environs—from the . . . consent of the barons and the king in his feudal capacity.[2]

THE LANGUAGE OF COMMON LAW

The language of the common law today and the terminology, "the words of art," used by the legal profession reveal the great

---

[2] Walter Ullmann, *Principles of Government and Politics in the Middle Ages* (New York, 1961), pp. 166–67.

antiquity of the system. Much of the terminology used in the twentieth century can be explained only by a description of medieval society. Such a phrase as "the seisin of a freehold" immediately takes one back seven or eight hundred years to a time when a very sharp division between "free" and "unfree" property interests characterized feudal society.

If the modern layman is bewildered by the language of the legal profession, he can blame William the Conqueror for his confusion, for the Norman Conquest made French the language of the royal household and the language of the royal courts. Anglo-French, or "law French," was used in pleading in the English courts, and the lawyer was forced to learn it as a second language.[3] He had to learn Latin as well, for Latin was the language employed in the Middle Ages for formal written records. Anglo-French was a dialect from which the English legal profession first developed a precise vocabulary for the expression of legal concepts. Words such as *plaintiff* and *defendant* are of French origin. As the English language evolved, it moved away from the Anglo-French, once the "king's English," but we will have occasion to use some of the medieval terminology which the common law retained. Those who are now impatient with this terminology may find some comfort in the knowledge that in the early history of the common law, at least, the language of oral arguments in court was close to the conversational language of the people.

We are concerned here with much more than the growth of professional jargon and definition of legal terms; we are concerned with the expanding jurisdiction of the royal courts and a dramatic increase in the number of legal rights they were prepared to recognize and to protect. For example, as feudalism declined during the thirteenth century, property interests not clearly related to feudalism were given protection.

---

[3] A. K. R. Kiralfy and Gareth Jones, compilers, *General Guide to the Society's Publications: Volumes 1–79*, The Selden Society (London, 1960), pp. 35–36; for a full discussion of Anglo-French, see F. W. Maitland's introduction to his edition of *Year Books 1 & 2 Edward II (1307–9)*, Selden Society, Vol. 17 (1903).

Leasehold and other so-called "chattel interests" in land eventually secured as much protection from the common law as freehold, a property interest of the highest dignity and quite suitable for a feudal class. More about this follows in Chapters 8 and 9.

STABILITY AND CHANGE: A PARADOX CONSIDERED

In every generation both lawyers and laymen seem to have been drawn toward two desirable but widely separated and contradictory goals. The first of these is the goal of permanence, stability, certainty in legal doctrines. The second is the goal of flexibility or adaptability, permitting adjustment of the law to social necessities. The result of the pull in these two directions has been an unresolved tension between the search for stability and the desire to make the law serve its own age. The tension here is not necessarily a conflict between factions, parties, or groups of men; not always a tug-of-war between conservatives and radicals. The dual objectives can exist in the legal thought of a single jurist.

The pull toward permanence in the law is particularly strong whenever real property interests are involved, whenever land, buildings, or real estate are at stake; for these interests often span long periods of time and may affect two or three generations. A long-term lease for a period of ninety-nine years ordinarily touches the use of land. Such a lease, properly drafted and clearly designed to endure into a distant future, will not be disturbed by a common-law court save for exceptionally good reasons. What was just and right in one generation—so argument may run—should not be disturbed in another generation; otherwise, men will not plan their affairs for the future with confidence that arrangements will hold up in court.

Another force contributing to permanence and stability in the law emerges from the doctrine of *stare decisis*, or the practice of looking to precedents while formulating a legal principle. The doctrine of *stare decisis* assumes that court decisions have been reasonable, that what was reasonable in one century may be reasonable in another—even though in the meantime the most revolutionary social and political changes may have occurred. The important word here is *reasonable.* Ever since the Roman law spread through the Mediterranean world, European legal systems have made much of the reasonableness of law and have been influenced by the ideal of creating a body of legal principles which would be simple, stable, and consistent. Among jurists there have always been those who take delight in the strict logic of a closely reasoned argument and who wish to treat law as a science, not as abstract as mathematics perhaps, but similar to mathematics in the timeless certainty of its conclusions.

We need not examine all of the assumptions involved in the doctrine that the law is written reason, *ratio scripta,* but we can note that they approach a belief in an absolute justice or equity which the human mind can apprehend by reason. Faith in the eternal reasonableness of law is thus not far from the ancient Stoic view eloquently stated by Cicero:

> True law is right reason, consonant with nature, diffused among all men, constant, eternal. . . . It needs no interpreter or expounder but itself, nor will there be one law in Rome and another in Athens, one in the present and another in time to come, but one law and that eternal and immutable shall embrace all peoples and for all time and there shall be as it were one common master and ruler, the god of all, the author and judge and proposer of this law.[4]

In the Middle Ages there was the notion of a permanence in the law imparted by its connection with immemorial custom. Law was not "made," according to this medieval view; it was

---

[4] C. H. McIlwain, *The Growth of Political Thought in the West* (New York: Macmillan, 1932), pp. 111–12, quoting from the *De republica.*

"declared" by those familiar with the custom of a certain territory. Bracton, a thirteenth-century English judge and author of a remarkable treatise on the laws and customs of England, explained that "while they use *leges* and a written law in almost all lands, in England alone there has been used within its boundaries an unwritten law and custom. In England legal right is based on an unwritten law which usage has approved. ... For the English hold many things by customary law which they do not hold by *lex.*"[5] Bracton was incorrect in attributing the use of custom to the English alone, but he was quite right in observing that in his own time customary law, approved by use, carried the greatest authority.

The other desirable objective which attracts the attention of lawyers is adaptability of the law to meet new social conditions. Attorneys make a living by knowing the law of their own day. They must prepare to advise clients in the light of both the most recent legislation and the most recent court decisions, no simple matter in the twentieth century, when almost continuous legislation swells the statute books and steady reporting makes available the decisions of hundreds of common-law courts. Nevertheless, the modern attorney must follow as best he can the constant changes in the law affecting his clients. The lawyer is aware that permanence and stability must give way again and again to pressures from society. And in the opinion of more than one eminent jurist, this is as it should be. John Chipman Gray, in his *Nature and Sources of the Law,* observed that "opinions of judges in the Common Law and of jurists in the Civil Law on what society needs have profoundly influenced the law and for the better. And what could be a happier state of affairs than that judges and jurists should approach the law from the

---

[5] Bracton, *De legibus et consuetudinibus Angliae,* ed. G. E. Woodbine, 4 vols. (New Haven, 1915–41), folio 1a. See also the edition with translation by Sir Travers Twiss, Rolls Series, 6 vols. (London, 1878–83). For the medieval view of law generally, see the excellent account by McIlwain, *Growth of Political Thought,* pp. 167–200.

side of public welfare and seek to adapt it to the common good?"[6]

Gray's comments illustrate, incidentally, the tension between stability and change. Having approved adjustment of the law to social needs, he turns to remarks about the permanence of certain legal concepts: "One should remember, though most legal conceptions alter, and there may be few which are so based on eternal principles that they cannot change while the order of nature continues, yet their change is often exceedingly slow and many of them go back as far as we have a clear knowledge of human affairs, and show to our eyes no signs of decay."[7]

Any encounter with the common law may reveal this tension, this polarity, between the permanent and the expedient. Courts resort to a legal fiction or grasp at a mere hint of an analogy—anything to avoid open confession that they are pouring new wine into old bottles. A legal fiction, of course, is an assertion which the court permits and allows no one to challenge during a trial; thus the court achieves a desired result. For example, the court of Exchequer formerly allowed a plaintiff to bring before it an action of Debt if the plaintiff asserted that by reason of the debtor's default the plaintiff-creditor was less able to pay what he owed to the Crown. The plaintiff's obligation to the Crown may have been nonexistent or so slight that failure of the debtor to pay up would have been immaterial. Simply by asserting he was less able to pay to the Crown, the plaintiff could get his case before the royal Exchequer. Fictions were not so frequent in the twelfth and thirteenth centuries as later, for early growth of the common law was marked by a certain frankness and directness.

When foundations of the common law were being established, especially in the years between 1154 and 1307, obviously

---

[6] John Chipman Gray, *The Nature and Sources of the Law* (New York: Columbia Univ. Press, 1909), p. 3.

[7] Ibid., p. 5.

the royal courts were not as clearly guided as they are now by statutes and judicial precedents. Beyond question law was what judges declared it to be. The common law was the body of rules enforced by royal judges; to be effective, a system of legal rules must have courts and enforcing agencies to give it life. A cause of action or a legal right is more than a matter for the plaintiff to assert; the plaintiff in any legal dispute must convince a court that he deserves a hearing. Indeed, a legal right might be defined as a power to act or to refrain from acting which the courts will recognize and the executive authority will enforce. A legislature may enact statutes setting forth rules of law, but statutes must be interpreted and applied in specific cases by judges in court. Even a constitution, the most solemn and permanent enactment that can be devised, must be interpreted finally by judges. Therefore, in any discussion of the growth of common law in medieval England, one must keep in mind the jurisdiction of royal courts, the character of royal judges, and the willingness of English kings to enforce the decisions of their courts.

ROYAL WRITS AND THE REGISTER OF WRITS

In a time before there was much parliamentary legislation, where would royal judges find the common law? An answer to this question leads directly to the writ system and to the Register of Writs, which grew in the thirteenth century with dramatic rapidity. There is no better evidence for the growth of the common law in the Middle Ages.

First, what was a writ and what could it do to initiate legal action? George Spence has defined the original, or originating, writ as

> an order from the king under the Great Seal, addressed to the sheriff of the county in which the cause of action arose or where the defendant resided, commanding him to cause the party complained of to appear in the king's court at a certain day to answer

the complaint. Every writ was founded on some principle of law, *regula juris*, which gave the right on which the action was founded and the facts were stated with so much detail only as to bring the case within such principles of law.[8]

Each order, or writ, acquired a name. For example, to secure enforcement of an agreement, a plaintiff would obtain from Chancery, the writ-issuing bureau, a writ called Covenant; to collect a certain sum of money lent, the plaintiff would bring the action of Debt; to recover personal property or chattels illegally taken, the plaintiff would obtain a writ of Replevin. The number of writs increased from about thirty-nine in the time of Glanvill (ca. 1189) to more than four hundred in the reign of Edward I (1272–1307); it is unnecessary here to name all of them. Sometimes a writ took its name from a Latin word or phrase; the writ of Right, called *Praecipe*, mentioned in Magna Carta, Chapter 34, was so named for the first word following the salutation clause of the writ. The entire formula of the *Praecipe quod reddat* can serve as an illustration of an original royal writ.

> The King to the sheriff, greeting. Command [*Praecipe*] N. that justly and without delay he render to R. one hide of land in such a vill, whereof the said R. complains that the said N. deforces him. And if he does not do this, summon him by good summoners that he be before me or my justices on the morrow of the second Sunday after Easter at such a place to show why he did not do it. And have there the summoners and this writ.
> Witness   Ranulf de Glanvill   At Clarendon[9]

There is more compressed into such a formula than the layman might imagine. Elements essential for any trial are either plainly stated or clearly implied. First of all, notice that the aggrieved man takes the initiative; he actively seeks aid from

---

[8] George Spence, *The Equitable Jurisdiction of the Court of Chancery* (London, 1846–49), I, 225.

[9] F. W. Maitland, *The Forms of Action at Common Law*, A. H. Chaytor and W. J. Whittaker, eds. (Cambridge Univ. Press, 1954), p. 82; for a brief discussion of this writ see Maitland's account, pp. 22–24.

the royal courts in the recovery of his property. The plaintiff goes to Chancery and complains that he has been deforced of one hide of land (about 120 acres). He states the facts of the case, and they are concisely embodied in the writ, which tells the sheriff who allegedly took land, how much land, and where the land is located. In this particular writ the defendant is ordered to obey the king's command. If he refuses, a certain time is set for the beginning of a trial at a certain place. At that time and place the sheriff will "return" the writ so that the court will have the facts of the case and the grounds for an action with any additional information the sheriff may need to supply. The writ implies that the court will move to a decision, determining whether the plaintiff or the defendant has the better right to the disputed hide of land. Also, by implication, this writ reveals a concern on the part of the king that men throughout the realm shall enjoy undisturbed possession of property to which they have a right and that to accomplish this purpose the royal authority will act, when called upon, through the royal Chancery, the sheriff, and the courts of justice. Finally, it is implied that the sheriff, a royal agent, will execute the decision of the court.

During the twelfth and thirteenth centuries the tendency was in England to create an appropriate writ for the protection of every private right or interest recognized by the royal courts. Then, at the end of the thirteenth century, the lush growth slowed, and the time soon came when the plaintiff whose case could not be brought within the scope of one of the common-law writs might be compelled to seek a remedy elsewhere than in a common-law court, perhaps by means of a petition to the king's council, perhaps by a petition to the chancellor. For the writ system hardened and set in the fourteenth century. Thereafter a plaintiff might brood on the maxim, "No writ, no remedy."

The formulas employed by the Chancery were collected and arranged to suit the convenience of the clerks or attorneys using them. These form-books, or catalogs of writs, were known as *registers*, and the twelfth-century treatise called Glanvill *(De legibus et consuetudinibus regni Angliae)* may well be the earliest collection.[10] From Glanvill onward, until the nineteenth century at least, the Register of Writs was one of the most valuable sources a lawyer could consult to determine legal remedies available at common law, for the early "writs of course," the commonly known formulas, embodied the law of England fully as much as did later statutes of Parliament. Yet, surprisingly enough, official texts of the Register do not exist. Even in the Chancery, copies of the Register were not uniform in arrangement; perhaps it was enough for a clerk to be able to find in his own private collection the proper model of a writ when he needed it. Ultimately the court before which a case was tried had the final word on the suitability of a writ; if it did not fit the facts of a case, a writ might be quashed. In this, as in all matters involved in trial procedure, the litigants seeking royal justice had no alternative but to accept the ruling of a royal court or to petition the king and his council for a remedy.

GROWTH OF THE WRIT SYSTEM

We have noted the extremely rapid increase in the number of writs during the thirteenth century—from thirty-nine writs in the treatise called Glanvill to four hundred and seventy-one about a hundred years later. What produced such an increase, and what did it mean for the legal rights of Englishmen? There are no simple answers.

Some of the original writs clearly fall into groups, or families, within which the formulas are closely related because they are grounded on a single principle; variations embodying the prin-

---

[10] R. C. Van Caenegem, *Royal Writs in England from the Conquest to Glanvill*, Selden Society, Vol. 77 (London, 1959), p. 11.

ciple thus swelled the Register of Writs. The writs of Entry, for example, are all founded on the fact of a recent flaw in a title to real property. Various situations can create a recent flaw—a wrongful enfeoffment, or transfer of seisin, by a bailiff, guardian, lessee, or tenant for life; this act and those of other unqualified persons might produce disputed titles. Consequently, the writs of Entry multiplied, and by the reign of Edward I there were eighteen of them.

The action of Trespass was "that fertile mother of actions."[11] Trespass against land, trespass against the person, and trespass against goods were all variants of a principle involving the misuse of force—"by force and arms" the wrongdoer has committed a fault. Before this writ was framed and accepted by the royal courts about 1252, a man might have been expected to act on his own behalf in defense of his own goods or lands or person.[12] Those persons pursuing and catching a "hand-having" or "back-bearing" thief were allowed to execute him on the spot. G. G. Coulton has described an incident recorded on the Northumberland assize rolls for 1255. A certain "foreigner" (*extraneus*), Gilbert of Niddesdale, met a hermit on the moors of Northumberland, "beat him and wounded him and left him half dead, and stole his garments and one penny, and fled away." Gilbert was caught. The hermit asked for his stolen penny. But he was told to observe the custom of the county: to recover his stolen chattels a man must behead the thief with his own hands. Determined to regain his penny, the hermit mustered enough strength to get it by the custom of the country.[13]

Such rough justice was a necessity in a society lacking police officers. The population of England, totaling about two million

---

[11] Maitland, *Forms of Action*, p. 48.
[12] James Barr Ames, *Lectures on Legal History: and Miscellaneous Legal Essays* (Cambridge, Mass.: Harvard Univ. Press, 1913), pp. 50, 56.
[13] G. G. Coulton, "Some Problems in Medieval Historiography," The Raleigh Lecture on History, 1932, *Proceedings of the British Academy*, XVIII, 17–18; for the full record of this case see Surtees Society, LXXXVIII (1891), p. 70.

in the thirteenth century, lived for the most part in rural villages.[14] Towns or boroughs were small in size by modern standards. London itself at that time contained about 50,000 residents. Good roads were scarce and communications poor. Neighborhoods enforced the peace by the frankpledge system, which made each man in a group of ten neighbors responsible for the good behavior of the other nine. All of England was thus organized to police itself. Even so, many persons were incapable of standing on the boundaries of their own land to resist the trespasser; for these, and others unwilling to counter force with force, the ability to invoke majestic royal authority by the action of Trespass must have been a great benefit. The writs of Trespass were a genuine innovation, clearly increasing the legal rights of Englishmen.

In England the old forms of action have been largely abolished as the result of nineteenth-century legislation.[15] And in most of the United States there is usually but one action, called an action at law and equity. A knowledge of the old writs is still useful, however, for understanding common-law principles. Royal writs were crisp, concise formulas. Their clarity, formality, and brevity made it possible to master them as instruments in the conduct of legal matters. Even today the practicing attorney may speak of Covenant, Debt, Replevin, Trespass, or Account in ways which would be familiar to his medieval precursors. "The forms of action we have buried," Maitland wrote, "but they still rule us from their graves."[16] Lawyers today speak of numerous causes of action at law although they no longer draw on the armory of writs supplied by the medieval Register. As recently as the middle of the nineteenth century, and after the abolition of large parts of the old writ system, Henry John Stephen stated in his magisterial treatise, *Pleading in Civil Actions* (1843), that no case was then

---

[14] A. P. Usher, *Industrial History of England* (New York, 1920), p. 89.
[15] Maitland, *Forms of Action*, pp. 7–9.
[16] Ibid., p. 2.

within the scope of judicial remedy unless a remedy might have been initiated by means of "some known original writ. . . . The enumeration of writs, and that of actions, have become, in this manner, identical."[17]

In the Middle Ages the writ system was the very heart of the common law. Bracton observed that "there may be as many kinds of writs as there are kinds of action"—*tot erunt formulae brevium quot sunt genera actionum.*[18] W. S. Holdsworth, an eminent modern historian of the common law, has pointed to the essential role of the medieval writs. "The common law," he declared, "grew up round the royal writs. They formed the ground plan upon which its builders worked. . . ."[19]

ROYAL JUDGES AND COUNCILORS

The authority of the Crown, both in theory and in fact, contributed enormously to the growth of the writ system. Medieval theories of kingship made administration of justice one of the principal functions of monarchy, and if he chose to exercise it, the king in his council had a wide field for inventiveness in legal matters. To create a new writ or a new remedy for a new and difficult case was a serious business, as Bracton has explained; nevertheless it was an accepted function of the royal council.[20] And the king in council had the right, Bracton went on to say, to provide a suitable remedy for every wrong. Litigants were not compelled to seek the king's justice; only in matters touching freehold did the Crown enjoy a monopoly over judicial busi-

---

[17] Henry John Stephen, *A Treatise on the Principles of Pleading in Civil Actions,* 5th English ed. (1843), reprinted and edited by Samuel Williston (Cambridge, Mass., 1895), p. 9.

[18] Bracton, folio 413b.

[19] W. S. Holdsworth, *Sources and Literature of English Law* (Oxford Univ. Press, 1925; reprinted 1952), p. 113; see also *Diversité de Courts,* edition of 1561, f. 117: *"Nota que les briefs sont les principals et premier choses en nostre ley."*

[20] Bracton, folio 1b, "Si autem talia nunquam prius evenerint, et obscurum et difficile sit eorum iudicium, tunc ponantur iudicia in respectum usque ad magnam curiam, ut ibi per consilium curiae terminentur."

ness. But because English subjects gave them business, gradually the medieval royal courts starved out, rather than crushed out, their competitors.

Thus by the end of the thirteenth century the royal courts were rapidly becoming courts of first instance for free men of the realm. They provided the best justice available, for several reasons. First, the medieval jury, a body of neighbors sworn to give evidence under oath, was preferable to older modes of trial such as ordeal, combat, or compurgation. Second, the professional skill of royal judges was superior to that of feudal lords and manorial bailiffs. Such royal judges as William Raleigh, Bracton, Pateshull, Thurkilby, and Robert Burnell were sophisticated jurists, truly learned in the laws of the realm. Third, the incontestable validity of royal records was preferable to the records and fallible memories of suitors of local courts. Finally, decisions of the royal courts were enforced by an authority with wealth and power of a magnitude not to be challenged by any English subject. One can observe again and again the initiative and leadership of English monarchs and their judges and ministers in developing and enforcing rules of the common law.

Members of the king's council, which included judges of the royal courts, were constantly involved with feudalism. They displayed no hostility to feudalism as a system of land tenure; on the contrary, the *Curia Regis* was quick to protect the possession of feudal property. But in a fashion almost unique in Europe the English king could govern the land through the institutions of the counties without depending entirely on the political services of the feudal class. The royal Chancery and the royal Exchequer acted directly on English subjects through sheriffs, commissioners, and judges operating through the institutions of the county. Royal judges, traveling about the realm in the course of a general eyre, or itinerary, carried the majesty of the king's court into the county courts without the intervening assistance of feudal lords.

Consequently, from the time of William the Conqueror, save

for one or two inglorious exceptions, English kings were un-usually successful in making their authority prevail through-out the realm. Possibly only in the Norman Kingdom of Sicily before 1250 did monarchs exercise an authority comparable to that of English kings. Elsewhere in medieval Europe feudal lordships frequently surpassed the royal domain in size and wealth. In France the great lordships of Flanders, Normandy, Burgundy, Champagne, Poitou, and Gascony were so powerful and so deeply entrenched that not until the end of the fifteenth century could it be said that the king of France governed them effectively. Not until the ministry of Richelieu in the sev-enteenth century did royal authority in France command obe-dience of the French nobility in a fashion comparable to that of Henry II ruling twelfth-century England. These facts bear on the early maturity of the common law, which could not have developed without a formidable royal authority working through nonfeudal institutions in all parts of the realm.

During the thirteenth century the community of English feudal barons attempted on at least two great occasions to hold in check the legal inventiveness of the king's council. So long as the council might invent a new formula for a writ or recognize the propriety of a new cause of action, the baronial and all other local courts were in danger of losing the fees, fines, and amerce-ments obtained from the administration of justice. In the course of the rebellion which produced Magna Carta (1215), King John was forced to promise that the writ called *Praecipe* should not be issued in such a way that a feudal lord would lose jurisdiction. But all too soon the writs of Entry were de-vised to determine questions of title, and in a sense the promise in Chapter 34 of Magna Carta was circumvented.[21] Again, in the Provisions of Oxford (1258), during the rebellion led by Simon

---

[21] William S. McKechnie, *Magna Carta: A Commentary on the Great Charter of King John* (Glasgow, 1905), p. 405: "The writ which is called *praecipe* shall not for the future be issued to anyone, concerning any tenement whereby a freeman may lose his court."

de Montfort, the barons tried to curb the chancellor's power, as agent of the king, to issue new writs. The Provisions stated:

This the Chancellor of England swore. That he will seal no writ, excepting writs of course, without the commandment of the king and of his council who shall be present. . . . And that he will seal nothing which may be contrary to the ordinance which is made and shall be made by the twenty-four or by the major part. And that he will take no fee otherwise than what is given to the others. And he shall be given a companion in the form which the council shall provide.[22]

By the end of the thirteenth century baronial opposition to the growth of the common law seems to have faded. At any rate, according to the eminent legal historian Frederic W. Maitland, the Statute of Westminster II, Chapter 24, seems to encourage Chancery initiative: "Men are no longer clamouring about the multitude of new writs. Parliament has to urge the Chancery not to be pedantic, but to grant new writs when new cases fall under old principles."[23] Maitland is referring here to the passage in the statute instructing the Chancery clerks.

Whensoever from henceforth it shall fortune in the chancery, that in one case a writ is found, and in like case [*in consimili casu*] falling under like law, and requiring like remedy, is found none, the clerks of the chancery shall agree in making the writ, or shall adjourn the plaintiffs until the next parliament and write the cases in which they cannot agree, and refer them to the next parliament, and by the consent of men learned in the law, a writ shall be made, lest it might happen hereafter that the court should long time fail to minister justice unto complainants.[24]

For all of the urging, the Statute of Westminster II produced no remarkable activity in Chancery. After the door was wide

---

[22] *S.C.*, pp. 384–385.

[23] *Select Pleas in Manorial Courts*, F. W. Maitland, ed., Selden Society, Vol. 2 (London, 1889), pp. lix–lx.

[24] G. B. Adams and H. M. Stephens, *Select Documents of English Constitutional History* (New York: Macmillan, 1921), p. 76; *Statutes of the Realm*, Record Commission, 11 vols. (London, 1810–28), I, 71.

open to extension of the law by analogy, apparently Chancery officials did not take advantage of their opportunity. Thus the clause *in consimili casu* was not responsible for important additions to the forms of action at common law.

COMMON LAW AND ROMAN LAW

The chancellor and his Masters in Chancery, *magistri cancellarii*, were often ecclesiastics trained in both canon and civil law. Why should not the Chancery staff and the royal judges round out the law of the royal courts by drawing on the more complete Roman system? The possibility of a medieval "reception" of Roman law or of canon law in England is so obvious that legal historians have sought to determine precisely the extent of Roman influence.

The Roman law available in the Middle Ages was not the entire body of the Roman law known in the days of either the Roman Republic or the unified Empire. Rather, it consisted of two kinds of Roman law. The first, called the "vulgar Roman law" of the West, was the law surviving in the western portions of the empire after Germanic invasions of the fifth century;[25] the second was the corpus of Roman law compiled at the order of the Byzantine emperor Justinian (A.D. 527–565). By appointing commissions of able jurists to do the work, he salvaged, preserved, and made available, both for his own time and for later centuries, something of the best of Rome's achievement in jurisprudence. Justinian's codification, the *Corpus Juris Civilis*, with subsequent additions made by glossators, could be mastered by serious and able students. The compilation had a clear-cut plan of organization consisting of four parts: first, the *Codex*, a collection of imperial edicts, *leges*, and constitutions,

---

[25] On this point generally, see Ernest Levy, *West Roman Vulgar Law*, Memoirs of the American Philosophical Society, Vol. 29 (Philadelphia, 1951); Max Conrat, *Geschichte der Quellen und Literatur des römischen Rechts im früheren Mittelalter* (Leipzig, 1891).

comparable to statutory law; second, and most important for jurisprudence, the *Digest*, or *Pandects*, carefully selected extracts from the writing of outstanding jurisconsults, among whom the names of Gaius, Ulpian, Papinian, and Paulus are preeminent; third, the *Institutes*, a textbook for students; and fourth, the new laws, *Novels*, or *Novellae*, added to bring the compilation up to date. This was the form in which great teachers such as Irnerius at Bologna (ca. A.D. 1100–1130) appropriated and transmitted Roman law to modern Europe.

About a century ago a scholar of great reputation, Henry Sumner Maine, credited Bracton, the medieval judge, with a heroic plagiarism, "putting off on his countrymen as a compendium of pure English law a treatise of which the entire form and a third of the contents were directly borrowed from the *Corpus Juris.*"[26] And in much the same vein, Kenelm Digby, another nineteenth-century legal historian, observed that "the direct effect of the Roman law upon the law of England is not . . . very conspicuous till the reign of Henry III, when its influence appears in almost every line of Bracton's great treatise."[27]

Maitland refused to accept such extensive borrowing in Bracton's *De legibus et consuetudinibus Angliae*. After careful study of Bracton's *Note Book* of English cases and after comparing Bracton with Azo, a contemporary glossator, Maitland flatly contradicted Maine, branding his remarks about Bracton's plagiarism as a piece of "stupendous exaggeration." Further, Maitland concluded that "the amount of matter that Bracton borrowed from the *Corpus Juris* is not one third, is not one thirtieth" of his treatise.[28]

Since Maitland was able to find marked cases in the early

---

[26] Henry Sumner Maine, *Ancient Law*, 5th ed. (New York: Henry Holt, 1888), p. 79.

[27] Digby, *Introduction to the Law of Real Property*, 3rd ed. (Oxford, 1876), p. 66.

[28] *Bracton's Note Book: A Collection of Cases Decided in the King's Courts during the Reign of Henry III, by Henry of Bratton*, ed. F. W. Maitland, 3 vols. (London, 1887); *Selected Passages from the Works of Bracton and Azo*, ed. F. W. Maitland, Selden Society, Vol. 8 (1895), p. xiv.

plea rolls which matched some two thousand cases collected in Bracton's *Note Book,* there is no question about Bracton's firsthand familiarity with the decisions of other contemporary English judges. What, then, did Bracton take from the law of Rome? Roman law supplied the sense of form and arrangement which a law book should have, that is, how to arrange rules under headings such as persons, things, and actions—all of which he could have taken from the system of classification in the *Institutes.* But within a Romanized scheme, according to Holdsworth, Bracton set forth a body of rules for the most part thoroughly English.[29]

Even the great authority of Maitland, however, did not settle the matter of Bracton's Romanism. As the controversy now stands, the burden of proof seems to rest on those seeking to demonstrate a large amount of direct borrowing from the *Corpus Juris*—not only on the part of Bracton but also on the part of his fellow English judges, who did not always follow Bracton's liberal views. Some borrowing from Roman law cannot be denied; it will account for at least four or five forms of action in the Register of Writs. These touched three subjects not to be handled lightly in the royal courts: recovery of seisin of real property, the majesty of the Crown, and the relation between the lessor and the lessee.

CHANCERY PROCEDURES

Could Chancery clerks have engaged in law-making simply by agreement among themselves on the propriety of issuing new writs of course? Certainly if they took a writ devised for a special case and allowed it to swell into a writ of course available for anyone requesting it, the effect was legislative. For what had been special, particular, and exceptional would thereafter be general and common. And the shift from exceptional to com-

---

[29] W. S. Holdsworth, *Sources and Literature of English Law,* p. 29.

mon remedy did occur; how it happened we do not know. Without explicit reason a notation may appear in the margin of a thirteenth-century enrollment, *Hoc breve de cetero erit de cursu* —this writ in the future will be a writ of course.[30] Or again, there may be simply a marginal notation of one word, *Forma;* here, too, the effect was to open up a new cause of action for plaintiffs requesting it.[31] We are not dealing with a bureau insisting on written authorization for all of its acts.

Whatever its validity, the argument for bureaucratic contributions to the Register should not be pressed too far. Such brief marginal notes as the foregoing may represent the conclusion of solemn but unrecorded discussions in the king's council, at which the chancellor sat with judges and other royal officials. Royal judges, moreover, were always in control of judicial procedures. Chancery clerks, acting solely on their own, were in no position to create a new remedy. Unless royal judges were prepared to accept a new writ, it would fail at the opening of a trial.

ALIEN MERCHANTS AND MONEYLENDERS

Possibly the king in council, the royal judges, and the Chancery clerks were all merely the clerks of thirteenth-century social and business morality; perhaps they all adapted the common law to new circumstances and to new ideas brought into England by foreign trade. This is an attractive argument, likely to receive every consideration in the present, when economic factors are so often given top rank among all determinants of change in society. There is no difficulty in establishing the fact that English wool sold readily over much of Europe; that in the thirteenth century Italian merchants came to England from Florence and Genoa; that French merchants came from Bor-

---

[30] This notation appears on the Close Roll, 6 John, m. 18, *in dorso.* It makes a writ of course of a formula for Entry *sur disseisin.*

[31] Close Roll, 16 John, m. 2.

deaux to compete with Flemings from Bruges, Rhinelanders from Cologne, and Hansards from Lübeck. It is much more difficult, however, to establish that foreign merchants prevailed in securing recognition of legal doctrines new to the common law. This is not all. To prove contributions by alien merchants to the common law one must show that new and exceptional remedies, first obtained by aliens, were subsequently granted as a matter of course to all English subjects seeking justice at common law.

How could an alien merchant induce the king's council to grant him an exceptional legal advantage? The power of money may be one answer. Both Henry III (1216–1272) and his son Edward I (1272–1307) were frequently in need of large amounts of money. They both spent heavily on ambitious projects overseas as well as in the British Isles. They both outran the income from the royal domain. Royal treasury balances could drop remarkably low;[32] for example, on February 29, 1286, King Edward had a balance of £2 8s. 1d. ; again, on July 16, 1289, Edward had £2 13s. 8½d.[33] Consequently, the man with money to lend to the Crown was in a position to ask the king's council for exceptional protection in his other business affairs. Understandably enough, Edward favored the Italian merchant-bankers, organized in family societies controlling highly fluid capital. The Frescobaldi of Florence lent the English Crown more than £120,000 over a period of twenty years.

The position of the alien merchant was always insecure. A sovereign makes a poor creditor—by reason of the familiar maxim, "No writ runs against the king," no one can sue him for collection of a debt. Ability to assist in supplying the royal financial necessities in the future must have been the alien lender's best guarantee of repayment by the Crown. The high risks of lending to royal debtors may explain, in part, the high

---

[32] R. J. Whitwell, "Italian Bankers and the English Crown," *Transactions of the Royal Historical Society*, N. S. XVII (1903), pp. 175–233.

[33] Ibid., p. 183.

rates of interest sometimes demanded and paid; Henry III once borrowed at 120 percent *per annum*.[34]

Aliens secured exceptional treatment from the king.[35] When an alien moneylender accepted a lease for a term of years as security for a loan to an English subject, the debtor got hard cash immediately; the creditor got the right to collect the revenues from the leased property for a certain number of years. Out of the revenues the creditor recovered his principal sum and also the interest on the loan. The charge of usury could not be brought against the alien creditor; he did not ask for the return of a certain sum of money; principal and interest blended indistinguishably in the revenues from the leased property. This made a convenient arrangement for both borrower and lender so long as the creditor-lessee was not disturbed in his possession.

Until sometime after the middle of the thirteenth century, however, a leaseholder, whether English or alien, was not satisfactorily protected in the enjoyment of the lease. He could not use legal remedies available to the freeholder, because in the opinion of common-law judges he had only a covenant, an agreement, with the borrower. The primary concern of the royal courts in the time of Glanvill was to protect seisin of a freehold; this mysterious blessing of seisin was never to be conferred upon the leaseholder. Glanvill observed (ca. 1190) that royal courts would hear cases of Covenant only if the king wished them to be heard there.[36] It required an uphill struggle

---

[34]   Ibid., p. 195.

[35]   Ibid., p. 203. Whitwell cites the case of Gregorio Palmieri (of Siena?), who was granted royal protection in the lands and revenues of Robert Passelewe which he had from Robert for the payment of a debt. The protection was to last until the debt was paid. Gregorio then at once demised and leased these lands to Alexander de Dorset and Walter de Stavel; Patent Rolls, 11 Henry III (1227), m. 4, *De Protectione pro Alexandro de Dorsete*. This is an example of a gagee assigning his interest to lessees, who enjoy exceptional protection while in possession of the leasehold.

[36]   Glanvill, *De legibus et consuetudinibus regni Angliae*, ed. G. E. Woodbine, Yale

against the doctrine of seisin before leasehold gradually obtained protection at common law comparable to that enjoyed by freehold. By the end of the thirteenth century the leaseholder could use the remedy of Covenant to force the lessor to keep his part of the agreement. Also the leaseholder could use the action *Quare ejecit infra terminum* against a lessor who arranged, or gave his consent to, the ejectment of the leaseholder by a third party before expiration of the lease. Finally, with the remedy of Ejectment, an action designed for the benefit of the leaseholder, the process was complete, and the leaseholder could sue anyone who disturbed him in his possession of the lease.

That the alien moneylender played a role in the gradual development of remedies for the leaseholder is more than a possibility. He sometimes secured a special royal protection in the enjoyment of lands and leases. This royal favor was recorded on the rolls of Chancery, where no one could dispute it. Whether it was a favor granted by reason of the alien's wealth or simply as a response to a well-managed request, the repeated protection of property interests in the hands of aliens may have taught the royal judges the reasonableness of protecting all leases and other chattel interests in land by remedies enforceable in the common-law courts.

Discussion here of alien merchants and moneylenders, and their influence on remedies finally obtained by all leaseholders, has touched on two elements essential for legal change in medieval England. The first is a self-assertive, alert, and influential group of men pressing for a new remedy or

---

Historical Publications, Manuscripts and Texts, XIII (New Haven, 1932); and English trans. by John Beames, ed. J. H. Beale (Washington, D.C., 1900), X. c. viii: "Upon this subject it should be remarked that the King's court is not in the habit of giving protection to or warranting private agreements [*privatas conventiones*] of this description concerning the giving or accepting of things in pledge or others of this kind, made out of court, or even in any other court than that of the King."

procedure which could be justified by comparison with a similar remedy in another legal system or by analogy. By their requests, petitions, and efforts to protect their own interests, the initiating few make themselves heard in the courts. A second element is recognition and acceptance by the courts; they open the door for the granting of a new remedy available to all plaintiffs.

The common law dealt with a complex, uneven, and dramatic growth dominated by the English monarchy, its councilors, sheriffs, and judges. To set the early common law in its proper relation to the society in which it flourished, Chapters 2 and 3 examine the character of the monarchy which enforced it. Next, Chapters 4 and 5 describe the social structure of England because, as observed, the medieval common law served the needs of a dynamic society. In Chapters 6 and 7 we shall turn to the relation of the early common-law courts to other contemporary courts of county, hundred, and borough; and while dealing with institutions, we shall examine the structure and function of Chancery, the great writ-issuing bureau. Then we shall consider in Chapters 8 and 9 the nature and sources of the common law, placing particular emphasis on the law of Property. Finally, in Chapter 10 we shall note those medieval developments destined to grow and to flourish in later centuries. Here we will consider the law-making activities of medieval parliaments before 1307, the medieval use of judicial precedents, the medieval legal profession, and the emergence of courts of equity, which supplemented the common law and, in effect, made possible the continued growth of legal remedies in a royal court.

PART ONE
THE POLITICAL SCENE

Chapter 2
Royal Centralization
and Absolutism

The growth of early common law is inseparable from the events of English political history. The first Angevin rulers, Henry II, Richard the Lionhearted, and John, along with their ministers and judges, created the legal system; political crises in the thirteenth century permanently determined its character. Exceptional power in the hands of English rulers enabled them to operate centralized administrative machinery, and royal power, combined with administrative skill, moved in the direction of absolutism. Henry II acted with almost absolute power as he devised procedures to collect taxes, raise military forces, keep records, police the countryside, and administer justice. In the most remote counties of England royal judges, sheriffs, and commissioners drilled Englishmen of all classes in the procedures of the royal government and in the law of the land. Regalian rights which other monarchs in Europe could only hope for were freely exercised by Henry II. The exceptional strength of Angevin monarchy was essential for the development of a body of common law for the entire realm.

But the successors of Henry II met opposition when they reached for absolute power. They were forced to recognize that, although they might continue to rule as supreme administrators, they could not invade the customary legal rights of their subjects; the king is under law, is limited by the law. Legal concepts now clustered about the phrases "rule of law" and "due process" trace back to the quarrel of King John with his baronage. The granting of Magna Carta did not settle the issues between advocates of royal prerogative and their opponents. The long series of political crises, disturbing English government in every century between the twelfth and the eighteenth, lie beyond the scope of the chapters which follow. Here the account deals first with the political scene in the time of Henry II, a period of foundations; next with political contests before the death of Edward I.

HENRY II: SUPREME ADMINISTRATOR
OF THE REALM

The personal force and attention to public affairs of Henry II go far to explain his success as supreme administrator of the realm. The founder of the common law, Henry, duke of Normandy and of Aquitaine and count of Anjou, was crowned king of England on December 19, 1154. A monarch of exceptional abilities, he promptly began to set in motion administrative procedures and judicial practices on which his successors would build for centuries.

Although the affairs of his French lands kept Henry on the Continent for twenty-one of his thirty-four years as king of England, his absences from the realm of England did not indicate indifference about English affairs nor neglect of his prerogatives as *dominus et rex*. In fact, in spite of his absences, it was in England that Henry had his great successes and made his reputation as a wise and skillful political administrator. Intensely practical and possessive, he was determined to enjoy to the full every feudal and royal right, power, and prerogative he could obtain. While securing his own interest, he gave his subjects the incidental benefit of an orderly government.

At twenty-one Henry was a tall, clean-shaven man, thickset, muscular, bullnecked. Dignified in bearing, he cared little about appearance, wore his reddish hair close-cropped, and for freedom of movement preferred a short cloak to longer garments. Restive and impatient, he could not be quiet during church services and often whispered and scribbled during mass. He had the quick, violent temper of the Angevins; his energy and restlessness fatigued his entire household, for he was constantly on the move throughout his lands. Where he was, there was his capital; and he amazed his own subjects as well as his enemies by the rapidity with which he traveled, encumbered by his household and by packhorses carrying documents, records, and supplies for transacting the business of government. In an age when twenty-five to thirty miles a day was the normal distance on horseback, Henry once covered one hundred and seventy miles in two days.[1]

Although Henry was well educated in the arts of war, he was more than a soldier. He could read, speak, and write Latin, and he enjoyed the conversation of such a learned man as John of Salisbury, the foremost humanist of the twelfth century, who was often at his court. Henry was only twenty-one years of age at the time of his coronation, but he was no apprentice in the arts of government. Four years earlier he had acquired from his father, Geoffrey of Anjou, the administration of the duchy of Normandy; after his father's death he had inherited the county of Anjou. Aquitaine came to him by his marriage with its duchess, Eleanor. These were rich and powerful lordships in France.

The marriage of Henry of Anjou and Eleanor of Aquitaine augmented the central problem of the French monarchy in the

---

[1] C. H. Haskins, *The Normans in European History* (Boston, 1915), p. 92.

Middle Ages, namely, mastery over the great feudal lordships of France. Strong only in the Ile de France, King Louis VII now had to deal with a vassal in control of more than half the realm of France, governing a territory extending continuously southward from the English Channel to the Pyrenees. Although Henry properly did homage for his French fiefs, he possessed within them an aggregate of power unattainable by the king of France.

The legal problems confronting Henry II would have dismayed a less energetic and high-spirited man. Simply to maintain law and order in French lordships and to collect there his feudal dues and services demanded great strength and skill. Each duchy or county in France had developed its own dialect and customs. Somehow the Normans, Bretons, Poitevins, and Gascons had to be brought within the framework of a single administration. In England, Henry faced the problem of restoring order to a demoralized kingdom filled with the unlicensed castles of masterless barons who had profited by decades of civil war and weak rule under Henry's predecessors.

Like every ruler in medieval Europe, Henry confronted on all sides the claims of the Church of Rome, which asserted that spiritual authority was superior to secular authority throughout Christendom. Relations with the Church tested Henry's political skill more than all other problems of kingship. After the Norman Conquest, William I had separated English ecclesiastical and secular courts. Then the Investiture Controversy in the reigns of William II and Henry I disturbed relations of Church and state, as the papacy encouraged churchmen to demand freedom from secular interference in the election of bishops. A compromise in 1106 between Anselm, archbishop of Canterbury, and Henry I settled the investiture question until 1135. Then King Stephen enlarged the freedom of the Church from secular control. Henry II could not have foreseen the defeat he was to experience in attempting to redefine the jurisdiction of ecclesiastical and secular courts.

POLICIES OF RESTORATION

Henry II looked backward to the time of his grandfather, Henry I. He treated the reign of his predecessor Stephen as a period of unlaw, because civil war had troubled it. He returned to the time of Henry I in some of his best-known declarations of "the recognized customs and rights of the kingdom," the Constitutions of Clarendon (1164) and the Assize of the Forest (1184). The preamble of the Constitutions of Clarendon describes the document as "this record and recognition of a certain portion of the customs and liberties and rights of his ancestors—namely, of King Henry, his grandfather, and of others—which ought to be observed and held in the kingdom."[2] In the Assize of the Forest, Article I, Henry declares that "he wills that full justice shall be had as was had in the time of King Henry, his grandfather."[3]

Realizing that the men who knew best the machinery of government were those who had served in Henry I's administration, Henry II enlisted the service of some of these men. For efficient operation of the Exchequer, he employed Richard fitzNigel, son of a former treasurer and grandson or grand-nephew of Roger, bishop of Salisbury, who had established Exchequer practices in the time of Henry I. Richard fitzNigel later drew on his familiarity with the Exchequer to write in 1177 a famous treatise, *Dialogus de Scaccario*, explaining how the sheriff's accounts were audited and enrolled twice annually at Easter and at Michaelmas. Richard's bureaucratic skill was valuable to Henry. During the reign of Stephen, royal revenues had dropped from £66,000 annually to £22,000, and a smoothly working Exchequer was obviously essential for the restoration of royal finances.[4]

---

[2] S & M, p. 73.

[3] Ibid., p. 87; and *Calendar of Patent Rolls* (1155–57), p. 63; Henry confirmed to the burgesses of Barnstaple all good customs which they had in the time of his grandfather and abolished "omnibus pravis consuetudinibus post avum meum ibi elevatis."

[4] William Stubbs, *Constitutional History of England* (Oxford: Clarendon Press,

Henry II was at home in the procedures of the English royal Chancery. He made excellent use of the formal royal writ.[5] All his documents were remarkable for their regularity and for their crisp and precise style. Once royal officials had been trained in the terminology of the charters and writs of Henry's Chancery, they were able thereafter to carry out the king's orders without doubt or confusion about the meaning of royal instructions.

CONTROVERSY WITH BECKET

Theobald, archbishop of Canterbury and a man loyal to the memory of Henry I, brought to the attention of Henry II the name of Thomas Becket, son of Gilbert Becket, a London merchant. Thomas Becket was then archdeacon of the See of Canterbury. In the course of travels on the Continent, he had studied Roman and canon law at Bologna and at Auxerre. In 1155 Henry II made Becket his chancellor and principal counselor. Persuasive and forceful in personality, Becket was an energetic administrator with as much capacity for the work of government as King Henry himself. He could turn diplomat or soldier, as the king's need required. When Theobald died in 1162, Henry compelled the English clergy to accept Becket as the new archbishop of Canterbury. Some of the clergy murmured at the king's choice, for Becket was not ordained when Henry made his decision and other well-qualified men desired the position. Becket did not seek the highest church office in England; indeed, he protested that as archbishop he would not be able to support the royal policies toward the Church.

1880), I, 435. But note Henry's ability to collect from all his lands the impressive sum of about £180,000 in 1159 for the subjugation of Toulouse, ibid., I, 517.

[5] R. C. Van Caenegem, *Royal Writs in England from the Conquest to Glanvill*, Selden Society, Vol. 77 (London, 1959), p. 166; see also Leopold Délise, *Recueil des Actes de Henri II concernant les provinces françaises et les affaires de France* (Paris, 1909), Introduction, p. 1.

Henry's will prevailed. Friendship between Henry and Becket was then so strong that Henry clearly expected the new archbishop, while still serving as chancellor, to promote a cordial relation between ecclesiastical and secular authority in England. In this hope he was soon disappointed.

Once Becket had been ordained priest and installed as archbishop, he suddenly changed his behavior. Formerly the king's most loyal servant, he now became an ascetic zealot and defender of the rights of the clergy, opposing royal acts with imperious willfulness. Becket soon resigned his post as chancellor and thereafter devoted all of his energy to affairs of the Church. In all accounts of the contest which developed, events are clouded by partisan emotions. The principal issue, however, was clear—was the Church to have exclusive jurisdiction over all clergymen in all circumstances? Was a clergyman suspected of murder to be accused in a royal court and possibly punished by a royal court? William of Newburgh, a chronicler living at the time of the controversy, stated that Henry's decision to act on the matter of "criminous clerks" was prompted by the fact that he had learned of a hundred murders committed during his reign in England for which churchmen were answerable.[6] If brought to trial in an ecclesiastical court, criminal clergymen could look forward to nothing more severe than being deposed from their orders and put in prison on a restricted diet, because an ecclesiastical court could not give a sentence of death.

To obtain a declaration of the proper relation between Church and state, Henry summoned a council at Clarendon— "on account of the dissensions and disputes that had arisen between the clergy and the justices of the lord king and the barons of the realm concerning customs and rights."[7] His pol-

---

[6] *Historia rerum anglicarum (1016–1198)* in *Chronicles of the Reigns of Stephen, Henry II, and Richard I,* Vols. I and II, ed. R. Howlett, Rolls Series (London, 1884–85), I, 140.

[7] See the preamble of the Constitutions of Clarendon in S & M, p. 73.

icy of restoring the customs of the time of his grandfather meant that in ecclesiastical as well as in secular affairs he would set aside arrangements established in the intervening period. Becket's criticism of this policy was that to ignore events of Stephen's reign was not to reconstruct but to innovate, to create an entirely new situation beyond the Church-state relation established in Stephen's reign. Stephen had granted to bishops justice and power over ecclesiastical persons and their possessions.[8] This jurisdiction, Becket said, should continue.

Archbishops, bishops, clergy, earls, barons, and magnates of the realm met with Henry at Clarendon, a hunting lodge, to make their declarations, which were set out in sixteen articles forming the Constitutions of Clarendon.[9] Three of these articles were highly important in development of the common law. In the first article, touching advowsons, Henry's side won without dispute. Henceforth the right of advowson, the right to name the candidate for a vacancy in a parish church, belonged to the landowner, while the right to install the new man belonged to the bishop. Advowson was a temporal property right, and any dispute over it came into royal court. The later common-law action of Darrein Presentment is a refinement of Article 1 of the Constitutions. By this action a royal court would identify the patron who had presented the last parson, whose death created a vacancy. This patron, or his heir, could then present again.[10]

Still another point won for the temporal courts was their right to determine a preliminary matter of competence on

---

[8] See Stephen's Second Charter, *Statutes of the Realm, Charters*, p. 3.

[9] *S.C.*, pp. 170–73, gives the Latin text; see S & M, pp. 73–76, for an English translation.

[10] The treatise called Glanvill, *De legibus et consuetudinibus regni Angliae*, ed. G. E. Woodbine, Yale Historical Publications, Manuscripts and Texts, XIII (New Haven, 1932), appearing about 1187–89, clearly shows (XIII, 18–22) the persistence of the right of advowson.

whether a property in land was to be treated as "free alms," an ecclesiastical tenure, or "lay fee" (Article 9).[11] Whether the common-law action and writ subsequently known as *Utrum* was first based on the Constitutions of Clarendon is uncertain. But Glanvill, writing about fifteen years after the Constitutions, mentions the "recognition," that is, the testimony of twelve lawful men on whether *(Utrum)* a certain property is lay fee or ecclesiastical; and he describes the same procedure as that set down in the Constitutions of Clarendon.

As for Article 3, the most bitterly contested article of the Constitutions of Clarendon, since it was preeminent in the quarrel between Henry and Becket, it is quoted here in full.

> Clergymen charged and accused of anything shall, on being summoned by a justice of the king, come into his court to be responsible there for whatever it may seem to the king's court they should there be responsible for; and [to be responsible] in the ecclesiastical court [for what] it may seem they should there be responsible for—so that the king's justice shall send into the court of Holy Church to see on what grounds matters are there to be treated. And if the clergyman is convicted, or [if he] confesses, the Church should no longer protect him.[12]

This article requires explanation, for it describes a procedure which is far from obvious. Maitland has a succinct account.[13] A clergyman suspected of a crime is to be accused before a temporal court. Here he will either plead his innocence or confess the truth of the charges. If he pleads his innocence, he will be sent to the ecclesiastical court for trial; there, if found guilty, he will be deposed, by churchmen, from his orders. A layman now, he will be brought back to the temporal court; royal officers will have been present at his trial and will see that

---

[11] "... utrum tenementum sit pertinens ad elemosinam sive ad feudum laicum. ..." For the distinction between these tenures, see below, pp. 101–103.

[12] S & M, p. 74.

[13] P & M, I, 448. For a fuller account see F. W. Maitland, "Henry II and the Criminous Clerks," *English Historical Review*, VII, 224.

he does not make his escape; when they have brought him back to the temporal court, he will then—perhaps without further trial—be sentenced to the layman's punishment, death or mutilation.

Becket claimed that this procedure would amount to a double punishment, violating the maxim *Nec enim Deus iudicat bis in idipsum* (for even God Himself does not judge twice in the same matter). Even though the trial went forward in an ecclesiastical court, a temporal court would first hear the accusation, royal officers would be present at the ecclesiastical trial, and the deposed clerk would be punished by the temporal power.

The very tone of the Constitutions of Clarendon was probably as offensive to Becket as the content of any particular article. Henry II seems to have assumed that he had the responsibility for seeing justice done throughout the realm in all save purely spiritual matters; furthermore, he and his council would decide where the lines were to be drawn between Church and state jurisdictions.

Although at first he agreed, Becket finally refused to give his formal assent to the Constitutions of Clarendon, thus adding to the very difficulties that the meeting at Clarendon had been expected to solve. In the long-drawn-out and tragic dispute which followed, Becket behaved like a man without a temporal ruler. He refused to be governed by the royal authority. At a council at Northampton, shortly after the Clarendon conference, he would not admit that the king might judge him or the royal curia try him for contempt. He would obey, he said, only the pope. Enraged by Becket's defiance, Henry deliberately sought to compel Becket to resign as archbishop. He took away from Becket the income and the office of archdeacon of Canterbury; he ordered Becket to account for all of the fees which he had earlier received in the Chancery—a request impossible to fulfill.

Becket fled to France, where he could rely on the sympathetic interest of King Louis VII while threatening Henry II with excommunication. In 1170, after an apparent reconciliation, Becket returned to Canterbury. Immediately he renewed his hostility toward the king's agents and friends. He excommunicated three bishops who had participated in the coronation of the "Young Henry," son of Henry II; on Christmas Day he excommunicated Ranulph de Broc, the sheriff of Kent. When news of Becket's treatment of his bishops reached Henry in France, he was so furious that he uttered the fateful words which four knights took literally. Whatever Henry II may have snarled in his anger, he implied that he was served by cowards, who were afraid to rid him of a low-born priest. Reginald Fitzurse, Hugh de Moreville, William de Tracey, and Richard le Breton secretly left the court of Henry, crossed the Channel from Normandy, and made their way to Canterbury, where they were joined by Ranulph de Broc, the newly excommunicated sheriff. The armed men easily found Becket in his cathedral at vespers. He made no effort to escape; on the contrary, he sought martyrdom.

After the murder the popular reaction was all in Becket's favor. Pilgrims began to come to his tomb in Canterbury, bringing at least the pilgrim's penny as a gift to Becket's church. The martyred archbishop was looked upon as being more than a man; he was the great champion of the Church. Within two years Becket was canonized, and Henry II himself was driven, either by his own conscience or by a sense of expediency, to make a pilgrimage to Becket's shrine. Dressed as a penitent, barefoot, Henry walked through the streets of Canterbury and into the church where his former friend and recent opponent had fallen. St. Thomas in his tomb seemed to have the victory. Having abrogated the Constitutions of Clarendon (1172) and having now done penance for the rash words in Normandy which led to Becket's murder, Henry then turned his attention to other matters involved in the government of his empire.

Actually, in the years after Becket's murder, Henry gave up only the jurisdiction of the temporal courts over ecclesiastics accused of a felony. "Benefit of clergy," as it came to be called, was the right of a clergyman in England, ordained or un-ordained, to be tried in an ecclesiastical court for a felony less than treason. Treason and all misdemeanors by clergymen remained within jurisdiction of the temporal courts. In that period many persons—students for example—came under protection of the Church, and benefit of clergy gradually widened in its application until by the sixteenth century it applied to all who could read, or pretend to read, a certain verse in the Bible, the opening lines of the 51st Psalm: "*Miserere mei, Deus*—Have mercy upon me, O God, according to thy loving-kindness: according unto the multitude of thy tender mercies blot out my transgressions." This was the "neck verse," or "noose verse," by which many an English felon escaped capital punishment—once. On a second offense felons could not claim benefit of clergy. Even within this limitation, benefit of clergy was a dark stain on the administration of criminal law in England until 1826, when it was abolished by statute.[14]

The career of Henry II seems to have aimed at creating an elaborate concert of principalities over which he would exercise a supervisory control while members of his family, guided by his policies, would govern the component parts of a harmonious, integrated structure. If a man's life is to be judged by its aim, then Henry II failed completely. Later centuries, however, have not judged Henry in the light of his own aim; rather, they have admired the excellence of the man as an administrator and organizer, particularly in England. There he made such good use of the royal courts, the writ system, the sworn inquest (or jury), and administrative bureaus that he established the common law and laid the foundations for its future growth. These remarkable achievements were the by-products of Henry's sense of orderly procedure and his exceptional skill

---

[14] 7 and 8 George IV, c. 28, s. 6. In the United States, by act of Congress, April 30, 1790, s. 30, benefit of clergy was not to be allowed or used upon conviction of any crime for which by statute of the U. S. the punishment is death.

in adapting for the government of England the practices of his Norman predecessors.

RICHARD THE LIONHEARTED: ABSENT KING

Richard the Lionhearted, the elder of the two surviving sons of Henry II and Eleanor of Aquitaine, inherited the Angevin empire and demonstrated conclusively that his father had created a superb administrative machinery of government in England. It could operate in the king's absence; it could operate in war or in peace; it could operate under the strain of repeated, heavy, financial demands.[15] While Richard's Crusade to the Holy Land makes an interesting narrative, it has bearing on the law and institutions of England at only one point—finances.

After a Crusade, perpetual wars, and the construction of a magnificent fortress in France, England had been squeezed dry. If Richard had lived a few years longer, it is quite possible that he, rather than his successor John, would have faced a baronial rebellion such as that which produced Magna Carta. For all his reckless, spendthrift character, Richard had the capacity to win and hold the loyalty of the barons of his time, who admired his prowess in combat and his capacity for magnanimous generosity. Richard's chief minister, the justiciar Hubert Walter, might resign in despair as Richard ordered him to raise more money, but we do not find among Richard's officials or barons expressions of fear or hatred of the king. That was to come in the reign of John.

JOHN: IRRESPONSIBLE ABSOLUTIST

In a medieval monarchy the personality of the ruler made itself felt wherever the monarch was present to exert his prerogative

---

[15] W. S. Holdsworth, *Sources and Literature of English Law* (Oxford, 1925), p. 16.

to direct the process of government. And the character of King John is central for any explanation of the course of events during his reign (1199–1216).[16] Along with the realm of England, John assumed the government of lands on the Continent which his father and brother had retained despite the efforts of King Philip II of France to splinter the Angevin holdings. At the time of his coronation John was about thirty-two years of age. He was not lacking in intelligence, energy, or the determination to be, like his predecessors, wealthy and powerful. Whereas Richard had neglected public affairs, John was industrious and attentive to details; he was often present in the law courts and at the Exchequer. John, however, had none of Richard's excellence as a soldier; and, more important, he was suspicious of all men, jealous of his barons, devious in pursuing his objectives, and calculatingly cruel. Even members of his own family were not safe. With good reason John was accused of arranging, in 1203, the murder of his nephew, Arthur of Brittany, who might have inherited the throne of England by the strict rules of primogeniture. John appropriated the private revenues of his own mother, Eleanor of Aquitaine, as well as those of his sister-in-law, Berengaria, the widow of Richard. These great ladies appealed vainly to the pope.

On occasion he mistreated hostages; in 1212 he hanged the sons of twenty-eight Welsh chieftains. John was so much mistrusted by his barons that one of them, Robert fitzWalter, once arrived at court with five hundred armed knights to see justice done in a case touching his son-in-law. This same Robert fitzWalter was to be the marshal, or leader, of the armed rebellion which broke out in 1215. John's name will always be associated with this rebellion, which forced him to grant what was known to contemporaries as the Charter of Liberties, or the Charter of the Barons, and to later ages as the Great Charter

---

[16] For a full account of this period, see Sidney Painter, *The Reign of John* (Baltimore, 1949).

(Magna Carta). The English barons should have been John's most dependable subjects, but he had made personal enemies among them and lost their support long before the treaty at Runnymede in 1215.

LOSS OF NORMANDY, MAINE, ANJOU, AND BRITTANY

A connection exists between the loss of Normandy and the obvious ability of the English baronage to draw together some ten years later to present John with their formal demands for the correction of his misrule.[17]

John was unfortunate in his enemies; he had failed, some years before 1215, in contests with powerful opponents beyond the realm of England. The first failure was in France against an exceptionally able monarch, Philip II. John gave Philip an excellent pretext for war by preventing the marriage of Isabella of Angoulême, daughter of one of his vassals, and Hugh of Lusignan, another of his French vassals. John became enamoured of Isabella, set aside her formal betrothal with Hugh of Lusignan, and married her himself. The infuriated fiancé appealed to Philip II, John's overlord. When Philip summoned John to appear in the French royal court, John ignored the summons and his French lands were consequently declared forfeited. Philip then executed the sentence of his court by going to war. First he seized control of the regions of Anjou, Maine, and Brittany. The murder of Arthur of Brittany had produced anything but loyalty among John's French barons, and thus with comparative ease Philip went on to take Normandy and soon thereafter the county of Touraine. By the end of 1204 John had lost all of his French territory north of the Loire River.

He was not the only loser in this series of events. Many of

---

[17] On this subject generally, see F. M. Powicke, *The Loss of Normandy* (Manchester, 1913).

John's barons had fiefs in France as well as in England. They now had to choose whom they would serve, John or Philip. Those barons who chose to keep their English tenures were not cheerful about giving up what they had previously held in France. John's failure in Normandy did not improve his popularity in England; justly or not, he acquired the nickname "Softsword." But the effect on John's reputation was neither the only nor the principal result of the loss of Normandy. Those English barons who had given up French tenures now identified themselves more clearly with other English barons. There appeared among them a sense of community, of common interest. Whereas before the loss of Normandy these men were usually called "the barons of England," after 1204 they were often designated as "the English baronage."

QUARREL WITH POPE INNOCENT III

Soon after the debacle in France, John began a long quarrel with Innocent III, probably the most powerful pope of medieval Christendom. Troubles began in the course of electing an archbishop of Canterbury to succeed Hubert Walter, who died on July 13, 1205. The monks of Christ Church, Canterbury, decided to assert an exclusive right to choose the next archbishop, although the practice had been to allow the bishops of the province of Canterbury to participate in an election. Without royal permission and in a hasty secret caucus, the monks chose Reginald, their superior, who was quietly dispatched to Rome to receive papal confirmation. But Reginald's vanity was too much for him; he could not remain discreetly silent about his good fortune; he boasted along the way. The news soon came back to John, who flew into a rage, declared the election of Reginald void, and ordered the monks of Canterbury to elect a royal favorite, John de Gray, bishop of Norwich. The monks obeyed, the suffragan bishops concurred, and John then invested his own candidate—who also set out for Rome!

Confronted by the rival candidates, Innocent III set aside

both elections. He then asked the monks of Canterbury to send him a delegation, and he instructed the latter to elect Stephen Langton, an eminent English cardinal at the Roman curia. But John refused to accept the election of Langton; he confiscated the property of the archbishopric of Canterbury, expelled the monks of Christ Church, defied Innocent III, and forced Langton into exile. When Innocent III ordered John to accept Langton, threatening an interdict if John refused longer to obey, John replied that an interdict would lead him to expel the clergy from the realm and that he would put out the eyes and cut off the noses of all Romans whom he might find within the borders of England.

Nevertheless, the interdict followed (1208) and lasted four years before John capitulated. All church services were forbidden; the bells were silent. John himself was excommunicated but managed for a time to withstand this blow. As a final measure the pope declared John deposed from the kingship, absolved all of his subjects from their oaths of allegiance, and ordered Philip of France to conquer England and to place his son, Louis, on the throne. Philip willingly planned a campaign.

Suddenly and characteristically, John gave up completely and negotiated a reconciliation with Rome through the papal legate, Pandulph. He agreed to accept Langton as archbishop of Canterbury; he agreed to recall the exiled clergy and to restore Church property; he even agreed to make all of England and Ireland a fief of the papacy, paying an annual tribute of one thousand marks sterling. A remarkable change immediately resulted in the relations of John with the papacy, for the pope was now his overlord and zealous in his concern about his vassal's interests.

MILITARY DISASTERS AND THE BARONS' REBELLION

A military defeat in France led directly to the first serious check to royal absolutism in England. John began to organize an expedition into France by which, in alliance with Otto IV, Holy

Roman Emperor, and Baldwin, count of Flanders, he expected to crush Philip II and to recover Normandy and other land lost in 1203 and 1204. The allies developed a strategy designed to catch the royal French forces between two armies. The English were to move north and east out of Poitou while the Flemish and imperial advance moved south and west. In a single battle at Bouvines Philip smashed one jaw of the pincer-like maneuvers against him and shattered the coalition; John's campaign turned into a fiasco. He returned to England to raise money for another effort, and when he increased the rate of scutage from two to three marks on the knight's fee, the northern barons refused to pay on the ground that they were not obliged to serve in Flanders.

Refusal to pay scutage was a serious matter. Scutage was a money payment in lieu of the military service for which most vassals were responsible, the customary period being forty days a year at the vassal's expense and as long thereafter as the lord would pay the vassal's expenses. To refuse to pay scutage or to do the military service demanded by an overlord was to deprive him of the services for which a fief was originally granted. A vassal's refusal either to serve or to pay sums with which his overlord might maintain a mercenary force amounted to breaking the feudal contract.

Like his ancestors before him, John had about two hundred and thirty great noblemen who held grants of land directly from the Crown. These were the tenants-in-chief, who in turn distributed large portions of their holdings to sub-vassals. Theoretically this arrangement made available a military force of about 8,600 men trained from youth in the art of war and accustomed to fighting as heavily armed cavalrymen equipped with lance, sword, and shield. These barons and knights, holding land by military tenure, formed the aristocracy of English society. In 1215 they had not yet divided into the various ranks of nobility known later. If there was a line of demarcation within their ranks, it was the division between those who held directly from the Crown—the *barones*, the magnates, the tenants-in-chief—and all others.

From the time of William the Conqueror onward, the English kings had taken oaths of fealty, oaths of personal loyalty, from all free men. The entire military aristocracy, down to the humblest knight, owed service to the king as feudal overlord, and the oath of fealty to the lord king, *dominus et rex*, was not taken lightly in the thirteenth century. Many vassals felt that they could not honorably make war on John, much as they might sympathize with those barons who did rebel. The revolt which preceded the granting of Magna Carta built up slowly over several months, and the rebels took up arms only after John had failed three times to discuss with the leaders their requests for reassurance about their customary rights.

About forty-five barons formulated demands, which John refused to consider. They then, along with many others, formally renounced their allegiance by the procedure of *diffidatio*, chose Robert fitzWalter as the leader of their army, and marched on London, the principal walled town of England, where the citizens cordially welcomed the rebels. Supported by the citizens of London, the barons seemed invincible as they moved from their strong base westward through the Thames Valley. John finally agreed to treat with them at Runnymede, a meadow beside the Thames River between Staines and Windsor.

MAGNA CARTA: "FIRST STATUTE OF THE REALM"

In the negotiations which led to the formulation of Magna Carta, Stephen Langton became a key figure. Archbishop of Canterbury and papal legate *ex officio*, Langton desired to protect and to strengthen the position of the Church. In the light of all that had happened in the way of Church-state controversy during the years since his election, Langton might have been expected to press for "free" elections to bishoprics, and in fact the first provision of Magna Carta touches this point. But Langton seems to have had the statesmanship to look beyond the interests of the Church and the particular grievances of the barons. He pressed for a general plan of reform which would recognize the special interests of ecclesiastics and barons while guaranteeing a royal administration which would deal predictably with all the realm. When the barons presented a fourth set of demands to John, they had the benefit of Langton's counsel. The result was a document known as the Articles of the Barons, which John accepted as the basis for negotiations and sealed with the Great Seal. Magna Carta grew out of a point-by-point discussion and rephrasing of the Articles of the Barons. In this treaty-making, Stephen Langton was a prominent spokesman in the baronial party, while William Marshall, earl of Pembroke, one of the few men in all England trusted by both the baronial and the royal side, represented royal interests.

This is not the place to discuss the various phases through which the Great Charter passed before reaching its final form in 1225. Suffice it to say that the Charter of 1215, granted in the midst of rebellion, was not the Great Charter subsequently confirmed and placed in the statutes as "the first statute of the realm."[18]

It should be remembered that although a few chapters became famous and were often quoted and interpreted, *all* of Magna Carta was important for the thirteenth-century law of England. From the beginning the Charter was an expression of the law which the king and his judges and other officials were not permitted to ignore.[19] The provisions, or chapters, as they later came to be called, can be grouped into four categories. In

[18] The Charter, as revised in 1217 and confirmed by Henry's regents in that year, was confirmed again in 1225. The issue of 1225 was the version of Magna Carta so often confirmed in later years. For a text indicating revisions of the 1215 version, see S & M, pp. 115–26.

[19] For detailed comment on the provisions of Magna Carta, see William S. McKechnie, *Magna Carta* (Glasgow, 1905).

the first, John granted freedom of elections to the Church. In the second he defined the relations of the king with his barons (thirty-two of the sixty-three chapters fall into this category). In the third and probably the most meaningful group of provisions, the king dealt with the national administration. Here are the statements which were later interpreted to support a much wider application than that intended in 1215. By the fourth group of provisions, the barons received the power to execute the terms of the Charter; a committee of twenty-five barons was to lead the entire realm into action against the king if he failed to keep his promises.

The Charter touched on a number of matters affecting the relation of the subject with the sovereign power. The opinion expressed in the later slogan, "No taxation without representation," has been read into Chapter 12, which says: "No scutage or aid shall be imposed in our kingdom except by the common council of the kingdom. . . ."[20] But the American Revolutionist and his English sympathizer in the eighteenth century were not saying the same thing as the thirteenth-century barons. Medieval and modern techniques of representation were far from identical. While the American colonists wanted representation in Parliament like other British subjects, the barons at Runnymede disliked arbitrary taxation imposed from above without the taxpayer having an opportunity to express his consent through any channel.

If one had to choose a chapter from all of Magna Carta to express the spirit and the principal idea embodied in the Charter, it would be Chapter 39 of the 1215 version: "No free man shall be taken or imprisoned or dispossessed, or outlawed, or banished, or in any way destroyed, nor will we go upon him, nor send upon him, except by the legal judgment of his peers or by the law of the land."[21] The modern doctrine of "due process

[20] S & M, pp. 117–18.

[21] Ibid., p. 121, n. 36; see also Paul Vinogradoff, "Clause 39," in *Magna Carta Commemoration Essays*, ed. Henry Elliot Malden (London, 1917), pp. 78–95.

of law" has evolved into a very sophisticated and complex concept, and we should not, of course, take Chapter 39 of Magna Carta as the sole foundation of all the elaborate modern doctrines about due process. Nevertheless, the many reissues and confirmations of Magna Carta established a principle which the English people invoked whenever they felt that the king was acting arbitrarily.[22] Henry III, John's son and successor, reissued the Charter three times and confirmed the issue of 1225 on three occasions. Edward I, following Henry III, confirmed the Charter three times;[23] eventually it was confirmed at least thirty times before the close of the Middle Ages. In effect, each confirmation of the Charter became a solemn assurance to the realm that the king would act with a regard for the welfare of all subjects. It was an assurance, moreover, that the king would act according to clearly established procedure; in short, the king, like all of his subjects, was under the law.

The negotiations which led to the granting of Magna Carta did not bring an end to the conflict between John and his barons; civil war continued. Indeed, the situation became even more complicated when Pope Innocent III, then John's overlord, declared the Charter void and "a shame for England."[24] The pope struck at the rebels with the ecclesiastical weapons of excommunication and interdict, which were enforced by Guala, a papal legate. Undeterred by this severe censure, the rebellious barons invited Louis, son of King Philip of France, to take the throne of England. Although Louis crossed the Chan-

---

[22] *Magna Carta Commemoration Essays*, p. 79.

[23] See C. H. McIlwain, "Magna Carta and Common Law," in *Magna Carta Commemoration Essays*, pp. 124–79. *S. C.*, pp. 490–93, gives both the French text and an English translation; the latter is quoted by S & M, pp. 164–65; and see *Statutes of the Realm*, I, 123.

[24] The bull of Pope Innocent III, dated August 24, 1215, concludes: "We utterly reprobate and condemn any agreement of this kind [i.e., Magna Carta] forbidding, under ban of our anathema, the aforesaid king to presume to observe it. . . ." McKechnie, *Magna Carta*, p. 55, citing Charles Bémont, *Chartes des Libertés Anglaises (1100–1305)* (Paris, 1892), p. 41.

nel in the spring of 1216 to join in the war against John, England was spared a long continuance of fighting. For John died in October of that year, leaving as his heir a nine-year-old boy, whose guardians and regents quickly brought an end to the disorders. They forced Louis to return to France and granted the most favorable terms to those English barons who would return to their former allegiance to the Crown.

Within the period between 1154 and 1216, the figure of King Henry II stands out most prominently as the founder of the common law. His sons and their councilors and judges continued to operate the administrative machinery which Henry II so effectively established; they continued to use the jury, the sworn inquest, and the itinerant justices that Henry had employed extensively. The negligence of Richard and the abuses of John failed to destroy the common law. Magna Carta limited the exercise of royal power, but without diminishing or impairing royal authority to the point of impotence. The king was still the head of the royal administration. He still enjoyed the royal prerogative to act at his own discretion in the large sphere of administration. He could still choose his own ministers, judges, and councilors. He was still the master of his own household. Magna Carta did not make the king of England powerless to govern. Consequently the administrative machinery and the common law continued to develop under the leadership of Angevin kings and royal councilors.

Chapter 3
Royal Prerogative and the Community of the Realm

During the thirteenth century the common law of England developed rapidly in the midst of political crises produced in large part by the financial demands of Henry III (1216–1272) and his son Edward I (1272–1307). Sharp contests between the royal prerogative and the community of the realm involved control of the country's foreign policies, control of the membership of the royal council, and control of the increasingly complex administrative machinery of government. These political controversies also affected the character of the law of the realm. By the end of the century, Parliament had emerged as a device frequently employed to obtain the counsel and consent of the realm for the operations of a government in which the royal prerogative in administration continued to exert an animating force.

Henry III and Edward I eventually made good their disputed claims to choose their own ministers and agents. At the same time the community of the realm, represented by great barons, prelates, knights of the shire, and townsmen, acquired the right in Parliament to approve and give consent to new laws and taxes beyond customary feudal dues and services. Repeated confirmations of Magna Carta, when demanded by the community and granted by the monarchs, reiterated the idea that the king, like his subjects, was under the law.

The working compromise achieved by Edward I, between government by royal prerogative and government by the consent and counsel of the community of the realm, was actually an uneasy truce between opposing theories of the source of authority. The absolute authority of a monarch, king by the grace of God, was nicely counterbalanced and restrained by a feudal theory of kingship strong enough to hold the king to the observance of contracts with his feudal tenants-in-chief, the great barons and churchmen. Precarious though it may have been, the Edwardian compromise operated effectively under Edward's leadership. For one thing, it resulted in the declaration of many rules of common law embodied in long and notable parliamentary statutes. Unquestionably the contest between royal prerogative and community of the realm had a direct bearing on the history of English law, for out of the controversy came many explicit rules for the governance of the realm.

HENRY III: DUPE OF ALIEN COUNSELORS

When John died on October 19, 1216, his heir was a mere boy nine years old. As *rector*, or regent, for the young Henry, a council of barons wisely chose William Marshal, earl of Pembroke, who clearly understood the baronial views of kingship even though he had not joined the baronial faction in arms against John in 1215.[1] This venerable warrior had already served three English kings, and he enjoyed the confidence of Guala, the papal legate, who worked closely with him in a program designed to bring peace to the realm by ending civil

---

[1] See Sidney Painter, *William Marshal* (Baltimore: Johns Hopkins Univ. Press, 1933), for a biography of the regent.

war. William restored order within a short time by following policies acceptable to the baronage. A generous amnesty brought disaffected subjects back to their allegiance to the Crown.[2] Within a year William had persuaded Louis of France to give up all hope of obtaining the kingship of England and to return to Paris. In cooperation with the papal legate, Earl William reissued Magna Carta with some modifications adjusting it to the new situation. Beyond the Channel, the regency made no bold and expensive ventures to recover former Angevin lands in France. These policies saved the throne for Henry and initiated an era of harmony between royal authority and the baronage. Harmony endured until 1232, when at the age of twenty-five Henry III assumed full personal control over the administration.

Soon after 1232 began a series of difficulties for Henry. These troubles stemmed in part from Henry's desire to exercise personal authority in the government, but they stemmed even more directly from Henry's character. Shrewd manipulators exploited his simplicity and his extraordinary devotion to the Church. He spent lavishly, and the people of England were asked to finance enterprises which benefited neither Henry nor them and seemed fruitless for everyone except a few self-promoting "aliens." He wasted men and money on ill-conceived military expeditions in France, he allowed relatives and other aliens to infiltrate his court, and he collaborated with the papacy in ambitious and unrealistic schemes to put his son Edmund in control of the far-off Kingdom of Sicily.

FOREIGN INFLUENCE AT COURT

The presence of foreigners in high positions angered the English baronage, who argued that the king should be advised by men familiar with the long-established customs of the king-

---

[2] Kate Norgate, *The Minority of Henry III* (London, 1912), pp. 278–80.

dom. In 1235 Henry married Eleanor of Provence, who was closely related to the prominent House of Savoy. She was abundantly supplied with Savoyard uncles, who managed to get lands, offices, and the highest positions in the Church in England. One of them, Boniface, secured with royal support the archbishopric of Canterbury, succeeding Edmund of Abingdon. Another, William of Savoy, obtained the leadership of the royal council. Still another of Eleanor's uncles, Peter of Savoy, was granted the cluster of properties known as the honour of Richmond.

The Savoyards were not the only aliens who thrived at court. Members of the House of Lusignan arrived from France confidently expecting that Henry III would not deny their claims of kinship through Henry's mother, Isabella of Angoulême. Papal legates, papal nuncios, papal tax collectors, and canon lawyers from Rome were also able to secure the cordial support of Henry III. A most devout son of the Church, Henry readily turned to Rome for guidance in the midst of his political problems.

Unquestionably Henry III was devout, kind, well educated, and appreciative of beauty, whether in the setting of a small gem or in the grandeur of a Gothic vault. Among many benefactions, he contributed heavily to the building of a great abbey church and chapter house at Westminster in the "new style" imported from France. But Henry III was a blundering king.

THE SICILIAN FIASCO

One of Henry's most disastrous undertakings was the Sicilian affair. On impulse Henry undertook a project to make his son Edmund ruler of the Kingdom of Sicily, a dominion including much of Italy south of Rome as well as the island of Sicily. After the death of Frederick II, Holy Roman Emperor, in 1230, and of his son, Conrad IV, in 1254, the succession of the Kingdom of Sicily became a confused issue. Pope Alexander IV sought to install a compliant monarch as a neighbor on the southern border of the Patrimony of St. Peter. Unfortunately for the success of Alexander's plans, Manfred, natural son of the great Frederick II, was already firmly established in Palermo, the Sicilian capital. Against this brilliant Hohenstaufen, Pope Alexander proposed to support Edmund of England, but only on certain conditions: Henry III was obliged to send a military force to Sicily and to repay the debts which Alexander had already incurred in Sicilian affairs. Henry agreed to these terms, even though a failure to pay the large debts would result in his excommunication and the laying of an interdict on England. It was a rash commitment, for Henry had neither soldiers to send to Sicily nor money at hand to repay the papal debts of 135,541 marks, a tremendous sum. As it turned out, Edmund never ruled a day in Sicily. But Edmund's failure to obtain the throne of Sicily did not release Henry from his obligation to repay the papal debts.

CROWN AND BARONAGE IN CONFLICT

The ineffective assertion of English claims to lands in France, the fiasco in Sicily, and a long domestic struggle between Henry III and his barons produced the critical events of 1258, which brought to the front an exceptional baronial leader, Simon de Montfort, earl of Leicester and brother-in-law of Henry III. Personal relations between Simon and Henry were seldom cordial. Henry's mismanagement and lack of resolution annoyed Simon repeatedly. After the failure of the French expedition of 1242, Simon as much as said that Henry III should be shut up like Charles the Foolish and have nothing to do with the government. "At Windsor there were houses with iron bolts good for keeping him securely within."[3]

[3] Charles Bémont, *Simon de Montfort*, English translation by E. F. Jacob (Oxford, 1930), p. 66.

In 1258 Simon's personal dissatisfaction with Henry's rule was matched by a widespread discontent among English barons and churchmen who had felt the pressure of repeated financial demands. From the beginning of Henry's reign, payment after payment had been requested and granted: scutage, carucage, aids for the recovery of Gascony, payments for the confirmation of charters, aids for a crusade, and numerous papal exactions beyond the thousand marks a year which King John had agreed to pay as tribute. And yet in 1258 Henry III was helplessly in debt; up to this point he had spent an estimated 950,000 marks in vain projects.[4] He was able to borrow only at extortionate rates when he turned to Italian merchants for money.[5] To extricate himself from his financial difficulties, in 1258 Henry asked a parliament at London for a tallage of one-third of all the goods of the realm. This request stirred up an angry protest and demands for the reform of the royal government.

THE PROVISIONS OF OXFORD AND THE BARONS' WAR

Many smoldering discontents burst into flame as the English barons began to air their grievances and to plan how they might be corrected. The result was a constitutional crisis which eventually culminated in civil war between royalist and baronial factions. Throughout this time of troubles (1258 to 1267), the barons were not doctrinaire constitutionalists seeking to enact a written constitution for England. Nevertheless, their opposition to an unrestricted use of the royal prerogative had its effect on the course of political developments. The years of controversy ultimately ended in fixing even more firmly in the English constitution the principle that the king is under the law.

[4] William Stubbs, *Constitutional History of England* (Oxford: Clarendon Press, 1880), II, 77, citing Matthew Paris, p. 948.

[5] R. J. Whitwell, "Italian Bankers and the English Crown," in *Transactions of the Royal Historical Society*, N.S., XVII (1903), p. 205.

In 1258 Henry III had no other course of action but to place himself in the hands of his barons and prelates. He was dependent upon them for money to conduct the government and to meet his commitments to the papacy for the payment of monies agreed on in the Sicilian affair. He was compelled to agree to a petition for reform and did so before the adjournment of the London parliament on May 5th. He also agreed to the creation of a body of twenty-four counselors, who were to be chosen in a parliament at Oxford early in June. Half of the twenty-four were to be named by the king, the other half by the barons.

The position of the barons is not easily described, but it may be roughly summarized. They felt that Henry had been persuaded by alien counselors to pursue the Sicilian will-o'-the-wisp. He had allowed himself to become involved in a situation from which he could not extricate himself save by the heavy taxation of the wealth and service of his magnates, who had not been consulted about the Sicilian affair. The English barons felt themselves to be the natural, proper advisers of the king in affairs touching the community of the realm, but they had been pushed aside for many years by the king's French relatives and by legates, nuncios, and tax collectors from the papal curia. They were determined to correct the government of the realm by placing their own representatives in the councils of the king.

In 1258 the barons were filled with reforming zeal. They went much farther in their demands than the baronial faction which forced Magna Carta from King John. In granting Magna Carta, John had promised that the royal administration would act in certain clearly defined ways, but the barons of 1215 had not asked to be associated with the Crown in the conduct of the government. However, at the Parliament of Oxford in 1258, the barons insisted upon an elective council of fifteen men, a standing council who should meet three times a year with another group of twelve elected barons. In these three annual "parliaments" the twelve elected representatives of the commonalty and the fifteen elected councilors were "to treat the wants of the king and of the kingdom."

Beyond the three parliaments each year, the Provisions of Oxford established baronial control over the great officers of royal government—the justiciar, the treasurer, and the chancellor were specifically mentioned, along with the guardians of royal castles. These officers were to be appointed for the term of one year, and each was to account for his office at the end of that term.

The reformers clearly wished to keep their hands on innovations in the law. By the Provisions of Oxford the chancellor of England swore "that he will seal no writ, excepting writs of course, without the commandment of the king and of his council who shall be present." In other words, the writs of course, initiating litigation for well-known causes, could be issued without supervision; but exceptional special writs could be issued only in the presence of the council. And elsewhere in the Provisions of Oxford the barons repeated that the chancellor is not to be inventive in legal matters or responsible to the king alone. Rather, he is to "seal nothing out of course by the sole will of the king. But that he do it by the council which shall be around the king."

Again and again the Provisions deal with the administration of justice. And while dealing with the power of the justiciar and bailiffs, the barons show their concern for procedure: "And let the writs be pleaded according to the law of the land, and in fit places." (*E les brefs seicut pledez solum lei de la tere e en leus deues.*)

Among the details of the Provisions of Oxford none was as extraordinary as the proposal of an elective council by which the barons made themselves partners in the exercise of royal authority and joined their wills with the will of the king. As councilors they were to have a voice in the appointment of the king's ministers. This was, of course, a deep invasion of royal prerogative and entirely out of line with contemporary political thought elsewhere in Europe. Nevertheless, under the leadership of Simon de Montfort and Richard de Clare, earl of Gloucester, the reforming barons attempted to operate the government of England according to their plan. Success depended on cohesion and unanimity among them in the conduct of business, but by 1260 several great lords had broken with Simon. In 1261 the pope absolved Henry III from his oath to maintain the Provisions. At this critical time only the unwavering adherence of Simon de Montfort kept alive the original baronial plan. To settle the differences between the growing royalist faction and the followers of Simon, both parties agreed to accept the arbitration of Louis IX, the saintly king of France, who had a great reputation as a judge.

In his award, given at Amiens on January 24, 1264, Louis IX held that the Provisions of Oxford, the heart of the English baronial program, were entirely null and void. He declared that Henry III might freely appoint, dismiss, and remove the justiciar, chancellor, treasurer, counselors, judges, sheriffs, and any other officials of his kingdom or his household. Louis quashed the statute that the realm of England should be governed only by natives and that aliens should leave. The award of Louis was a complete victory for Henry III.

Louis IX had decided in favor of a Europe-wide theory of medieval kingship by which the king was king by the grace of God, the sole administrator of the realm, without a peer, and free to take counsel from any person whom he wished to consult. Many people in England were prepared in 1264 to accept this theory of kingship.

But the Montfort faction regarded Henry III as a bungling monarch and themselves as the victims of his simplicity. They regarded control of the royal council as the key to good government, for the king in council could legislate. There he could give his approval to policies which committed the entire realm to war or peace. There he could give his approval to new forms of action and to new writs affecting the law of the land. If the royal councilors were not familiar with the existing law of the land, they might ask the chancellor to affix the Great Seal to startling and undesirable innovations. If they accepted the Award of Amiens, as they had sworn to do, Montfort and his followers could expect the complete annihilation of five years of struggle. They chose to break their oaths. The Award of Amiens was the signal for civil war.

The men who had drafted the Provisions of Oxford knew what they wanted, and for a time they had actually shared in the operation of the royal government. As events proved, however, they would not work like professional bureaucrats, giving sustained attention to day-by-day administrative details. Although the Earl Simon acted in lofty and disinterested ways and gained an ardent personal following, he could not hold the loyalty of all the barons. Consequently, the king could build a following to oppose the Montfort faction. When it became impossible for the royalist and Montfort factions to work together, the result was a resort to force in January of 1264. Simon initiated the military action.

In the fighting which followed, Simon won a brilliant tactical victory at Lewes, May 14, 1264, where he took prisoner Henry III, his brother Richard, and another member of the king's retinue, Henry of Germany. The young Prince Edward, Henry's eldest son, was given up as a hostage, security for the observance of Henry's promises to observe the Great Charter and the Charter of the Forest as well as the Provisions of Oxford. Henry III promised to reduce his expenses and to live within the revenues from the royal demesne. A complete amnesty for Simon and other baronial leaders completed the terms of victory dictated by Simon.

Using his opportunity to revive the plan of an elective council, Simon restored with extensive changes the constitution of 1258–59. It was still a government by king and council, but Simon was, in fact, the troubled master of England. Although he drew support from the knights of the shires, the lower townsfolk, and some of the clergy who were opposed to the exactions of Rome, the lords of the Welsh march were irreconcilable and so was the Roman curia. As he tried to construct a base of support for his formula of government, in January, 1265, Simon called a special parliament more remarkable for its composition than for its actions. For the first time representatives from the towns and for the second time representatives from the shires were summoned to meet for deliberations on the affairs of the kingdom. The parliament was an opportunist measure designed to draw to the Earl Simon all the friendly support he could marshal. The subsequent development of the House of Commons, in later centuries, has given Montfort's parliament of 1265 an importance not attached to it by its contemporaries. Simon himself was a great nobleman, not a man of the people, and he did not contemplate government of the people by the people.

Simon de Montfort was drawn into military action in the west of England along the border of Wales, where his good fortune ran out. The young Prince Edward, then twenty-six years of age, escaped from Simon's custody, joined forces with Gilbert de Clare, earl of Gloucester, and a strong royalist force quickly gathered. At Evesham on August 3, 1265, surrounded by a small group of devoted followers, Montfort lost his life in a battle with forces commanded by Edward and Gilbert. After Simon de Montfort's death the baronial cause seemed to be completely overwhelmed by the royalist victory.

THE DICTUM OF KENILWORTH

A commission of four bishops, two earls, and six other barons drafted a settlement known as the Dictum of Kenilworth (1266). They confronted the fact that Henry III had survived his enemies and that he could insist on the freedom to exercise the royal prerogative unimpaired by the will of elected baronial councilors. Once more the precarious balance between royal prerogative and community of the realm had been restored—this time in favor of the king, as the Dictum of Kenilworth made clear. But in its first two articles we still find a concern for the proper administration of the law, the proper use of royal writs, and the appointment of disinterested judges:

1. We declare and provide that the most serene prince Henry, illustrious king of England, shall have, fully receive, and freely exercise his dominion, authority, and royal power without impediment or contradiction of anyone, whereby, contrary to the approved rights and laws and the long-established customs of the kingdom, the regal authority might be offended; and that to the same lord king and to his lawful mandates and precepts full obedience and humble attention shall be given by all and singular the men of the same kingdom, both greater and lesser. And all and singular shall through writs seek justice in the court of the lord king and shall there be answerable for justice, as was accustomed to be done up to the time of the recent disorders.

2. Furthermore, we ask the same lord king and reverently urge his piety that, for doing and rendering justice, he will nominate such men as, seeking not their own interests, but of those of God and the right, shall justly settle the affairs of subjects according to the praise-worthy laws and customs of the kingdom, and shall thereby strengthen with justice and restore the throne of royal majesty.[6]

EDWARD I: "HAMMER OF THE SCOTS" AND RELUCTANT CONSTITUTIONALIST

Spectators at Edward's coronation ceremonies at Westminster saw a king schooled in all the medieval arts of ruling. He was then thirty-five years of age, tall, vigorous and well proportioned, handsome in appearance and regal in bearing. An expert in the most violent and strenuous physical activities of the

---

[6] *Statutes of the Realm*, I, 12–17; *S.C.*, pp. 407–11; S & M, pp. 149–50.

feudal aristocracy, he delighted in the joust, or mock battle, and in hawking and hunting. By the year of his coronation Edward had gained almost twenty years of experience in public affairs. First he had served in Gascony, later along the Welsh borders. During the course of the Montfort rebellion, he had been at the very center of the royalist factions. Following the victory at Evesham, Edward had assumed the leadership in policies of royalist restoration, contributing to the good order of his father's last years. From all of these experiences, and particularly from the clash with Simon de Montfort and his party, Edward had learned much. He had never accepted the baronial view of kingship; on the contrary, he vigorously opposed it or ignored it whenever he could. But during his participation in the clash with Montfort, Edward had observed how readily the great Earl Simon had enlisted support among the feudal class and to what a plight Henry had been brought by baronial opposition. When Edward himself met with the serious opposition of his great barons and prelates, he avoided a possibly fatal clash with them so that he might enjoy the reality of power rather than the open recognition of his own personal views about the royal prerogative.

Edward's compromises profoundly affected English law. To secure men and money for large and ambitious projects, Edward had the good sense to make concessions to the feudal theory of kingship. For example, in a constitutional crisis in 1297 he confirmed Magna Carta and emphatically declared what was so generally understood in the thirteenth century, namely, that Magna Carta was to be observed as common law; that on no account were aids, taxes, and prises to be taken from the kingdom "except by the common assent of the whole kingdom and for the common benefit. . . ."[7] Edward also identified himself with his people in the midst of differences with Pope Boniface VIII and explained to the See of Rome that "it is the

[7] S & M, *Confirmatio Cartorum*, pp. 164–65.

custom of the realm of England that in all things touching the state of the same realm there should be asked the counsel of all whom the matter concerns."[8]

Edward frequently summoned parliaments to obtain the support of his subjects and, above all, to obtain their wealth. These meetings served several purposes: 1) to inform the nobility, the clergy, and representatives from the English shires about royal policies, administrative procedures, and matters affecting the safety of the realm; 2) to secure the consent of the community of the realm to legislation; and 3) to secure consent to taxes to meet royal necessities. In short, Edward was well aware of his prerogative, and he was prepared to exercise personal, discretionary power as administrator of the government and king *gratia dei*. But he was prudent enough not to base his authority upon this essentially theocratic view to the exclusion of the baronial view expressed in Magna Carta.

Edward I was a lawyer-king in an age peculiarly conscious of law and of the rights guaranteed by it. Whether or not Edward alone deserves credit for the extraordinary burst of statutory legislation which began shortly after his coronation, the legislation seems to have been in accord with his lawyer's temperament, and much of the legislation was designed to serve the interests of the Crown as well as the interests of the subjects. At any rate, Edward I called the parliaments during a decade of statute-making scarcely to be matched in significance by the legislative activity of any other comparable period in English history, unless it be that of reform legislation in the nineteenth century.

In any discussion of Edward's legislation, it is well to remember that in the thirteenth century "statute" was a collective term applying to all the enactments of a single parliament. Consequently, some of Edward's statutes contain many articles which, standing alone, conform to the modern under-

---

[8] Stubbs, *Constitutional History of England*, II, 165.

standing of "statute." The Statute of Westminster I (1275) represents the work of a codifying parliament touching many facets of the substantive law in no less than fifty-one clauses.[9] Edward possessed a strong sense of order; he worked toward well-organized procedures and sought to extend and enlarge the area in which the English law was operative. The Statute of Westminster I was in line with royal policies. Here and in other declaratory legislation were set down, often in minute detail, authoritative statements of the law of England, much of which had been treated hitherto as immemorial custom. Such declaratory statements, incidentally, were not "passed" in Parliament by formal vote. It was not then necessary to secure the formal consent of representatives of the community of the realm to the precise wording of the statute as finally drafted by Edward's councilors, judges, and Chancery officials. If the English people had accepted the enforcement of these customary rules in the courts for a number of years, obviously they had already given their consent to them. Custom, approved by use, carried the greatest authority in the Middle Ages. But new laws and taxes were different matters altogether. A parliament, or something like it, was essential for obtaining a grant of taxes, and this is true of the parliament enacting the Statute of Westminster I. It granted Edward a tax on wool, woolfells, and leather. Medieval legislation and consent to taxation usually went hand in hand.

RELATIONS WITH WALES, SCOTLAND, AND FRANCE

Edward I always needed money, and he could get it only by parliamentary grants. Again and again his energy led him into foreign enterprises far beyond the ordinary revenues of the Crown. Consequently, he sought money from his subjects to finance policies in Wales, Scotland, and Gascony. From a firmly established base in England, he endeavored to exercise effec-

---

[9] *Statutes of the Realm*, I, 26.

tive overlordship along the English borders as well as in southwestern France. Beginning with his stay in Gascony in 1273–74 until the time of his death in a campaign against the Scots in 1307, Edward was preoccupied with the affairs of one or another of these regions. He aimed at much more than military conquest. He sought the extension of firm administrative control, and—in Wales, at least—the extension of English law as well.

He tried to accomplish his purposes by constructing within Wales and Gascony elaborate fortifications conjoined with towns to serve the needs of the garrisons. Military campaigns were expensive in themselves, but the construction of fortified towns—or *bastides* as they were called in France—sometimes required years to complete. Two campaigns against Llewelyn of Wales brought the submission of the Welsh in 1284. Then followed the building of castle-towns such as Flint, Rhuddlan, Builth, Conway, Caernarvon, Harlech, and Beaumaris—to name only some of the more prominent. These castle-boroughs clinched the submission of the Welsh princes and provided centers from which English influence and administrative orders spread out among a people who clung desperately to every shred of independence they could maintain. Edward clearly needed the garrisoned fortresses, for when he turned his attention elsewhere, the Welsh rebelled against his authority.

The Scottish problem was far from simple, and Edward never solved it. By his entanglement in Scottish dynastic rivalries, Edward added to his already large military expenses and commitments and to his reliance on the community of the realm in matters of finance. Parliaments not only provided his subjects with opportunities to present petitions for the redress of grievances but also repeatedly confirmed the feudal concept of kingship, insofar as it limited the power of the king to tax.

Edward asserted his right to arbitrate the disputed succession in Scotland. When the Scots would not obey him, he was led into a long series of campaigns, marked by success on the battlefield and by failure in breaking the resistance of the Scottish clans. The Scottish menace, combined with the costs of a French war, created such opposition in England that Edward was forced to confirm Magna Carta and to make other promises to avoid a rebellion at home.

Edward's policies in Wales, Scotland, and Gascony are clearly related to his legislation and administration in England. Edward could hope to become strong abroad only by being strong in England; hence his concern for quieting and eliminating the causes of tension and clamor among his English subjects. He wished always to find in England military power for the extension of his lordship beyond the borders. Thus his legislation and administration reflect his desire to bring into a proper and harmonious relationship with the Crown those classes in English society upon which his hopes depended— namely, the clergy, the landed aristocracy, and the town merchants.

Anything like a complete analysis of Edward's statutes would mean setting forth almost in its entirety the medieval English common law; and not once but repeatedly, because medieval English statutes recapitulated the laws of the realm— even the most ancient laws—in a fashion which modern jurists would label absurdly redundant. Discussion here will be limited to Edward's handling of certain deep-seated and continuing causes of grievance and complaint which he sought to remove by means of royal writs and parliamentary statutes. In this process the interests of the Crown were not neglected.[10]

ROYAL COMPROMISES WITH CLERGY,
BARONS, AND MERCHANTS

Already centuries old by the time of Edward I, the clash between priestly and civil authorities was—and remained—a

---

[10] See generally, T.F.T. Plucknett, *Legislation of Edward I* (Oxford, 1949).

continuing problem of Christian society from the late Roman Empire onward. In theory, the priestly power and the power of kings should gear together smoothly for the purposes of Christian salvation. In reality, difficulties between priestly and royal authority stemmed from the widespread acceptance of a few fundamental principles which, on occasion, have shaken all Europe. They can be briefly stated in a few oversimplified propositions for which Christian faith supplied the foundations:

First, the Christian Church is universal; its mission is nothing less than the spiritual salvation of all mankind.

Second, Christendom is one society, whatever may be the political units into which it is divided for the regulation of temporal affairs.

Third, secular rulers cooperate with the Church by policing Christendom to create a well-ordered Christian commonwealth.

Fourth, the Church of Rome administers its own affairs under the leadership of a divinely ordained monarch, the pope, who acts through a hierarchy of officials living under their own system of law, judged in their own courts, and supported by their own revenues.

This meant that the thirteenth-century Englishman lived under two authorities, one ecclesiastical, the other royal. Both claimed his obedience; both taxed him; both judged him. Moreover, adding to the complexity of Church-state relations was the fact that secular officials were members of the Church and were born into it, just as ecclesiastics, in turn, were born into the community of the realm. And this is not all. In the Middle Ages ecclesiastical and royal authorities recognized and admitted the divinely ordained character of each other and recognized that each needed the other in order to function most effectively. The royal government needed the bolstering support of the prestige, administrative experience, wealth, and educated leadership which prelates of the Church could usually supply. The Church, for its part, relied entirely on the military force and protection which only a strong monarch could provide. Thus priestly and royal powers could not avoid dealing with the same body of subjects and with each other.

Unfortunately, whatever medieval theorists might say about ideal relations between the Church and temporal rulers, the spotted actuality was always an uneasy truce or an open contest for supremacy between two evenly matched contenders for the obedience of the same persons. One does not easily dictate borderlines of jurisdiction to a supranational authority claiming a divine mandate. For a king to delimit successfully the spheres within which ecclesiastical and royal power would each function demanded the complete accord of the pope and the Church hierarchy; this was not easily obtained.

The relations of Edward I with the Church were not lacking in drama and in serious risks for the monarchy. Edward's law-making on ecclesiastical property interests began quietly enough with the Statute of Mortmain (1279), sometimes called the Statute *De Religiosis*. The intention of this statute was to prevent the Church from acquiring lands in such a way that the king and other principal lords lost feudal services and dues. In its opening lines the statute expressed a concern lest "services which are owed from fiefs of this sort, and which were originally established for the defense of the kingdom should be wrongfully withheld."[11]

A corporation could easily avoid rendering customary feudal services and payments. A corporation never rides out fully armed and prepared for battle in the service of an overlord. A corporation, civil or ecclesiastical, never dies intestate; its lands never escheat to an overlord. A corporation is never a minor heir; its lands are never administered by an overlord as a wardship. Unlike an individual, a corporation never seeks permission—or pays for permission—to marry. A corporation never dies; it never pays relief like the heir who seeks thus to reconstruct *(relever)* his ancestor's feudal contract with an overlord.

---

[11] *Statutes of the Realm*, I, 51; *S.C.*, pp. 451–52.

Edward I was the feudal overlord of the entire realm; like any other feudal overlord, he stood to lose knight services (or their monetary equivalents), escheats, wardships, marriages, and reliefs if lands fell into mortmain *(manus mortua)*, the "dead hand" of a corporation. The Statute of Mortmain served, then, the interests of the king fully as much as those of his barons. Henceforth no corporation, civil or ecclesiastical, could hold land in England except under certain conditions: a) by a grant made prior to the statute; or b) by a royal license; or c) by the authority of an act of Parliament.

The Statute of Mortmain looked backward, forcefully restating a well-established principle, certainly as old as Chapter 43 of the reissue of Magna Carta in 1217. It was aimed at preventing an ancient practice, namely, the collusive grant of a fief to a religious corporation on the understanding that the grantor might resume it again with the corporation as his new overlord. The Statute of Mortmain thus had the effect of stabilizing the number of tenures between the king and the tenant holding the fief in demesne. In this respect it was in line with a later statute, *Quia Emptores* (1290), which regulated the sale of land.[12] In general, Edward sought to prevent the addition of new rungs in the ladder of tenures.

Some years after the Statute of Mortmain, Edward acted on the numerous complaints of churchmen about royal interference in the jurisdiction of ecclesiastical courts. The king could stop a trial in an ecclesiastical court by issuing a writ of Prohibition ordering the ecclesiastical court not to proceed further with the matter.[13] But when was the writ of Prohibition justified? Edward was neither giving away any of his traditional royal prerogative nor diminishing the authority of the Crown when he issued an ordinance in 1285 assuring undisputed ecclesiastical jurisdiction over matrimonial and testamentary cases.

---

[12] *Statutes of the Realm,* I, 106; *S.C.,* pp. 473–84; S & M, *Quia Emptores,* p. 174.
[13] For the form of the writ of Prohibition, see S & M, p. 85, a translation of the Latin writ in Glanvill, XII, 22.

In the next year he went further by means of an admonishing prerogative order or writ, *Circumspecte Agatis* (1286), directing certain royal justices then on eyre in Norwich to act circumspectly when handling matters of a purely spiritual nature *(quae mere sunt spiritualia)*.[14] He defined for them what was "purely spiritual" by enumerating matters for which the Church customarily exacted a penance but for which the secular authority then had no penalty. To this list Edward also added matters touching relations between churchmen and the administration of church buildings and the adjoining churchyards. The entire document reads like royal answers to a number of specific ecclesiastical requests, and the answers are boldly hedged about with some reservations. In general, however, so long as the court Christian did not impose a pecuniary penalty to be paid to the Church, then the trial proceedings might not be stopped by royal intervention.

By *Circumspecte Agatis*, Church courts could take jurisdiction of pleas involving correction of sin, breach of faith, defamation, tithes, obventions, oblations, mortuaries, church buildings, churchyards, pensions paid by a rector to a prelate, and laying violent hands on a clergyman. Edward's writ must have been useful in its time as a means of settling disputes about ecclesiastical jurisdiction, for the writ, issued by the authority of royal prerogative, later swelled into the dignity and title of a statute.

The Statute of Mortmain regulated a thorny aspect of ecclesiastical property interests, and *Circumspecte Agatis* clarified an equally thorny matter of ecclesiastical jurisdiction. Much more hotly debated was Edward's taxation of churchmen in England. Edward insisted that the English clergy should contribute to the defense of the realm and to the costs of a war with France. Troubles with France began with fighting

---

[14] *Statutes of the Realm,* I, 101; *S.C.,* pp. 469–70, *Circumspecte Agatis*).

in the Channel between men from Normandy and men from the Cinque Ports located along the English Channel coast. The French king, Philip IV, summoned Edward to his court and after Edward's nonappearance declared forfeit the land in Gascony which Edward held as a vassal of Philip IV.

Even before a decision on war had been reached in Parliament (1294), Edward began to raise money by confiscating property. Impetuously he took all wool then in the possession of English merchants, restoring it only after a payment of from three to five marks on each sack. He also seized whatever money and treasure his agents could find in the sacristies of cathedrals and monasteries.

Thoroughly aroused by the perils of dealing simultaneously with insurgent Welshmen and the menace of an alliance between Scotland and France, Edward was in no mood for prolonged bargaining when he called together the clergy of England to ask for money. Angered by their delays in responding to his request for a grant, he was furious when he heard what the clergy proposed to give him—two-tenths of their annual revenue. He refused to accept their grant, informing them that they would either pay half their entire annual revenue or be outlawed. Edward towered so high in his rage that he terrified the ecclesiastical assembly; the dean of St. Paul's died of fright in Edward's presence.[15] The clergy, nevertheless, tried to bargain; they sought to gain some advantage, large or small, out of obedience to the extraordinary demand for money. They asked for the repeal of the Statute of Mortmain. Edward refused. A few days later a royal order went out to collect the requisition of one-half of the ecclesiastical revenue.

The next development in the taxation issue followed the arrival in England of a papal bull, *Clericis laicos* (1296), in which Pope Boniface VIII firmly declared that clergymen who paid and officials who exacted grants, taxes—whatever—would all

---

[15] Stubbs, *Constitutional History*, II, 137.

be punished by the pope. Laymen would be excommunicated and clergymen deposed if they made payments without the license of the bishop of Rome. The clergy in England were hard pressed to know whom they should obey. Archbishop Winchelsey notified Edward that papal orders clearly prevented the clergy from making a grant of any kind. A provincial council of the archdiocese of Canterbury supported Winchelsey's position. Once more Edward threatened to put the clergy of England beyond the protection of the law. Although this resulted in the capitulation of several individual clergymen, the clergy as an estate did not come to terms with Edward. He proceeded to confiscate the lay fees of the Church within the archbishopric of Canterbury.

At this stage, the whole taxation issue began to widen out so that eventually Edward had to confront not only the opposition of the clergy but that of the barons and merchants as well. Edward was high-handed with all of his subjects. He seized the wool of merchants; he ordered the collection of thousands of bushels of wheat and large supplies of beef and pork for the provisioning of an expeditionary force. In May of 1297 he called to military service all who held lands worth £20 a year. Some of the great barons asserted that they were not obliged to go to Gascony unless in the company of Edward himself and that they had no obligation whatever to go to Flanders, where Edward planned a campaign. There was talk about a confirmation of Magna Carta. But Edward's resolution was so strong that he set out for Flanders with an incomplete force, leaving behind him a regency which was soon powerless to withstand the critics of Edward's determination to carry the war to French soil. England was on the edge of another baronial rebellion.

Edward had scarcely embarked when the aggrieved clergy and barons joined to put tremendous pressures on the regent, Edward's son. They insisted on the king's confirming the Great Charter of Liberties and the Charter of the Forest, as well as his granting firm assurances that he would not in the future demand extraordinary services and money without first obtaining the consent of the community of the realm. When these requests, together with seven articles condemning Edward's recent exactions, were presented to him in Flanders, he complied without reservations. The resulting documents, *Confirmatio Cartarum* and *De Tallagio non Concendo*, reaffirmed a well-worn medieval principle: "No tallage or aid shall be levied by us or our heirs in our realm, without the good will and assent of the archbishops, bishops, earls, barons, knights, burgesses and other free men of the realm."[16]

Edward's sensible, although reluctant, compliance in confirming the charters avoided civil war in England. And the crisis was also lessened by a papal bull releasing the English clergy from their unhappy position between the demands of an imperious king and the orders of an equally imperious pope. In the bull *Etsi de statu* (1297), Boniface VIII withdrew from the position he had taken earlier in *Clericis laicos;* he qualified his earlier statement by allowing clergymen to contribute to the royal necessities in a "defensive" war. Since the Scots were then in arms on the northern border of England, the English clergy with good conscience could make grants toward royal campaigns in a defensive war.

But Edward's first confirmation of the charters was not enough to quiet all doubts about his future course of action. He was asked repeatedly to give reassurances that he would not resort to arbitrary taxation or to government without consultation and consent. Consequently, the principle of Magna Carta was confirmed in 1298, 1299, 1300, and 1301. And every

---

[16] *Statutes of the Realm*, I, 125; *S.C.*, pp. 493–94; for English translation see G. B. Adams and W. M. Stephens, *Select Documents of English Constitutional History* (New York, 1901), pp. 88–89. The *Confirmatio Cartarum*, c. 6, contains the same limitation in slightly different language; ". . . for no business from henceforth we shall take of our realm . . . aids, tasks, nor prises, but by the common consent of all the realm, and for the common profit thereof, saving the ancient aids and prises due and accustomed."

confirmation reinforced the view that the Great Charter of Liberties was part of the common law of England. In his confirmation of 1297, Edward had promised that "judges, sheriffs, mayors, and other officials who under us have to administer the law of the land shall allow the said charters in pleas before them and judgments in all their points, that is to say, the Great Charter of Liberties as common law."[17] This view was not altered by later confirmations; indeed, they only rooted Magna Carta more deeply in its fundamental position as a statement of English law.

Thus the royal taxation of the clergy, when joined with the extraordinary taxation of the merchants and demands for baronial service in Gascony, culminated in a limitation of the royal prerogative. Standing alone, or even with papal support, the clergy of England could not have established the principle that what touches all shall be decided in Parliament. The war with France brought other estates into the dispute over taxes, so that ultimately Edward was compelled to negotiate not with one estate but with representatives of the community of the realm.

The growth of the common law in the thirteenth century represents in large part the definition of established customs. In the form of writs, judicial decisions, treatises, royal ordinances, and parliamentary statutes, the common law emerged into explicit written form and formal procedure.

The forces at work to bring formal rules out of the shadowy vagueness of customary usage are not always apparent, but certain elements cannot be disregarded. For one thing, the Angevin kings of England began and maintained a splendid

---

[17] "...C'est a savoir la grande charte des franchises cume loi commune." For the text and English translation, see *S.C.*, pp. 490–93. See also C. H. McIlwain, "Magna Carta and Common Law," in *Magna Carta Commemoration Essays* (London, 1917), pp. 122–79. And see the discussion above in Chapter 2, pp. 51–55.

practice of record-keeping. It is impossible to imagine the development of the common law without the literacy of royal judges, sheriffs, commissioners, and clerks. The entire machinery of administration depended on good records and rolls.

Also, we cannot avoid mentioning the effect of controversy and dispute in the courts of England. Controversies occasionally forced a definition of the law and frequently resulted in written statements on well-kept records. When the controversy touched a large and difficult matter, the case was usually referred to the king in council to be determined by the most experienced and learned men such as the royal judges. When it was a matter affecting the community of the realm, the king called in those prelates, magnates, merchants, or others without whose counsel he was unwilling to proceed to a settlement. Ultimately, the result of a deliberation by representatives of the community of the realm might be embodied in a statute containing many chapters specifically defining the law.

If the king would not hear the discussion of grievances or petitions "in his council in his Parliament," if he would not take the counsel of prelates, magnates, and others, he ran the risk of armed rebellion in which the rebels themselves would undertake the definition of the law of the land. Controversies and rebellion produced a definition of the relations of the monarch with his people as well as definitions of their relations with each other. The records of legal development show an English populace thoroughly trained by the Angevin monarchy, which brought them to an awareness of the law of the realm and the procedures for its enforcement. In the midst of the tensions between the royal prerogative in administration and the rights of the community of the realm, the barons, the great freeholders, played a prominent part. In the following chapter we shall deal with their legal rights and obligations and their position in the medieval social order.

PART TWO
THE SOCIAL ORDER

Chapter 4

Free Tenures and
Their Obligations

The common law of England developed in a stratified society thoroughly accustomed to a hierarchy of classes and the property interests ordinarily associated with them. Medieval royal judges were always interested in the status of a litigant appearing before them, because the common law maintained a sharp distinction between "free" and "unfree." After the middle of the twelfth century the Crown had a monopoly over all cases involving freehold tenure.[1]

Although tenure and status did not always go together, the relationship was a potential factor in any civil action. Even in the administration of criminal justice there was a distinction between tenures. Most of the class distinctions of medieval England had their foundations in the institutions of feudalism and were not, of course, peculiar to England. Indeed, over all of Latin Christendom men of the twelfth century recognized the status and privileges of the free classes—especially those of the military aristocracy and of the clergy—who were largely supported by the labor of the agricultural workers, the peasants.

---

[1] Glanvill, *Tractatus de legibus et consuetudinibus regni Angliae*, ed. G. E. Woodbine (New Haven, 1932), I, 1, 2.

THE THEORY OF THE BODY POLITIC

Social thought throughout the Middle Ages adhered with incredible persistence to an organic theory of social classes. Each class performed a function contributing to the well-being of the entire society. This theory, clearly stated in John of Salisbury's *Policraticus* (Book V, Chapter 2),[2] actually continues to appear in other literature from the twelfth century well into the nineteenth.

The main argument of John of Salisbury is fairly simple. The state is more than an aggregate of persons; it is a kind of organism. Just as the body in good health depends on the harmonious action of many parts, so does the social order. The clergy are its spirit, or soul, having predominance over the whole body. The monarch is the head providing direction. The military class corresponds to the arms and hands, providing defense. The tillers of the soil are like the lower limbs and the feet "ever cleaving to the ground"; the peasants, like the feet, support the weight of the whole body, keep it erect, and enable it to move.

The remarks of John of Salisbury about the functions of the professional soldier are relevant to a discussion of common-law rules touching free tenures. In his *Policraticus* (Book VI, Chapter 8), this humanist and churchman sets forth a list of obligations tinged by contemporary ideals of chivalry. The man-at-arms should protect the Church, revere the clergy, defend the poor, maintain peace, carry out the decrees of judges "wherein each man follows not his own judgment but that of the angels of God and of men from the dictates of equity and the public weal. . . . It is the office of the judges to pronounce sentence, in like manner also it is the duty of these men [the military class] to execute it. . . ."[3] In this same chapter

---

[2] John of Salisbury, *Policraticus*, trans. C.C.J. Webb, 2 vols. (Oxford, 1909), II, 22–23.

[3] Ibid.

John of Salisbury also suggests, in a rather vague but note-worthy way, that the military class has a general responsibility for maintaining the laws against their abuse by the monarch. This idea was to be fully expanded by Bracton in the thirteenth century. But John of Salisbury merely comments that "if very little freedom is allowed to the supreme power, nevertheless, he that presides over the laws is subject to no man and should be more closely guarded from that which is unlawful."

There are good reasons for selecting John of Salisbury as the spokesman for social theory in twelfth-century England. He was often at the court of King Henry II, where he represented the humanistic learning of his day, and he died as the bishop of Chartres, where the cathedral school was noted as a great center of learning. Beyond question, John of Salisbury was in the main current of the thought of his time. And he was not quickly forgotten. When the English barons, headed by Simon de Montfort and Roger Bigod, expelled foreign prelates in the crisis of 1258, they justified their action in a letter to the pope by quoting John of Salisbury, saying that the state should be an organic unity and that harmony should reign between the members of a body.[4] Not long after this, the anonymous author of the *Song of Lewes* also employed the metaphor of the har-monious functioning of organs of the body in the course of explaining views of the barons who were then in rebellion against Henry III.

Whenever men in the Middle Ages called for social reform and for justice, they were apt to invoke the organic theory of society by demanding that each class, each part of the "body politic," should serve the commonweal. Not until the sev-enteenth century did such reformers as the Levellers in En-gland seriously criticize the class structure and the property interests and obligations associated with it. Before the sev-

---

[4] Frederick Hertz, *Nationality in History and Politics* (Humanities, 1944), p. 288, n. 2.

enteenth century, social criticism was aimed principally at selfishness and lack of responsibility on the part of men who failed to perform the functions expected of their class. In the view of such critics as William Langland, John Gower, and Geoffrey Chaucer in the fourteenth century and John Hales and Thomas Cranmer in the sixteenth century, the commonweal consisted of classes mutually dependent upon one another, and the commonweal would thrive only so long as each class properly met its obligations to the others.

SOCIAL THEORY AND LEGAL DEVELOPMENT

Links between social theory and the law are not difficult to find. Ideas of justice and equity are closely connected with what men feel they have an obligation to do, and the sense of obligation can involve unwritten rules of customary social behavior as well as formal law. Whenever customary behavior is challenged or violated, the ensuing controversy may easily produce a written statement of a rule or law controlling future social behavior; thus the customary obligation becomes transformed into an explicit legal obligation enforced by the courts.[5] Social theories such as those expressed by John of Salisbury reveal an awareness of social conditions and customs which "ought to be," as well as an awareness of customs already in existence. The *Policraticus* is in no sense a law book, but it indicates what an educated man of the twelfth century might think about the obligations of clergymen, monarchs, judges and councilors, professional soldiers, and many more, including the cultivators of the soil. From the *Policraticus* to formal legal declarations about obligations and duties is not a long step.

---

[5] These links between moral obligation and legal obligation have been treated in masterly fashion by H.L.A. Hart in his book, *The Concept of Law* (1961). Professor Hart's analysis is particularly useful for the historian of the medieval common law who confronts the evolution of formal legal rules out of customary social rules.

SOCIAL THEORY, CHRISTIAN DOCTRINE,
AND THE *POLITICS* OF ARISTOTLE

Before leaving medieval social theory to proceed with a discussion of the various tenures recognized by the medieval common law, it may be useful to examine an apparent contradiction between medieval social theory and Christian doctrine. Was John of Salisbury inconsistent when he advocated a society of classes? Can a society of sharply divided classes be reconciled with Christian teaching about the inestimable worth of each individual soul? Did not Christianity teach that all men are sons of God and brothers in Christ? Can a social theory of classes be reconciled with the teaching that all persons are equal in the sight of God?

To grasp medieval answers to such questions one must put aside ideas of social reform advocated since the French Revolution and the Industrial Revolution; medieval concepts of justice or early Christian social teachings may appear strange from a modern perspective. The social thought of the Apostolic Age did not lack a doctrine of the bond uniting all men in a common humanity, nor did it lack a doctrine of the grace of God appearing to all men. Nevertheless, the New Testament also contains a tough-minded acceptance of the fact that people differ in sex, age, wealth, social position, authority, and responsibility. Some are masters, others are servants; some are Jews, others are Gentiles; some are Greeks, others barbarian; some are bond, others are free—"the body is one, and hath many members" (I Cor. 12:12). And though all mankind might be and should be united in religious faith, even then, servants should obey their masters—and masters should be just and fair to their servants. The social teachings of the New Testament propose no sharp alteration in the class structure; rather they demand charity, consideration, kindness, and tact from those who are in power, and obedience, respect, and cheerful service from those who are subject to authority. The amelioration of the class structure in this world—the here and now—was not the primary thrust of New Testament social doctrine. The Christian writers of the Apostolic Age believed that the only ultimate justice was to be dispensed in eternity.[6]

If the drama of salvation in eternity was the great theme of Christian literature before the nineteenth century, then we should not expect John of Salisbury or John Gower or any other medieval commentator on the social order of his time to go farther than the New Testament writers to whom they probably looked for instruction. Modern social values and modern ideas about the purpose of human life disagree with those of the Middle Ages, but medieval Christian social commentators cannot be accused of inconsistency when they urge that each class should do its proper tasks. The Christian of the Middle Ages was neither a hypocrite nor a crooked thinker if he accepted a social order of sharply defined classes. A society of classes did not upset his ideas about the chief end of man.

Recovery of the complete writings of Aristotle by twelfth-century scholars in Latin Christendom could only bolster ideas of class divisions and the preeminence of the professional military class. In his *Politics*, Aristotle assumed that every viable political community contains classes of men performing different functions essential for the life of the community. "A state," he observed, "is not a mere aggregate of persons, but a union of them sufficing for the purposes of life. . . . There must be husbandmen to procure food and artisans and a warlike and a wealthy class, and priests and judges to decide what is just and expedient" (VII, 9). In a section immediately following this, Aristotle goes on to remark that "it is no new or recent discovery of political philosophers that the state ought to be divided into classes and that the warriors ought to be divided from the

---

[6] The New Testament abounds in clues about social ideas and obligations; the following are illustrative: I Corinthians 7:22 and 24; 12:13–14; Ephesians 6:5–8; Colossians 3:10–11; 4:1; I Timothy 6:1; Titus 2:9; I Peter 2:17–18; 3:8; Romans 10:12; 12:4; 13:7.

husbandmen." Equality, for Aristotle, merely consists in the same treatment of similar persons (VII, 14).

FEUDALISM: LORD AND VASSAL

Having noted that the medieval English common law divided all society into two groups, "free" and "unfree," it is time to examine free tenures and their obligations. This leads directly into the world of feudalism and its rules of social relationships and property, which left a permanent mark on the English law of Property.

Much scholarly ink has been spilled on the relationships within feudalism. Any account of feudalism, however full and detailed, will fail to describe with precision the rich variety of relationships created over a period of several centuries in widely separated parts of Europe. No historian has yet found the typical fief for feudalism, just as no one is likely to find a typical manor for manorialism. The term "feudalism" is so imprecise that at least two eminent English legal historians would gladly abolish it.[7] Yet, until a better term emerges, modern historians must accept "feudalism" with all of its vagueness. Like medieval lawyers, one must generalize, as best he can, about the crazy quilt patterns of medieval relations between lord and vassal.

Feudalism in Europe developed over a very long period during which central governments were powerless to meet problems of defense and to maintain order. Late Carolingian rulers of the ninth and tenth centuries resembled brothers quarreling about the ownership of a field while their neighbors were lighting grass fires all over it. During the ninth and tenth centuries Europe suffered repeated raids: Norsemen came to the

---

[7] H. G. Richardson and G. O. Sayles, *The Governance of Mediaeval England* (Aldine, 1963), p. 30.

coasts and river valleys in long ships; Magyars rode their small horses out of the grasslands of central Asia; Muslim pirates crossed the Mediterranean from Africa to pillage the shores of France and Italy. Destructive raiders struck deep and unpredictably into the heart of Europe. Their hit-and-run tactics, employed by small forces, meant that each locality had to defend itself as best it could.

Under these frightening conditions, men turned helplessly to a strong patron, a lord, a defender, someone who could provide land for subsistence and security in time of danger. Such a man might have a few experienced fighters at his command. He controlled one or more primitive but useful strongholds, fortified by an encircling moat and earthworks surmounted by a palisade. Understandably enough, in the iron age of feudalism the principal military figure of a locality would easily assume certain political powers over the lands and people of the countryside which he undertook to defend. Although he might not take the title of king, being content with that of count or duke, he would administer justice according to the custom of the locality, collect taxes, and possibly treat with neighboring lords like a sovereign authority.

In a period of terrible insecurity, feudalism sprang up among the ruins of the Carolingian empire as a substitute for strong central government. Power came into the hands of great families which might trace their descent from a warrior renowned for his resistance to "foreign" raiders. The feudal lord, whatever his title, became linked to the people of his locality by several ties—personal, proprietary, and political. Consequently, it is possible to view feudalism as a system of personal relationships between lord and vassal, or as a system of land tenure, or as a system involving the wide distribution of political powers ordinarily exercised by kings or emperors.

The personal relationships between lord and vassal were at the very heart of other institutions. Modern connotations of the word "vassal" create a hurdle which must be cleared away to get at the medieval meaning of the word. In modern usage, "vassal" has a melancholy sound implying someone completely subservient, almost a slave. But in the Middle Ages vassalage was entirely honorable and entirely voluntary, a relationship between members of the nobility. Even a king might accept vassalage without impairing his dignity and title. A king might voluntarily place himself in the position of vassal, as did John during negotiations with Pope Innocent III. Note the voluntary element in vassalage. It cannot be emphasized too strongly that the man who may choose his lord is a free man. The man who may travel at will or work at will is free. He may be poor in land and wealth, but he is free. The system worked both ways: just as there was no compulsion on any man to become a vassal, there was no compulsion on a lord to accept the homage of a man who was displeasing to him.

Tacitus, the Roman historian, described the Germanic custom of a free warrior attaching himself to fight and, if need be, to die in the company of an admired chieftain. Unquestionably, the custom of the early German *comitatus* persisted into later centuries among the Germanic peoples who invaded and settled in the Roman Empire. The Anglo-Saxon *thegns* of a later time were not unlike the companions of a Germanic chieftain of the age of Tacitus. Among Frankish peoples, particularly in the Carolingian period (the eighth and ninth centuries), we begin to hear of vassals and vassalage. Vassals are, above all, skilled men-at-arms, trusted agents of the king.

Twelfth- and thirteenth-century custom expressed the honorable personal relationship with formal ceremony symbolizing an agreement of the greatest importance. Carl Stephenson, a modern American scholar, has noted how influential the ideals of vassalage remained in the vernacular literature of medieval France. "Almost invariably," he wrote, "the action in the *chansons de geste* turns upon the mutual faith of lord and vassal or, conversely, upon the failure of one to do all that he should for the other."[8] If men who listened attentively to the

---

[8] Carl Stephenson, *Medieval Feudalism* (Ithaca, 1942), p. 21.

epic poetry of the *Song of Roland* genuinely believed that loyalty to one's lord, good faith, and trust were admirable qualities, it follows that for them treachery and disloyalty to one's lord were the greatest of crimes. When feudalism was at full tide, it was clearly much more than a system of providing legal title in land; indeed, the sense of mutual personal obligation beween lord and vassal may have been even more essential than the granting of fiefs in return for promises of services. At any rate, homage and fealty always preceded a grant of land to a vassal.

Rendering homage and swearing fealty were parts of a solemn public ceremony. The free man wishing to become the vassal of a lord appeared unarmed and bareheaded in the presence of the lord. Kneeling before his lord, he placed his hands between those of his lord. Next, with formal oath he swore fealty, promising that he would be faithful to his lord against all other men. Then the lord, in equally solemn words, accepted the homage, raised the vassal to his feet and kissed him.

Once the lord-vassal relationship had been established, there remained the matter of providing property or livelihood for the vassal. The lord might promise to pay a certain sum out of money then at his disposal. But when land was more abundant than money, the vassal usually received a fief, a grant of land, to be held by the tenure of military service or of knight service. Again, there might be a symbolic act, an act of investiture by the lord, who would place in the hands of the vassal, the feoffee, a bowl of earth or a small bundle of twigs, something representing the fief and the transfer of seisin from lord to vassal. An even stronger claim to the fief might be established by taking the vassal to the land and there putting him in possession, in seisin, which meant that the vassal would be "seated" on the land, in a position to live there, to enjoy its revenues and produce, and to collect its services and rents as the tenant of a freehold.

The vassal expected to find peasant cultivators already at

work on his fief, for without people to till the soil, a fief would be useless to a vassal. His profession was war, not agriculture. Even if a tenant by military service had been willing to cultivate the soil with ox team, plough, and spade, his duties to his lord would have interfered with agriculture. In medieval society a vassal was not a man with a hoe; rather, a vassal was a free man-at-arms.

TENURE BY KNIGHT SERVICE AND ITS OBLIGATIONS

Assuming that a twelfth-century English lord had granted a vassal a knight's fee, what were the mutual obligations of lord and vassal? So long as the vassal performed his services faithfully, the lord was obliged to protect him and warrant him in the undisturbed enjoyment of seisin of the lands granted. Furthermore, the lord maintained a court for the administration of justice for his vassals. Land, protection, justice, and honorable treatment—these were the far from insignificant obligations of the lord under the feudal contract.

The vassal's obligations were more detailed and were subject to agreements so various that generalizing is dangerous. But foremost among the vassal's duties was that of military service at his own expense for a period of perhaps forty days each year and for a longer period if the lord assumed the expenses of military campaigning. Medieval knights used equipment beyond the financial means of all but a few. Probably the knight's armor, weapons, and trained war-horse were as far beyond the reach of a medieval peasant as a modern tank and its guns are beyond the means of a twentieth-century factory worker. The bit, bridle, reins, breastplate, saddle, and stirrups for the war-horse; the long hauberk, or shirt of mail, welded links of iron over a leather base; the conical helmet with nose piece; the metal-covered shield; the iron-tipped lance; and the long, cross-hilted sword were all necessary for the fully armed knight. And to fight well with them required strength, skill, and practice. Thus the vassal's obligation to do service annually for forty days in the field or possibly for three months in a castle garrison was no small consideration under the feudal contract.

The holder of a knight's fee owed to his lord much more than military service. He must attend his lord's court and occasionally pay sums of money. Certain events in the life of a feudal lord involved exceptional expenses toward which the vassal was asked to contribute. When the lord's eldest son attained the age of twenty-one, vassals were expected to contribute an "aid" for the ceremony of knighthood. When the lord's eldest daughter married, vassals were expected to contribute to her dowry. If the lord were taken captive and held for ransom, his vassals owed a contribution toward the ransom sum. Should the lord and his household visit the vassal's fief, the vassal must offer hospitality. Should the lord need supplies, the vassal must sell them at a reasonable price. And every vassal and lord knew that when the vassal died the fief was still expected to produce services.

When a vassal died leaving a son under age, the lord would assume wardship of the minor heir and also wardship of the fief. Until the heir came of age, the lord was under obligation to provide for his upbringing and training for the profession of arms. By being placed in the household of a nobleman, the young man could observe the etiquette of his class and at the same time learn how to manage a horse and how to use sword, lance, and shield. During the wardship of the fief, the lord expected to get enough money from it to employ, if need be, a landless, mercenary knight. These men were always in abundant supply, for younger sons were more numerous than the fiefs available. The lord of a wardship had a valuable property right which he might sell to the highest bidder, who would be thereafter the guardian of the heir.

Suppose that a vassal died leaving only a widow or a marriageable daughter. The lord again had a source of revenue. He might sell to the highest bidder the privilege of marrying the widow or the daughter. Moreover, there was always the chance that the lord might obtain money from a widow who wished to live without a husband and would pay handsomely to avoid marriage with a man chosen by the overlord. Either way, the fief contributed to the financial strength of the lord. When an heir came of age, he was allowed, after Magna Carta at least, to have his inheritance without paying relief or any other offering or composition, the assumption being that the guardian of the inheritance had already taken enough during the wardship. It was quite otherwise if a vassal died leaving an heir of an age to inherit immediately. Such a man was expected to pay, according to his status, what amounted to an inheritance tax. Again Magna Carta made a specific regulation:

> If the heir is of full age he shall have his inheritance for the ancient relief: namely, the heir or heirs of an earl £100 for a whole barony of an earl; the heir or heirs of a baron £100 for a whole barony; the heir or heirs of a knight 100s at most for a whole knight's fee. And let whoever owes less give less, according to the ancient custom of fiefs.[9]

RESULTS OF SUBINFEUDATION

Chapter after chapter of Magna Carta makes clear the concern of the English barons to regulate and protect the incidents of tenure by military service: wardship, marriage, and relief. Long after men of this class began to pay scutage, a money payment in lieu of rendering personal service in the field, they clung to the dignity of tenure by military service and to the occasional opportunities this tenure afforded them as lords to secure substantial payments from their own vassals. The legislation of Edward I did nothing to weaken feudalism as a system of land

[9] On these points, and Magna Carta generally, see the excellent commentary by W. S. McKechnie, *Magna Carta, A Commentary on the Great Charter of King John with an Historical Introduction* (Glasgow, 1905).

tenure; on the contrary, it seems to have strengthened it at a time when in all of England there were apparently only about five hundred feudal tenants who were fighting knights ready to serve in the wars of Edward I. By the close of the thirteenth century the Crown no longer expected the feudal class to make up the armies it would put into the field. However, it continued to look to the feudal landlords for military officers and men who could assist in the administration of justice. During the reign of Edward, the knights of the shire, as men of property acquainted with public affairs, became, possibly, more valuable to the Crown in the shire courts than on the battlefield. Tenure by knight service did not provide either the men or the money necessary for all of the military necessities of the realm; subinfeudation had corroded the effectiveness of the feudal class as a national military force. The mutual obligations of one lord and one vassal are complicated enough, but the whole problem of building a national military force on feudal tenures becomes even more complicated when we consider this process of subinfeudation, by which a vassal himself grants land to men who in turn become his vassals. Subinfeudation splintered fiefs into fractions, and long chains of tenure obscured the responsibilities of the tenants to their overlords. Take a specific case in the reign of Edward I:

> Roger of St. German holds land at Paxton in Huntingdonshire of Robert of Bedford, who holds of Richard of Ilchester, who holds of Alan of Chartres, who holds of William le Boteler, who holds of Gilbert Neville, who holds of Devorguil Balliol, who holds of the king of Scotland, who holds of the king of England.[10]

For another example we have the subinfeudation of half a knight's fee:

> In Redmarley, a hamlet in Worcestershire, there was half a knight's fee which Adam of Redmarley holds of John son of Geof-

[10] P & M, I, 233.

frey, John of William of Beauchamp, William of Beauchamp of William de la Mare, William de la Mare of the earl of Gloucester, the earl of the lord king.[11]

Theoretically, it should have been possible for each baron who held lands from the Crown to know exactly how much knight service he owed to the king. Theoretically, the process of subinfeudation did not destroy the power of the lands of a barony to produce knight service at the royal summons. But, in fact, when men began to hold by long chains of tenure a twentieth of a knight's fee or a fortieth of a knight's fee, their obligations were difficult to calculate exactly. The commutation of service to scutage might help, but it could not entirely solve the difficulty. If a scutage of two pounds were levied on the knight's fee, then, in theory at least, each tenant by military service knew his obligations and would pay even if he owed no more than a shilling. And the Crown endeavored to make the commutation system operate. It was inevitable, however, that ultimately taxation for military purposes would have to rest on another base. By the middle of the thirteenth century there were tenants who did not know how much service they owed:

> The muster roll of 1245 contains many examples of tenants who stated that they did not know how much service they owed to the king. . . . In 1285 it was stated that the service due from Belvoir . . . was unknown; in 1303 the jury said that the number of knights who should appear for the barony of Tattershall, Lincs., was not known; and when Gilbert de Gant, Lord of Folkingham, Lincs., died in 1274 the only information in the inquisition was that the lands were held by the duty of going with the king to the army for three weeks.[12]

The English barons as well as Edward I would support the Statute of *Quia Emptores* to prevent further growth of the

---

[11] A. L. Poole, *Obligations of Society in the XII*[th] *and XIII*[th] *Centuries* (Oxford, 1946), p. 5.

[12] I. J. Sanders, *Feudal Military Service* (Oxford, 1956), p. 72.

festoons and thickets of tenure already created by subinfeudation.[13] As a system of land tenure, feudalism was too
deeply rooted to be seriously modified, even by such a powerful king as Edward I. There is no evidence that he attempted to
undermine it; rather, his legislation endeavored to make feudal
tenures manageable for Crown and baronage alike. Although
tenure by knight service had long ceased to be the most effective source of military power in the realm, it endured for centuries after the reign of Edward I. Not until the Restoration was
this institution abolished in the course of seventeenth-century
reforms.[14]

There were other "free" tenures—sergeanty, socage, burgage, and frankalmoin—but no neat, well-ordered hierarchy of
free tenures existed. Rather, the common-law courts dealt with
a variety of free tenures and expected that one man could hold
several of them concurrently. Information about tenure and its
accompanying services can assist only in determining whether
a man was free or unfree in the Middle Ages. His exact position
in the social hierarchy is more difficult to establish. One case
should make further elaboration on this point unnecessary:

> On the day of his death in 1286 Sir Robert de Aguilon . . . held
> lands at Greatham in Hampshire of the king at a rent of 18s.; he
> held lands at Hoo in Kent of the abbot of Reading at a money rent;
> he held lands at Crofton in Buckinghamshire of William de Say by
> some service that the jurors do not know; he held a manor in
> Norfolk of the bishop of Norwich by the service of a sixth part of a
> knight's fee and by castle-guard; he held a manor in Sussex of the
> earl of Warenne by the service of one knight; he held a manor in
> Hertfordshire of the king in chief by the serjeanty of finding a
> foot-soldier for forty days; he held tenements in London of the
> king in chief socage and could bequeath them as chattels.[15]

---

[13] Plucknett, *Legislation of Edward I* (Oxford, 1949), pp. 102–104.
[14] *Statutes of the Realm*, 12 Car. II (1660), Chapter 24.
[15] P & M, I, 296, citing the *Liber de Antiquis Legibus*, pp. lxxi–lxxvi.

Obviously Robert de Aguilon was a free man, a tenant-in-chief of the king. He was also a tenant by payment of money rents, a tenant by knight service, a tenant by sergeanty service, and the holder of several socage tenures in London. But how should he be classified in the social order—as leaseholder, feudal knight, sergeant, or burgess? The complexity of property interests in this instance makes it unwise to insist on a rigid formula equating any one of the several free tenures with social position or status. The property interests of Robert de Aguilon and of others like him suggest that by the end of the thirteenth century in England men were thinking about freehold tenures as forms of wealth to be accumulated in any profitable combination.

TENURE BY SERGEANTY

Every interest in land in the Middle Ages carried with it an accompanying obligation of services or payments to a grantor of the interest. In fact, a lord usually granted land to obtain the tenant's services; this was true of both free and unfree tenures. What, then, were the distinguishing obligations of tenure by sergeanty?

Tenure by sergeanty seems to have been a grant of land in return for the performance of some *special* service. It might have been an occasional service—cooking a dinner when the king hunted in a certain forest or holding the king's head when he crossed the Channel—the special services were unbelievably diverse. Maitland used the word "servantship" to describe the servient character of sergeanty; in his opinion this was the essential element. One may accept Maitland's views and still believe that sergeanty eluded Maitland's powers of analysis. No one can describe clearly a tenure which in one instance may resemble tenure by knight service and in another instance may resemble the tenure called socage; sergeanty is cloudy. The heterogeneous services of medieval sergeants make amazing reading, and the only way to understand this tenure is to look at examples of it.

We learn that "Henry II enfeoffed Boscher, his servant, with the manor of Bericote in Warwickshire with a mill and pertinences worth £5 a year by the light service of keeping a white hound with red ears and delivering it to the king at the end of the year and receiving another puppy to rear."[16] The manor of Bericote and the mill may sound like lavish rewards for the keeping of a hunting dog, but if they were worth no more than £5 a year, then sergeant Boscher received something between 3d. or 4d. a day—about the same wage as that of the hearthman, a servant in the royal household, who built the fire in the hall and received 4d. a day.[17]

Other sergeanty service was merely occasional or annual. For example, a certain Rolland, sergeant and tenant of Hemingstone, rendered annually in the king's presence on Christmas Day what must have been entirely unpredictable clowning as festive service for a freehold.[18] Few sergeants, when performing their services, depended as heavily as Rolland on their extraordinary natural talents. Much more common were the huntsmen, falconers, tailors, and ushers who held lands by sergeanty.

A man could hold two tenures by sergeanty for performing two different services. A royal falconer, Henry, son of Henry de la Wade, received his land at Stanton for keeping the king's falcons. He was also on occasion the king's cook and received another sergeanty at Bletchingdon for the service of preparing a dinner of roast pork when the king hunted in Wychwood forest.[19] Kennelman, buffoon, falconer, cook—all had free tenures by sergeanty.

---

[16] A. L. Poole, *Obligations of Society*, p. 62, citing *Book of Fees*, p. 1278.

[17] D. M. Stenton, *English Society in the Early Middle Ages* (Penguin, 1952), p. 27.

[18] *Debuit facere die Natali Domini singulis annis coram domino rege unum saltum et siffletum et unum bumbulum* (Make a leap, a whistle, and a fart), A. L. Poole, *Obligations of Society*, p. 66; citing *Book of Fees*, pp. 136, 386, 1174, 1218.

[19] A. L. Poole, *Obligations of Society*, p. 69; citing *Book of Fees*, pp. 103, 253, 1374, 1397.

There were also sergeants who were obliged to render military service for forty days in the field, equipped with horse, doublet, steel cap, and lance. It may have required a very keen eye indeed to distinguish the sergeants from the knights when a mingled group rode together along a highway. By the close of the thirteenth century the services of two sergeants were equated with the service of one knight;[20] at this point "servantship" clearly begins to impinge on another tenure and to lose any distinctive quality.

Lacking a readily identifiable character, tenure by sergeanty suffered badly in the general decline of feudalism, but it may have disappeared for another reason. The partitioning of sergeanties made the services increasingly difficult to collect. Theoretically and logically, neither the alienation nor the partitioning of a sergeanty could be accomplished. In theory one could as readily partition a soap-bubble as a sergeanty—but in fact it was done! Logically one cannot divide the service of being a huntsman or falconer or cook without destroying the service. Little more than a rent payment could be expected from a sergeanty partitioned; certainly servantship could not be obtained. A royal inquiry between 1246 and 1250 revealed that in one case a small sergeanty—that of Richard of Pirie in Cirencester—had been broken into no less than twenty-four particles.[21] If Richard of Pirie's tenure was splintered into so many pieces and if others were changing into money rents, then sergeanty was becoming merely a name, a vestige of another time. The future lay not with sergeanty but with socage tenure. The humblest and vaguest of all free tenures, it survived to swallow up the others.

SOCAGE AND BURGAGE TENURES

Socage tenure, in particular, has drawn vital force over the centuries from a medieval legal doctrine rooted deep in the

[20] M. Powicke, *The Thirteenth Century: 1216–1307* (Oxford, 1953), p. 548.

[21] *Book of Fees*, pp. 1188, 1248f.; E. G. Kimball, *Sergeanty Tenure* (1936), pp. 229ff.; A. L. Poole, *Obligations of Society*, p. 76.

English legal system by the Norman and Angevin kings. Norman kingship left a permanent mark on the English law of Property by imposing the concept of the king as supreme landlord of the realm. All property title, consequently, in one fashion or another derives ultimately from the Crown. And it plainly follows that every man of property in England has a lord from whom he holds; logically enough, the English common law recognized no allodial lands; all land in England was held by dependent tenure of one sort or another. Under their Norman and Angevin monarchs, Englishmen had every opportunity to grasp the maxim: "No land without its lord." Whatever may have been the concepts of tenure in England before the Norman Conquest, the conquerors systematized them and brought every real property interest under the control of a simple formula: "Z holds that land of the lord king."[22]

With the waning of knight service and sergeanty as living institutions, the residual tenure proved to be socage. This may be surprising, for it is the most humble and also one of the most ancient of tenures. In origin socage is the tenure of free tillers of the soil obliged to render payments in money or in agricultural labor such as ploughing the lord's demesne. The *sokemen* of the eleventh century lived among the tenants in villeinage; they were men of the village and of the cultivated fields, not men of the castle or the manor house. They held their land freely but without the incidental financial burdens of military tenure. Much later on we find socage tenure mentioned in Magna Carta (Chapter 37), along with fee farm and burgage tenure, which it closely resembled.

For all of its subsequent and present importance, socage tenure in the Middle Ages can be described only in terms of what it was not. Socage tenure was not military, it was not spiritual, it was not servient. Furthermore, it was not burdened by scutage, wardship, or marriage. It was not restricted to a certain class or occupation. The tenant by socage might hold

---

[22] P & M, I, 232, *Z tenet terram illam de . . . domino Rege.*

directly from the king or from the humblest lord. He might pay a nominal or a very heavy rent. Socage tenure possessed the merit of being adaptable and flexible, preserving the concept of dependent tenure, while permitting a wide variety of rent payments in kind, in money, or even in managerial agricultural services. Moreover, it was a free tenure without stigma, and it was inheritable. For all of these reasons it thrived throughout the history of real property interests. What was true in the Middle Ages is even more true in the twentieth century. Socage tenure has outdistanced all other tenures and since 1925 has become predominant in England.[23]

To go beyond the most general statements about burgage tenure would quickly lead into particular borough customs and away from our main subject, the common law. In England, as elsewhere in medieval Europe, the town-dweller wished to be justiciable only in his own town court. This was a notable privilege, frequently granted by charter, and it opened the way to the growth of many local variations in customs and procedures. Once established, the local borough customs might place holders of burgage tenements beyond the applications of uniform rules of common law administered by the royal courts.[24] The localism inherent in borough charters can be seen early, in the grant by Henry I to the citizens of London in the twelfth century. Among other things, they are to have

> a justice, whomsoever they please from among themselves, to keep the pleas of my crown and to try them, and no other man is to be justice over the said men of London. And the citizens shall not be impleaded in any plea outside the walls of the city.... And with regard to lands ... I will on their behalf maintain justice according to the law of the city.[25]

[23] See the modern legislation in the Law of Property Act (1925), the Settled Land Act (1925), the Administration of Estates Act (1925), and the Land Registration Act (1925).

[24] P & M, I, 295.

[25] S & M, pp. 62–63; on borough customs generally see Mary Bateson, *Borough Customs*, Selden Society, Vols. 18 and 21 (1904–6), and A. Ballard and J. Tait, *British Borough Charters*, 1216–1307 (1923).

The twelfth-century charter of Newcastle-on-Tyne also granted the burgesses immunity from pleas outside the borough with the exception of pleas of the Crown. Felonious crimes—treason, murder, arson, rape, highway robbery, and forgery—were always justiciable before a royal court. In Newcastle, a charter states:

> Pleas that arise in the borough [of Newcastle] must be held and settled there, except those which are crown pleas. If any burgess is accused in any case, he shall not plead outside the borough except through default of [justice in the borough] court. . . . a burgess may give or sell his land and freely and quietly go whither he pleases, unless a [legal] claim stands against him.[26]

Although Thomas Littleton in his authoritative treatise on tenures (first published in 1481) discussed burgage as a separate tenure, it would be quite proper, according to more modern authority, to classify it "as a special variety of socage, used where the tenants were the members of a corporation."[27] Magna Carta (Chapter 37) mentioned burgage tenure as a separate tenure without providing clues about its distinctive character, and Littleton warned his reader that "for the greater part . . . boroughs have divers customs and usages, which be not had in other towns."[28] While heeding this warning about diversity, we can point to one feature of burgage tenure which seems to distinguish it more than any other, namely, the right freely to sell it, give it, mortgage it, lease it, or dispose of it by last will and testament as readily as if it were a chattel.

FRANKALMOIN TENURE

During the twelfth and thirteenth centuries Church corporations frequently acquired land by the tenure of free alms

---

26 S & M, pp. 64–65.
27 Thomas Littleton, *Tenures*, Book II, X, sec. 165.
28 W. S. McKechnie, *Magna Carta* (Glasgow, 1905), pp.69–70.

(libera elemosina), or frankalmoin. Some service was expected in return for the grant, but it was usually a spiritual service, not secular—possibly prayers for the souls of the donor and his family—and it was indefinite and difficult to enforce. Sometimes, however, the donor specified an enforceable condition. For example, he might state that if he changed from the profession of arms and wished to become a monk, the monastery having earlier received his gift should also receive him.

The formula describing a gift "in free, pure, and perpetual alms" implied that the tenant owed no secular service to the grantor. But here as elsewhere one generalizes about tenures at his peril; exceptions rise up to weaken general statements. For example, a certain Ralph, son of William of Adewich, granting land to a monastery, began by saying that he gave to the monks of Kirkstall, "for the love of God and the safety of my soul," half a carucate of land (about thirty acres) in Bessacar, "in pure and perpetual alms free and quit of all earthly service and secular exaction." Then the donor blandly proceeded in the next sentence to contradict himself by setting out the specific and unquestionably earthly and secular terms of the gift:

> by rendering to me and my heirs annually for all service, eight shillings, four at Pentecost and four at the feast of St. Martin. And be it known that the monks shall do the forinsec service which belongs to half a carucate of land where twelve carucates make the fee of one knight.[29]

It is not clear what Ralph was trying to accomplish in this grant, but it may represent an effort to secure revenue from property while escaping from the services he previously owed to his overlord.

Ordinarily tenure in free alms gave control over the land to Church courts and to no others. Thus land which was unquestionably held by frankalmoin tenure lay beyond the jurisdic-

---

[29] A. L. Poole, *Obligations of Society*, p. 6; quoting W. Farrer, *Early Yorkshire Charters*, II, 165.

tion of the royal courts and the rules of common law. For obvious reasons no incidents of wardship, marriage, or relief could be obtained from the Church. Small wonder then that Edward I was concerned, as we have noted, to limit gifts of land to the Church, lest services "owed from fiefs . . . originally established for the defence of the kingdom should be wrongfully withheld."[30] The statutory limitation of grants to the Church could not alter, of course, the character of already existing grants lying beyond the reach of new legislation.

FREEHOLD AS A LEGAL CONCEPT

Confronting a welter of services rendered in a feudal age, the royal courts of England made a great division between "free" and "unfree" property interests. Within the free tenures there gradually appeared several categories only roughly defined by the services. The twelfth and thirteenth centuries were a period of definition and systematization in many fields, of which the law was one. The categories of tenure were defined then and became fixed for centuries. The concept of the greatest importance for the modern reader is probably that of freehold tenure as something apart from another form of tenure which was unfree. This division between free and unfree is entirely foreign to modern doctrines of property; yet the medieval distinctions managed to survive well into the twentieth century.

The doctrine of freehold tenure had its origins in the period when feudalism was much more than a system of land tenure. For at least a hundred years after the Norman invasion of England, the Norman and Angevin monarchs actually based their power on their tenants-in-chief and on the knight service of their great vassals, their magnates, whose prowess in arms was not then to be matched by any other group or class within the English realm. The well-equipped, able-bodied knight of the eleventh and twelfth centuries was unquestionably a dan-

---

[30] Statute of Mortmain (1279); S & M, p. 169.

gerous fighter useful to the Norman kings, who employed the services of heavily armed cavalrymen to hold the realm of England. In effect, the Crown quartered the principal military power of the realm on the English agrarian population. Beyond all doubt barons of the king were free men; likewise, beyond all doubt, their tenures were also free. Although the Norman and Angevin kings used the nonfeudal, Anglo-Saxon political machinery of the shire and hundred courts, they could not avoid the establishment of feudalism as a system of land tenure, and there is no evidence that later English monarchs were hostile to the perpetuation of feudal tenures. In medieval England, as elsewhere in Europe, everyone accepted a social order dominated by men-at-arms.

The best English kings were extraordinarily successful in their control of feudalism. They made all military service the royal military service; private war was illegal. They prohibited the construction of unlicensed castles. They retained jurisdiction over certain major crimes, the pleas of the Crown. They controlled the coinage of money and the regulation of weights and measures. They maintained a monopoly over all litigation concerning freehold property; no man need answer another concerning his freehold except in obedience to the king's writ.

And beyond the free tenure by knight service were several other tenures which acquired the same dignity in the eyes of the royal courts. To explain their peculiar qualities is not easy, as we have noted, but perhaps they can be distinguished from the unfree tenures by a test involving the degree of dependence on the will of the lord of the tenure. That is, if a man's services are so uncertain and so unpredictable that he requires constant supervision, or if they are so uncertain that "he does not know at night what he will do in the morning,"[31] then, in the eyes of the law his tenure is unfree, and the man's rights in land are subject to seignorial rather than royal justice. The test of dependence on the will of the lord or of his agent is not always

---

[31] Bracton, fol. 26, 208b.

easy to apply, but it is the best guide. And the royal courts, in line with the practice then common throughout Europe, did not endeavor to regulate relations between the holder of a free tenement and the villeins, or agricultural workers, who lived on it. Not until the sixteenth century did "copyholders," the successors of the medieval villeins, acquire the remedies available at common law in the twelfth and thirteenth centuries for the protection of freehold tenures.

In the Middle Ages the distinction between the man-at-arms and the tiller of the soil was more than a legal difference. When feudalism was at its height in the eleventh century, the classes of society were distinguished by their patterns of life and their work. The free man-at-arms was not a tiller of the soil; he ploughed not and planted not; he did not harvest. From the twelfth century onward, the social cleavage between man-at-arms and peasant widened until it became practically impassable. A man in the late fourteenth century, say, was born into his rank in society, and he could not easily leave it. Nobility, as well as serfdom, came to be thought of as something in the blood. As feudalism waned, the class structure nevertheless remained intact, each class developing and maintaining distinctive manners, dress, forms of recreation, and even foodstuffs.

INFLUENCE OF THE ENGLISH BARONAGE
ON THE COMMON LAW

There is no question about the influence of the baronial class in thirteenth-century legal matters. "Their importance," observed A. L. Poole, "their prominence, their power to dominate was at the height of the Middle Ages quite incommensurate with their numbers. They are the principal element in the feudal conception of society."[32] Even the clergy were affected by the pattern of

---

[32] A. L. Poole, *Obligations of Society*, p. 36.

life of the nobility. The upper clergy, bishops and abbots, were often chosen from and lived like the military aristocracy, while the parish priest was usually closer to the cultivators of his manorial village. Bishops and abbots were also barons, maintained large households, hunted in the royal forests with the permission of the king—and sometimes, apparently, without the permission of the king.[33]

Since we are concerned here with the ways in which any class or group in English society might influence the development of the medieval common law, the status of the knightly class is important. There is good evidence that the customs of the barons, the tenants-in-chief of the Crown by military service, influenced not only the content of the common law but also the manner in which the Crown would administer it and observe its rules. The loss of Normandy, and particularly the military disaster of Bouvines in 1214, created among the English barons a new sense of community and the determination on the part of some of them to resist arbitrary royal demands for service and money.

To speak of the baronage of England, as it was on the eve of Magna Carta, as a community is no exaggeration. Conscious of their own common interests and customs, they were prepared to act for their preservation. Above all, they wished to see the Crown observe the feudal contracts which gave the barons their fiefs and the Crown its tenants-in-chief. The feudal military class had everything to lose if the contracts by which they were related to the Crown and to one another were dissolved.

---

[33] Charter of the Forest (1217), Chapter 11: "Any archbishop, bishop, earl, or baron who crosses our forest may take one or two beasts by view of the forester, if he is present; if not, let a horn be blown so that this [hunting] may not appear to be carried on furtively." S & M, p. 131. For evidence that clergymen may have been hunting without permission, see the prohibition in the Assize of the Forest (1184), Chapter 9. "Item, the king forbids all clergymen to commit any offences touching his venison or his forests. . . . if [royal foresters] find such men committing offences, they shall not hesitate to lay hands on those men in order to hold them and put them under attachment. . . ." S & M, p. 88.

The barons of England, at Runnymede and elsewhere, forced the Crown to recognize their customary contractual relations as part of the law of the realm. In the early thirteenth century, the law of the land was principally land law, consisting of the rules, customs, and practices of those holding free tenures in a feudal society. When Bracton wrote that "the king is under the law" and that "law makes the king," he undoubtedly included the common law, which the barons expected to observe toward their own men just as they expected the kings to observe it in his dealings with them. Moreover, barons of the king quite properly expected that the king would assist them by legal procedures or by military force, if necessary, to obtain the customary services and monetary aids from their own sub-vassals.

As an administrator the king may have had no peer, but this lofty position, the barons maintained, did not permit him to alter at will the terms of feudal contracts or feudal custom without first obtaining the advice and counsel of those affected by the change. Rather, the king must act in certain matters only with "the common counsel of the realm," which meant in the early thirteenth century the counsel of the great prelates and barons.

Thus the common law of the twelfth and thirteenth centuries is in large part the law of land and tenures, the law of property rights and services together with rules of procedure for the administration of justice. A glance at the chapters of Magna Carta or at any collection of common-law writs will reveal the dominant concern with rights in land: the possession, or seisin, of land, the services owed for the tenure of land, the inheritance of land, the leasing of land, the wardship of land, the profits from land, the burdens on land,. and the wrongs to land.[34]

---

[34] See *Magna Carta*, Chapters 2, 3, 4, 5, 7, 9, 12, 15, 16, 18, 23, 29, 31, 32, 37, 43, 46, 52; S & M, pp. 115–25.

Although medieval tenants by knight service were very knowledgeable about their rights and customs, they did not consciously support a program of constitutional government for England; nor did they, as a class, seek to realize a deliberate long-term legislative policy. But consciously or unconsciously, the baronage asserted the supremacy of law. They secured the benefits of the rule of law, not only for themselves but for all free men.

Since royal taxation touched other free classes as well as the baronage, the doctrine of the supremacy of law was endorsed also by the clergy and by the townsmen. Thus in the latter half of the thirteenth century, the community of the barons joined with other communities to form the community of the realm, the *universitas regni*. Parliament eventually became the institution through which the community of the realm could treat with the king, but early parliaments in England, like representative governments elsewhere in Europe, served the political ideas of a feudal society. As Walter Ullmann has aptly observed:

> The emergence of the *communitas regni* in the thirteenth century may be viewed as the coagulation of the still amorphous feudal body that had brought John to his knees. The *communitas regni* was an abstract reflection of the feudal baronage expressed in the easily available legal terms: the *universitas regni* was merely another name for the same thing.[35]

In its beginning, Parliament was a device enabling the Crown to act with "the common counsel of the realm" in the solution of national problems. The procedures of Parliament saved both the royal prerogative in administration and the feudal contractual relationship between Crown and subject; both continued to exist under the doctrine of the sovereignty of law.

[35] Walter Ullmann, *Principles of Government and Politics in the Middle Ages* (New York: Barnes & Noble, 1961), p. 175.

Chapter 5

Unfree Tenures and
Their Obligations

Medieval English common law, like Roman law, recognized only two great classes of men—free and unfree. Royal judges administering the common law favored freedom in any disputed case, and common-law procedures placed obstacles in the path of anyone trying to press a man into serfdom.[1] The question of free status was always a matter for the royal courts. Although common law favored freedom, it is also true that common law maintained for centuries a distinction between free and unfree status and free and unfree tenure. The distinction, moreover, was not to be ignored in the twelfth and thirteenth centuries, for it delimited the jurisdiction of the royal courts and affected the remedies that could be obtained in them. On any matter touching his freehold tenure the medieval freeholder could secure the protection of the royal courts, but the unfree tenant in villeinage was barred from this benefit. At a time when perhaps nine-tenths of the population lived on the land, working in the fields of agrarian vil-

---

[1] See *Brevia Placitata*, ed. J. G. Turner, Selden Society, Vol. 66 (1947), p. cxlv, *De libertate probanda*, on the proving of freedom; Bracton, fol. 105b; *Fleta*, Book II, Chapter 51, on the Writ of Peace in favor of Liberty.

lages, the common-law distinction between free and unfree cut deeply into the fabric of English society.

The line between free and unfree touched both property and personal status because villeinage was both a tenure and a personal condition which jurists did not hesitate to label *servus*, the Roman word for slave. Gradually, in the late Middle Ages, villein tenure acquired recognition as a property interest by "the custom of the manor": it came to be said that a man held "by copy of the [manor] court roll"—hence, he was a "copyholder" with a tenure on record. By the sixteenth century the copyholder had acquired, from the rules of Equity, as much security in the enjoyment of his tenure as the freeholder himself possessed.[2] The long-term trend, then, encouraged and protected personal freedom and blocked the arbitrary exercise of seignorial authority. Nevertheless, while giving the copyholder the freeholder's remedies, the royal courts were extremely slow to obliterate the distinction between freehold and copyhold. The two tenures were only brought to a common legal ground in the twentieth century, when they were merged by statute.[3] Consequently, any backward glance at the rules of common law touching property may fall on terms such as "freehold" and "copyhold," and the distinction between them merits attention.

The legalities of unfree tenures and the various functions of the village community are very difficult subjects for historical study. This is, in part, the result of contradictions: formal rules of law are so often at variance with actual local practice. The historian Paul Vinogradoff observed that the gradual evolution of the villein's position in the direction of freedom was accompanied by occasional violations of the formal rules of law and

---

[2] For an account of this evolution generally see Charles Montgomery Gray, "The Development of Equitable and Legal Protection for Copyhold Tenants," Ph.D. Thesis, Harvard Univ., 1956; but see E. Lipson, *Economic History of England*, 10th ed. (1949), I, 154–59.

[3] The Law of Property Act (1925).

that "the passage from obligatory labor to proprietary rights is effected . . . without any sudden emancipation."[4]

An agreement between a villein and his landlord was not enforceable in a royal court; in practice, however, villeins did make covenants, expecting them to be honored. Thus villeins acquired leases for money rents and moved toward free status without any ceremony of formal emancipation.[5] Now the man who makes a covenant is ordinarily free; consequently, whenever serfs make covenants to pay money rents, they are on the road to an improved legal position. This evolution—actually part of a tremendous social revolution—is interesting to observe but impossible to describe with precision.

THE MARKS OF UNFREE TENURE

There is no simple or conclusive explanation for the fact that medieval English royal courts refused to hear cases touching the tenures and services of certain unfree persons holding "by fork and flail." In the late twelfth century royal courts could not have entertained all causes even if they had wished to do so. Although medieval English kings accepted a general obligation to provide justice and good order for all the people of the realm, this obligation did not imply the provision of justice for all in a nearby royal court before professional royal judges. There simply were not enough professionally trained and experienced judges available to hear all cases.

Rather, men were free, indeed compelled, to seek justice elsewhere—in the courts of counties, hundreds, boroughs,

---

[4] Paul Vinogradoff, *Villeinage in England* (Oxford, 1892), p. 214.

[5] For an example of commutation of labor service to money rent, see the case of John Albin of Littleport, who made an agreement in 1322 with the bishop of Ely to pay 30s. a year for one full land (24 acres?) and two half-lands which he held "of the bondage of the lord" and he is not any longer to be "in the lord's service." *The Court Baron*, F. W. Maitland and W. P. Baildon, eds., Selden Society, Vol. 4 (1890), p. 135.

and fairs, and also in the manor courts of freeholders.[6] While confining attention to cases touching the free men of the realm, the royal courts left the unfree to the jurisdiction of manorial courts. Such a division of judicial business had the merit of forcing landlords to participate with delegated authority in a necessary function of government.

The lord of a single manor controlled and administered a block of land, an estate, cultivated as an economic whole by a group of villagers who cooperated in the tasks of ploughing, planting, and harvesting. The lord's agent, or bailiff, together with the reeve, chosen from the villagers as a sort of foreman, directed the work. A manor was usually contained within a single village, but occasionally one village might have within it two or more manors. We can think of the manor as an estate, a manageable unit, cultivated by the labor of villagers who led an intensely collective existence under the jurisdiction of one lord.[7]

From the point of view of the lord of the manor, if he held by military service, the agricultural labor of the villeins working the demesne lands was essential for his existence and support as a man-at-arms. Without the labor of the villeins, the lord of the manor would have been impoverished unless he held a *fief rente* or some other source of income.[8] The labors of the villein enabled the feudal lord to perform the services and to make the occasional payments which he was obliged to render to his own overlord.

---

[6] *Fleta* (Book II, Chapter 53) comments that "the king also has his court in his counties, hundreds, and manors where he has no justices but where it is the suitors who pronounce judgments on plaints, made by gage and pledges only and without a writ, against contraventions of the peace of the sheriff and the bailiffs, such as beatings, light blows, debts wrongfully left unpaid and trifling wrongs of that kind."

[7] *Select Pleas in Manorial Courts*, F. W. Maitland, ed., Selden Society, Vol. 2 (London, 1889), I, xl.

[8] Bryce Lyon, "The Money Fief under the English Kings, 1066–1485," *English Historical Review*, LXVI (1951), 161–93.

Unless the lord of a manor could compel and direct daily the work of his agricultural tenants, they might, understandably enough, concentrate their labor on their own holdings, particularly in a bad season, while entirely neglecting the tillage and harvest of the lord's demesne. Not until the farming of the lord's demesne for money rents replaced obligatory labor services could a landlord safely give up the direction of the agricultural worker's daily tasks and the enforcement of rent services in one of the manorial courts. How else could he be assured of income?

Noting the uncertainty of villein services, Bracton says that the tenant in villeinage "does not know in the evening what he will have to do in the morning." It might be ditching, threshing, ploughing, carrying—whatever the lord's bailiff and the weather might command.[9] In any society the life of the tenant holding by the performance of agricultural services must be full of uncertainties. This extreme degree of uncertainty about the amount and kind of day-to-day agricultural services most clearly marks the unfree tenures in medieval England.

Gradually, in the course of the thirteenth century, detailed statements of payments and labor services replaced the vague terminology of the twelfth century, when inquiries about villein obligations had resulted in phrases like "whatever he is bid" or "whatever the lord commands" or "without measure" or "a day's work as the reeve shall assign it."[10] The more clearly his services were defined, the less the agricultural tenant needed to refer to the will of the lord or that of his agent. The agrarian worker paying nothing but an annual money rent refers not at all to the will of his landlord; hence he enjoys in practice a

[9] Bracton, *De legibus*, fol. 26, 208b.

[10] See Jean Birdsall, "English Manors of La Trinité," in *Haskins Anniversary Essays in Mediaeval History*, C. H. Taylor and J. L. LaMonte, eds. (Boston, 1929), pp. 43–44. For an eleventh-century effort at definition of services, see *Rectitudines Singularum Personarum*, published in *English Historical Documents (1042–1189)*, David Douglas and G. W. Greenaway, eds. (New York: Oxford Univ. Press, 1953), pp. 813–16.

degree of freedom unknown to the man paying rent by labor services.

Some definition of services may be attributed, in part, to the practice of making manorial surveys, or extents. Containing enumerations of persons and inventories of goods and stock on hand, the manorial extent served as a useful check on the account books of bailiffs and stewards. Two surveys, drawn up for abbots in the late twelfth century, illustrate various duties of agricultural tenants.

The survey of the manor of Stukeley in Huntingdonshire, made for the abbot of Ramsey, states that in Stukeley there were seven hides (approximately 840 acres). The village rendered seven pounds annually in the time of Henry I, but at the time of the survey, in the reign of Henry II, it was held at a rent of eight pounds by Adam, son of Henry the archdeacon:

> Two hides and one virgate, that is to say, 9 virgates, were then held by work and not by pay. And this is the service which each [holder of a] virgate then performed and now still performs:
>
> From Michaelmas to the beginning of August he works 2 days in each week and ploughs on a third, except at Christmas and Easter and Pentecost. And from the beginning of August until Michaelmas he works the whole week except on Saturdays. He gives four hens at Christmas.[11]

A more detailed survey, that of Boldon in 1183, was made for Hugh le Puiset, bishop of Durham. The Boldon survey points up, incidentally, some differences in agriculture and in terminology between the Midlands and the northern part of England:

> In Boldon there are 22 villeins each one of whom holds 2 bovates of land of 30 acres and renders 2 shillings and 6 pence of scot-penny and half of a scot-chalder of oats and 16 pence of averpenny and 5 wagon loads of wood and 2 hens and 10 eggs and works [for

---

[11] *Cartularium Monasterii de Rameseia*, W. H. Hart and P. A. Lyons, eds., Rolls Series (1893), II, 274.

the bishop] throughout the whole year 3 days in the week except Easter and Whitsunweek and thirteen days at Christmastide, and in his works he does in the autumn 4 days at reaping with his entire household, except the housewife, and they reap, moreover, 3 roods of the standing crop of oats and he ploughs 3 roods of oatstubble and harrows it. Every plough of the villeins, also, ploughs 2 acres and harrows, and then they have once a dole from the bishop and for that week they are quit of work, but when they make the great boon days they have a dole. And in their works they harrow when it is necessary and they carry loads, and when they have carried them every man has a loaf of bread; and they mow one day at Houghton in their work until evening, and then they have a dole. And every two villeins build one booth for the fair of Saint Cuthbert. And when they are building lodges and carrying loads of wood they are quit of all other works. There are twelve cottars there, every one of whom holds 12 acres, and they work through the whole year 2 days in the week, except at the three feasts aforenamed, and they render 12 hens and 60 eggs.

The villeins in their work in each year ought to make, if need be, a house 40 feet in length and 15 feet in breadth, and when they make it every man is quit 4 pence of averpenny. The whole village renders 17 shillings of cornage and 1 milch cow. The demesne is at "farm" with stock of 4 ploughs and 4 harrows and tenders for 2 ploughs, 16 chalders of wheat and 16 chalders of oats and 8 chalders of barley, and for the other 2 ploughs 10 marks....[12]

The account of villein services at Boldon shows how the villein tenant there customarily paid his rent for 60 acres of tillable land. Notwithstanding all of the detail in the Boldon survey, at several points the villeins were obviously dependent upon the will of the landlord. For example, "in their works they harrow *when it is necessary*"; and they build, "*if need be,*" a house 40 feet long and 15 feet wide. In determining matters of necessity, it is unlikely that the villeins at Boldon had the last

---

[12] G. T. Lapsley's translation of the Latin text (ed. by W. Greenwell, Surtees Society, 1852) for *Victoria County History: Durham*, I (1905), pp. 327–51; for a discussion of the text see pp. 259–317 in the same volume.

word. Consequently, for this and other reasons their tenures were not freehold, and in their relation to the bishop of Durham, the lord of Boldon, the agricultural workers were not free.

The Boldon survey does not supply answers to some other points which might have been raised in a medieval court endeavoring to draw a line between free and unfree status. Beyond the uncertainty of services were other marks of servitude by which a royal court determined a question of status. For example, has an agricultural worker paid tallages or other arbitrarily levied sums of money? If so, the man is unfree. Has the worker paid a sum of money, "merchet," to obtain the lord's permission for the marriage of the worker's daughter? If so, the worker is unfree.[13] Can the worker bring into court relatives who will swear under oath that he is a free man holding freely from his lord? The testimony of relatives will carry great weight, especially if they say that the worker claiming free status and his ancestors for many generations held their land freely.[14]

To state all of this more positively, medieval courts regarded unfree tenure as a tenure at the will of the lord; the unfree man received neither deed nor charter. He was bound to his lord by a personal and hereditary tie.[15] It was a tie which, in theory, somehow attached to his body from birth. The unfree tenant was liable to tallage and paid merchet for the marriage of his daughter. He was obliged, moreover, to render labor services two or three days of the week, working on the lord's demesne, and he might be asked to do more, especially at the harvest of grain and hay. The villein had no right of legal action against his lord unless it were a matter of life and limb, and he certainly could not secure for his villein tenure the protection of a com-

---

[13] In 1342 Justice Belknap observed that "there is no service in the world which so quickly proves a man to be a villein as making a fine for marriage." *Y.B.* 15 Edw. III (R.S.), xiii.

[14] *Fleta*, Book I, Chapter 40.

[15] Marc Bloch, "The Rise of Dependent Cultivation and Seignorial Institutions," in *Cambridge Economic History*, I, 242.

mon-law court. Rather, he was obliged to sue in the court of the manor, where the lord of the manor or his bailiff presided.

When the tenant "by fork and flail" died, his tenement reverted to the hands of the lord; it did not pass directly to the villein's relatives. This last point was always insisted upon in legal doctrine; inheritance was a mark of freehold. In strict legal doctrine, no man could inherit a villein tenement. The twelfth-century *Dialogue of the Exchequer* states plainly enough that "the lords are owners of the chattels and bodies of their *ascriptitii;* they may transfer them where they please and sell or otherwise alienate them."[16] Glanvill is equally clear when he says of the villein that "all his belongings are in the lord's power."[17] And Bracton confirms this when he says that "whatever is rightfully acquired by the serf is acquired for his lord."[18] The son of a deceased villein might ask for his father's tenement, but he had no legal right to obtain it. As one of the unfree, he was dependent upon the will of the lord. Dependence on the will of the lord and uncertainty about the amount and kind of agricultural services—these were the most distinctive badges of unfree status and unfree tenure.

PATTERNS OF AGRARIAN LIFE

Contrasts between medieval and modern England are so great that to understand medieval patterns of life requires a lively historical imagination. The whole aspect of the English countryside has changed. The hedgerows of modern enclosed fields now stride over the older ridge-and-furrow divisions of medieval open fields. Great cities with their suburban sprawl have obliterated many medieval villages. Networks of railroads and

---

[16] *Dialogus de Scaccario* (Oxford ed.), I, xi; II, xiv.

[17] Glanvill, *De legibus*, V, c. 5.

[18] Bracton, *De legibus*, fol. 6.

paved highways have replaced the footpaths and rutted pack-horse roads of another time.

The metropolitan area of London alone is now three or four times greater in population than the entire realm of England in the late thirteenth century, when somewhat less than three million people lived thinly scattered over the land in thousands of small villages. Large areas, especially in northern England, lay uncultivated in the Middle Ages. Whereas in France the land suitable for agriculture was fully settled and utilized by the late thirteenth century, the agricultural lands of England were not to be so well exploited until the seventeenth century.[19] Even London, the medieval capital city of England, contained no more than thirty or forty thousand inhabitants by 1300, and London then had no great rivals elsewhere in the country.[20]

The overwhelming majority of the population of medieval England lived in isolated villages located in the midst of open fields. These villages, varying in size, contained from about twenty to one hundred households, and the villages were fairly evenly spaced throughout regions lacking deep valleys and steep uplands to block cultivation.[21]

Around the cluster of peasant dwellings in each village lay arable land useful for the production of grains, such as wheat, oats, rye, and barley, which were planted in rotation in either two or three open fields, each containing several hundred acres. The rotation plan allowed an arable field to lie fallow while its neighbor was under cultivation. In the thin soils of

---

[19] A. P. Usher, *Introduction to the Industrial History of England* (Boston, 1919), pp. 89–92, provides tables of estimates of English population and densities per square mile between 1086 and 1801. For 1086 he estimates a mean density of 35.38 per sq. mi. and for 1327 a mean density of 43.73. By 1630 the mean density increased to 102.70 per sq. mi., which implies full use of land suitable for cultivation by medieval methods.

[20] Gwyn A. Williams, *Medieval London* (London, 1963), pp. 315–17.

[21] On the location of villages, see M. W. Beresford and J. K. St. Joseph, *Medieval England: An Aerial Survey* (Cambridge Univ. Press, 1958), pp. 75–76.

bleak chalk downs the two-field system persisted longer than in the Midlands, which could support more frequent planting. In general, the poorer the soil, the longer the interval between plantings.

A shift from two-field to three-field tillage seems to have occurred in many parts of the eastern and northern Midlands during the thirteenth and fourteenth centuries. The older two-field system nevertheless persisted in many places until the enclosure movement, which gained momentum after the opening of the sixteenth century and continued well into the eighteenth.[22] Some villages used open-field cultivation until very recent times. For example, at Laxton in Nottinghamshire about a thousand acres, divided into more than 1,200 separate parcels, were cultivated as late as 1933 by thirty tenants using the three-field system, by which one field lies fallow while two are planted.[23]

But arable land alone could not meet all the needs of the medieval villager. Although the peasant depended largely on grain for his own foodstuffs, he most certainly required pasture and hay for plough teams of oxen or horses. The provision of adequate forage for livestock was a central problem for English agriculture until the eighteenth-century agricultural revolution. Consequently, natural hay meadows were the most valuable land used by the medieval village and were commonly protected by a hedge watched over by a village official, the hayward.

In addition to the ploughed fields and hay meadows, the village used grasslands for common pastures and bordering "waste" lands of forest, which offered browze for cattle and mast for swine while yielding firewood, timber, and game. Fenlands produced reeds and rushes, fish and fowl. Thus the common pastures and waste land supplemented in many im-

---

[22] H. L. Gray, *English Field Systems* (Cambridge: Harvard Univ. Press, 1915), p. 406.

[23] See J. A. Venn, *The Foundations of Agricultural Economics* (London, 1933), p. 43, for Laxton and other survivals of older field systems.

portant ways the productivity of the arable fields. All of the land used by a village made up the territory of a township.

Although they were variously laid out, all villages had certain features reflecting the basic needs of their inhabitants. Houses were usually situated on both sides of a single street. Behind each house, or messuage, lay an enclosed strip of land called "toft," or "croft," a farmyard containing, perhaps, a few fruit trees, a vegetable garden, a pen for poultry, and small outbuildings for the stabling of livestock unless the family and animals lived together in a single dwelling—not an unusual arrangement. A common house plan was the two-room cottage, about twelve by twenty-four feet, with an outside door, and perhaps one window, for each room. If the animals did not use one room as a stable, then the peasant family could use one room for sleeping quarters and another for cooking and eating. The roof of the peasant cottage was covered with thatch, shingles, or turf. The floor was unpaved.[24] The villagers and their animals might all use the village pond as a source of water, and the same pond might also impound water used by the village mill for grinding grain. A large outdoor oven for the baking of bread and a blacksmith's forge for the repair of ploughshares and other tools were used by all of the villagers. Within or near the village stood a small church and the residence of the village priest.

The largest residence, although not necessarily an imposing building, would be the manor house, possibly standing somewhat apart from the village street. Here lived the lord of the manor or his bailiff. A great lord might draw revenues from several villages and the manors in them while regarding one manor as the head or chief residence. Not every lord of a manor lived grandly in a handsome fortified dwelling. In fact, the lord

---

[24] G. G. Coulton, *Medieval Village* (Cambridge, 1926), p. 99, shows diagrams of cottage plans. See also F. W. Maitland and W. P. Baildon, eds., *The Court Baron*, Selden Society, Vol. 4 (1890), p. 142, for the case of Richard of Maunteley, who "surrenders into the lord's hand a cottage 11 feet long by 24 feet wide...."

of a manor, as already noted in the discussion of tenure by sergeanty,[25] might have a very modest revenue from a manor and live in a necessarily modest fashion among the villagers.

External aspects of the village and outlying fields were deceptively simple. A picture of a medieval village gives no clues about the property interests and agricultural methods of the medieval villagers, their tangled relationships and obligations. The common law was concerned with these relationships because all over England freeholders lived and worked among the unfree villeins. Small freeholders, usually socage tenants, had their acres within the open fields of the manor. The common law protected the rights of all freeholders, great and small. Consequently common-law rules touched every aspect of manorial cultivation and village life.

Free cultivators, holding, perhaps, by long-term leases or by inheritable socage tenure, lived side by side on the village street with their unfree neighbors. They cultivated strips of land in the open fields alongside these unfree neighbors. Both classes attended meetings of the manor court and the village church services, and their patterns of daily life were in fact indistinguishable. Indeed, the only distinction between free cultivators and villeins of the community lay in the former's legal status and legal relationship with the lord of the manor.

In addition to intermingling of free and unfree cultivators in the same village, there was intermingling of various proprietary rights in the open fields and common pastures of the village. The average tenement of the peasant was about thirty acres of arable land, called a "virgate" or "yardland." He could not possibly build a continuous fence around these acres, for they were scattered as strips within the open fields. The peasant's narrow ploughlands, strips, or *selions*, were about 220 yards long and 5½ yards wide. Each strip of these dimensions would approximate one-quarter of a modern acre of 43,560 square

---

[25] Above, pp. 102–103.

feet. An effort to give each household an equal chance to cultivate some of the good land of the township along with the
poor may have produced the scattering of cultivators' selions
throughout the open fields. Any consolidation of holdings
might have produced inequalities by giving thirty acres of fertile valley land to one cultivator and thirty acres of infertile
hillside to another. Moreover, a consolidation of holdings
would have meant inevitably that some villagers would have
tilled land conveniently close to their homes while others
would have been compelled to walk to the very boundaries of
the township to reach their acres.

The strips—they were variously named—were usually
ploughed by teams of four or eight oxen, yoked in pairs hitched
in tandem. By modern standards the oxen were scrawny,
scrubby animals weighing about four hundred pounds each at
maturity, that is, at four years of age.[26] Eight of these small oxen
would scarcely match the draft power of a single pair of modern Percheron, Belgian, or Clydesdale horses. Each full tenement of thirty acres, or virgate, provided two oxen for the
plough. Thus eight oxen did the ploughing of 120 "acres" held
by peasant cultivators. Whether the oxen worked eight at a time
or four in the morning and four in the afternoon, the practice of
combining yokes of oxen to form a larger plough team united
the peasant cultivator with his neighbors. A villager clearly
required the cooperation of his neighbors to plough his own
tenement and to fulfill his labor service on the lord's demesne.

Along with their own ploughing, the villeins ploughed the
selions of the landlord's demesne. It was common for them to
work three days on their own land and three days on the land
of the lord under the supervision of the bailiff and the reeve,
who saw to the yoking of teams at daybreak for ploughing,
carting, or whatever the work might be. The reeve continued to
oversee the work throughout the day.

---

[26] J.E.T. Rogers, *Six Centuries of Work and Wages* (New York, 1884), pp. 77–8; 184.

In spite of the variety of property interests existing in the same open fields, the planting and harvesting were necessarily uniform. A field was planted in one crop—oats or wheat or barley or beans—so that the entire field would ripen at once. After the harvest the livestock of the village could be turned out to graze on the stubble, or aftermath. Both communal agriculture by the open-field system and the need for pasture effectively blocked individualism in the handling of scattered selions. Unless one cultivator planted the same crop as his neighbors, he would have to fence each strip to prevent livestock from eating up his unharvested crop when the village herds were in on the stubble of grain already cut. But the temporary fencing of many scattered narrow strips belonging to one peasant would have been prohibitively expensive. Yields from medieval agricultural fields were very low. If a man sowed two bushels of wheat per acre, he would not expect to harvest more than eight or ten bushels per acre. Building and maintaining a fence around each selion ordinarily would have taken all of the profit in a crop. It was far better to go along with the communal village practice. The free peasant was controlled by communal practice just as much as the unfree. Not until the enclosure movement created tracts of several acres within one fence was it possible for any cultivator to deviate safely from communal village practice in the rotation of crops.

Hand tools, the lack of chemical fertilizers, the lack of good seed, indiscriminate stock breeding—these and other factors limited the productivity of medieval agriculture. Everyone in the Middle Ages, whatever his rank in society, lived close to the edge of famine, because poor roads prevented the quick movement of grain into regions where crops had failed. Moreover, few areas produced grain surpluses. Peasant diet was simple, scant, and very low in meat. Only the strongest and best animals were kept through the winter. Swine were the principal meat supply.[27] Sheep as well as cows were used as dairy ani-

---

[27] E. Lipson, *Economic History of England*, 7th ed. rev. (New York: Macmillan, 1938), I, 84.

mals. Fish ponds were constructed on many manors, and the right to take fish from them was a carefully guarded property right.[28]

Landlords also jealously guarded hunting privileges in the forest to assure themselves of food for the table as well as enjoyment of the violent sports of deer hunting and boar hunting. Unlike the frontiersman in America, the medieval English peasant, whether free or unfree, was under the constant supervision of foresters or game wardens serving the landlord. Poaching in field or stream would be heavily fined in the manor court; the poacher might even be sentenced to corporal punishment in the stocks.

Among other evidence concerning the medieval peasant's wealth, the English historian G. G. Coulton provided two inventories of the goods of deceased persons whom he regarded as having been comparatively well off. By modern standards these people were very poor. In 1301 a certain peasant's tools consisted of "a hoe, spade, axe, billhook, two yokes for carrying buckets, and a barrel: total estimated value 10*d*. . . ." Another, Coulton observed bitterly, "points out how large a proportion went in legacies to the Church, funeral expenses, probate and lawyers' fees. The widow, who got most, received a cow worth 5*s*. by definite bequest, and 3*s*. ¾*d*. as residuary legatee; funeral, food and drink came to 8*s*. 8*d*.; draft of will and probate to 1*s*. 2*d*."[29]

No serious study of medieval peasant life can fail to note how the daily round stunted the mind and spirit of the rural worker. His entire family worked in the fields, especially in the harvest—little children, everyone.[30] The housewife might be allowed to keep the cottage, but field work might be demanded from all.[31] The average peasant probably knew fewer than two

[28] Maitland and Baildon, *The Court Baron*, p. 55.

[29] Coulton, *Medieval Village*, p. 101.

[30] *Cartulary of Ramsey*, I, 339, 358, 367, 385, 395.

[31] Walter of Henley, in his *Husbandry*, lists the duties of the peasant's wife: she is expected to winnow grain, make malt, wash, make hay, harvest grain, help her husband fill the muck wagon or dung cart, drive the plough, load hay or grain,

or three hundred persons in his lifetime. He seldom traveled beyond his township. (Chaucer's plowman on pilgrimage to Canterbury was certainly an exception!) His ideas were as limited as his horizon, and his vocabulary might not exceed a few hundred words. No one cared to improve either his lot or his mentality. Cut off from the society of educated men and women, he began to work at the age of four, and at fourteen he was regarded as being ready to take a man's place in the work of the village community.[32]

A kind of paternal authority on the part of the lord, combined with village custom, forced the peasant into a communal pattern of living. Under these pressures he had few options, few decisions to make. He was compelled to attend the manor court, which met at least once a month if not more frequently. Here he was drilled in the details of village custom. Moreover, he must do "suit" to the lord's mill, bake oven, and forge; that is, he must grind his grain at the lord's mill and not elsewhere, and so with the baking at the oven and the use of the forge. In the lord's court the villager might be ordered to do many things unrelated to the cultivation of the manor: for example, he might be told to refrain from gambling and quarreling and breaking the peace by drawing a knife; he might be ordered to remove dung heaps from the street in front of his house. Sometimes the manor court issued injunctions hopefully affecting future behavior throughout an entire township; at Hazeldean in 1375 "it was enjoined upon all the women in the township that they should restrain their tongues and not scold nor curse any man."[33]

---

and go to market to sell butter, cheese, milk, eggs, chickens, pigs, geese, and grain.

[32] *Select Pleas in Manorial Courts*, ed. F. W. Maitland, Selden Society, Vol. 2 (London, 1889), I, 120, 121; (Manor of King's Ripton, Huntingdonshire, 1295) "... (and the jurors say upon their oath) that ... the (full) age of a woman is thirteen years and a half and that the (full) age for males is fourteen years and a half...."

[33] Coulton, *Medieval Village*, p. 98

SEIGNORIAL COURTS

The jurisdiction of the lord of the manor gave him many powers over his tenants, both free and unfree, but in practice these powers were restrained by the custom of the manor. Sir Paul Vinogradoff has made clear that whatever the medieval law books might say about the lord being able to work his dependents at his will and pleasure, the custom of the manor tended to fix services and payments. The villein in the thirteenth century was called *consuetudinarius*, a "customer," and he had many opportunities in manorial courts to declare the custom of the manor. Vinogradoff also noted that villeins sued and were sued in the lord's court, using actions comparable to those in the royal courts, and that in manorial courts "a body of customary law is evolved . . . which keeps in close touch with the development of the common law and paves the way towards the ultimate recognition of the binding character of customs."[34]

However, granting the tendency for custom to become binding and a restraint on both lord and villein, it should be emphasized that in a contest between lord and villein on any matter affecting villein tenure, services, or payments, the villein was powerless to seek justice elsewhere than in a court presided over by the lord or one of his agents. This was the customary court, sometimes called a *halimote*, meeting either in the open air or in the hall of the manor house. The principal business of the customary court was the administration of the manor as an economic unit.

If the lord's jurisdiction over his villeins had been confined to the agricultural management of an estate, there would be less difficulty in describing the manor court. But estate management was not the sole area of seignorial jurisdiction. A number of other matters also came under the lord's jurisdiction, and

---

[34] Paul Vinogradoff, *The Growth of the Manor*, 2nd ed. rev. (London, 1911), p. 349.

either by charter or usurpation the lord of a manor often exercised a jurisdiction known as view of frankpledge and another, commonly joined with view of frankpledge, known as a court leet. Still another aspect of seignorial jurisdiction touched what was called a court baron, a court in which the lord administered justice to his freeholders alone and dealt particularly with conveyancing and title to land. The amalgamation or fusion of judicial functions in the manorial court, bewildering as it may seem to modern eyes, apparently created no problems for those living under it; the court of the manor could deal with at least three categories of causes: 1) those touching the customary rents, payments, and services of the unfree tenants; 2) police and criminal matters; and, 3) causes arising out of the tenures of freeholders.

OFFICERS OF MANORIAL ADMINISTRATION

Manorial courts involved several officials who appear prominently in the records. The lord of the manor could not always preside; when he was absent his steward or bailiff took his place. If the lord had several manors, he might be represented in their courts by a steward, who traveled from one manor to another, serving as auditor of the records of manorial bailiffs and reeves. In the absence of the lord a steward could preside at a session. The steward would visit each manor two or three times a year, carrying his rolls and records with him. In *Fleta* we have a full and detailed list of the steward's manifold responsibilities, all of which were intended to protect the lord's interests.[35]

If the manor were a large one, it would have a resident bailiff who supervised its operation from day to day. Like the steward,

---

[35] *Fleta*, H. G. Richardson and G. O. Sayles, eds., Selden Society, Vol. 72 (1953), pp. 241–43.

he was a free man and he was rewarded for his services by a monetary wage. His responsibilities could be large; he was obliged to keep careful records of all work performed, all income produced, and all expense incurred. On those occasions when neither the lord nor his steward was present, the bailiff presided over the manor court.[36] Although the bailiff represented the lord's interest in the operation of the manor and was often in daily contact with the villagers, he stood somewhat apart from the village community. Like the steward, he derived his authority from his lord's appointment, and he was not the holder of a tenement within the manor.[37]

Whatever the size of the manor, there was always one official, drawn from the peasantry, on whom the entire manorial administration turned. This pivotal man was the reeve, who was chosen from and by the villeinage, generally at Michaelmas (September 29), and installed in office by the lord or his steward for a term of one year. The reeve, usually the holder of one of the larger villein tenements, might be selected to serve year after year as chief of the peasants, responsible for the detailed direction of each man's work in every aspect of the manorial economy. Carrying this heavy burden excused him from his own customary services; he himself could not plough and plant and harvest and at the same time direct the labor of others. Sometimes a reeve sought to escape his arduous responsibilities and paid a substantial sum to be excused from the office.[38]

Chief among the reeve's burdens must have been the com-

---

[36] Ibid., pp. 244–47.

[37] H. S. Bennett, *Life on the English Manor* (New York, 1938), p. 163.

[38] *Select Pleas in Manorial Courts*, I, 23. William Ketchburn gives the lord 6s. 8d. that he may be removed from the office of reeve in Bedlow, Northamptonshire (1275). In 1293 the jurors of the manor of Brightwaltham, Berkshire, nominated four men for the office of reeve. The steward of the abbot of Battle chose one—Thomas Smith—who then made fine that he might be absolved from the office of reeve "and he gives the lord 40s." (Ibid., p. 168.) In 1296 John Robin of Ruislip, Middlesex, offered his lord, the abbot of Bec, a mark of silver for permission to retire from the office of reeve. (Ibid., p. 43.)

pilation of annual accounts of income and expenditure in terms of bushels of grain and workdays—no small task for an unschooled man. The reeve had to account for items in three categories: 1) grain in the lord's barn: how much wheat was used for seed, how much went to manorial servants, how much remained in the barn, and so with the other grains, rye, barley, oats, etc.; 2) livestock: how many horses, oxen, pigs; 3) "works": i.e., how many man-days of ploughing, reaping, carrying, etc., owed to the lord, were actually performed. Only a person familiar with the record-keeping of unlettered men can even imagine the situation of a reeve making a complete annual account of the agricultural operations on the manor. Perhaps he made marks on barn doors or granary walls, or notched tally sticks. On many a farm today one can find numbers, notches, marks, and scratches representing memoranda of crops harvested and livestock loaded. For the man who made them in the first place, a few marks were eloquent and sufficient reminders. But historians can only conjecture how the reeve, perhaps with the aid of notched tallies, dictated his annual account, which some clerk then entered on a roll in complete form.[39]

Beyond the steward, the bailiff, and the reeve, there were other offices of manorial administration such as that of beadle and hayward, or *messor*. The beadle served as policeman for the village, while the hayward served as overseer and guard of grain fields and hay meadows. "And in hay time," remarks *Fleta*, "he ought to be over the mowers, the making and the carrying [of the hay]. . . ."[40]

The full list of manorial officals would include ploughmen, carters, shepherds, and swineherds. Their duties are set down in medieval manuals of husbandry such as that by Walter of Henley, on which *Fleta* draws in part. For purposes of this

[39] Bennett, *English Manor*, p. 188.
[40] *Fleta*, Book II, Chapter 84.

study it is enough to mention the body of manorial servants, more closely related to the manor house than to the village community.

Among all of the officers and servants of the manor, the reeve stood out as the chief man of the village community. He, and sometimes the priest, together with four men of the village, represented the community at the hundred court and also at the county court; the reeve and the four "lawful" men of the township also represented the community at the sheriff's tourn, or view of frankpledge.[41] The reeve was clearly the man at the center of manorial administration and a link between the village and the law courts.

PUBLIC DUTIES OF THE VILL

Every medieval English manor was located within the territory of a township, or vill, the smallest political entity recognized by the royal administration. The connection between the public responsibilities of the vill in criminal and fiscal matters and the operation of manorial courts presented a strange blending of private lordship and public affairs. One of the curiosities of medieval royal administration is that it demanded special services from the community (*villata*) living in the village without recognizing a special court or assembly for the discharge of those community obligations. It is another curiosity that the manor, which was primarily an economic unit, a manageable estate in land, should have supplied the necessary machinery through which the village community performed its political functions. The consequences of such arrangements present almost insuperable problems of analysis. An amalgam of political matters and matters of estate management will not dissect

---

[41] *Leges Henrici Primi*, Chapter 7; Assize of Clarendon, Chapter 1; *Select Pleas in Manorial Courts*, I, xxxiii.

neatly. Seignorial rights, villein services and payments, the custom of the manor, and the public duties of the village community all appear in the same records of manorial courts.

Except for the palatine jurisdictions, such as those of Chester and Durham, and the quasi-palatinate of the Isle of Ely, thirteenth-century England was divided into counties, or shires, which in turn were divided into smaller units called "hundreds" in southern England ("wapentakes" in Yorkshire, Lincolnshire, and Derbyshire, and "wards" in the northernmost counties). The word "hundred" can safely stand for all the subdivisions of the counties. Each hundred contained a number of villages. Since the hundred was a very ancient Germanic institution, changes in population and the siting of villages over a long period led to extraordinary variations in the number of villages composing the hundred, which might contain as few as two or as many as twenty village communities. The county had its court, and the hundred also had a court, the latter meeting at three-week intervals to handle civil cases such as debts and trespasses.

Of an estimated 628 hundreds in England, by the end of the thirteenth century 358 had fallen into private hands as franchises or "liberties" obtained by royal grant as well as by usurpation and prescription, and 270 hundreds were still controlled by the Crown. Thus the fees and fines of the hundred courts, the profits of justice, were shared by the king and local officials with many lay lords and prelates, some of whom might even claim successfully the right to hold a view of frankpledge at a specially full meeting of the hundred court twice a year. However, it was common for the sheriff to displace the bailiff as presiding officer for the view of frankpledge because at the view, and only then, were serious criminal matters brought before the suitors of the hundred court.

In the Norman period, with a few exceptions, all Englishmen twelve years of age or older were forced to become members of a frankpledge group, a group of about ten men who swore allegiance to the Crown and assumed the duties of maintaining the peace and providing a sort of collective suretyship. Although the frankpledge system did not operate in Wales or in the northernmost counties of England, elsewhere it compelled the populace to police itself by what has been called "the most efficient police system in Western Europe."[42]

The hundred courts supervised the tithings at the sheriff's tourns, or views of frankpledge—the full meetings of the hundred held each year after Easter and after Michaelmas. The frankpledge system served a clear purpose: it was to supply the royal sheriff, or someone performing his functions within the hundred, with information about criminal acts, violations of the king's peace, or violations of royal rights. Furthermore, it was to identify the criminal and, if possible, to produce him in court. Finally, the frankpledge system was a guarantee that the Crown could always find a group of men from whom it could extract a fine, at least, if the criminal act of one member of a tithing were ignored by the others. Certain classes of men were exempted from membership in a tithing by reason of the fact that the Crown could find other surety for their keeping the peace: magnates, knights, clergymen, burgesses with property, and domestic servants within the "mainpast" of a household whose lord assumed responsibility for those living in it. In reality, by the time Bracton was writing, the frankpledge system, perhaps originally designed for free men, had become a system of surety for villeins.

At a view of frankpledge, as mentioned earlier, each vill was represented by a reeve and four other men of the vill. Each tithing was represented by its chief pledge, headman, or tithingman. It was also necessary to have at the view at least twelve freeholders from the hundred, who served as a jury of presentment after the chief pledges had answered under oath

[42] Bryce Lyon, *Constitutional and Legal History of Medieval England* (New York, 1960), p. 197.

the long list of inquiries comprising "the articles of the view." The jury of freeholders heard the responses of the jury of villeins. Then the freeholders endorsed or corrected the statements of the villeins by their verdict presented to the sheriff. The freeholders could not claim an exemption from their obligation to swear to the facts of the verdict, "since it is the king's day," declared *Fleta*, "and was instituted to promote peace" (Book II, Chapter 52).

The articles of the view of frankpledge were intended to draw out from the suitors of the hundred court whatever might assure the inviolable peace of the countryside and maintain the tithings in complete form. *Fleta* gives a long list of items to which the suitors must respond. They must tell under oath what they know about burglars, robbers, thieves, manslayers, burners of houses, and their accomplices. They must answer inquiries about outlaws, treasure trove, waifs, prison-breakers, rapists, poachers, usurers, heretics, traitors, thieves, the hue and cry wrongfully raised or improperly pursued, boundaries broken down, water courses diverted, roads and paths wrongfully blocked, false measures and weights, the breaking of the assize of bread and ale, alienation of the rights of the king, watches not kept, prisoners unlawfully detained. These are only illustrative of the matters on which the suitors must supply information; the even longer list in *Fleta* does not pretend to be exhaustive. Whatever was against the king's peace might be an article of the view.

When the chief pledges have given their precise answers to the articles and when the twelve freeholders under oath have served as a second jury of presentment, endorsing or correcting by their verdict what has been said by the villeins, then the sheriff must act. If he can, he must secure the arrest of men charged with a felony and either collect fines for misdemeanors or obtain surety for their payment.

Attendance at the hundred court through their representatives was only one political obligation of the men of a village.

They were also obliged in the same way to attend the court held by royal itinerant justices and the county court as well. The villagers were exposed to the operation of the common law. As a community the village was obliged to arrest malefactors and to capture anyone guilty of manslaughter within the township boundaries. It was obliged to raise the hue and cry and to follow the trail of stolen cattle. It was obliged to keep watch at night, elect a constable, and observe the royal legislation about the keeping of arms. In sum, the royal government compelled the villeins of agricultural villages to police their own townships and to participate in the administration of justice.

The vill, or township, was a community with clear political obligations; it could be fined in the hundred court or in the county court if it did not perform them. But, strangely enough, it had no specific political machinery for carrying out its obligations; it was compelled to rely upon manorial courts to supply the lacking township or village institution for such matters as the election of the reeve and the constable, arrangements for watch and ward, and all else expected of it. Yet a manorial court had no "constitutional" place in the scheme of English local government. What was the linkage between manor and vill? Even the great Maitland, apparently at ease with every aspect and period of English law, reconnoitered carefully and planned his attack before he was ready, as he remarked, "to go up against the manor."[43]

The lord of a manor could support on two grounds his claim to preside over political matters arising within a township. First, he could claim that he was exercising either an explicit or an implied power delegated to him by the Crown; second, he could assert a widely accepted principle that every lord was entitled to hold a court for his tenants, be they free or unfree. Moreover, it often happened that manor and vill were the same. If so, why should not the manor court discuss and determine

---

[43] P & M, I, 594.

the political obligations of the vill when all the suitors of the manor court were present?

But it simply was not true that throughout England one village always contained one manor. The facts were not so tidy; the facts would not always permit one manor court to regulate the economic life of the village community and the tenures of its inhabitants while serving simultaneously as the machinery for the administration of police and fiscal matters. The lord of the manor or his bailiff could not always preside over cases touching both the private and the public law for an entire township, because one township might contain "two, three, or four manors."[44]

Sources of confusion here are not hard to see. For example, each manor has a reeve, but which reeve of two, three, or four manors will head the representatives from the township when they attend the hundred court? The solution seems to have been an allocation of certain duties to particular tracts of land. The duties tended to become permanent, a fixed burden on land.[45] The complexities of jurisdiction on the lowest level have been little more than outlined here,[46] but even a brief examination of manor and vill shows the amalgamation of two powers of lordship in the manor court. One is the jurisdiction which the lord can claim as a delegated authority from the Crown; the other is the jurisdiction which the lord can claim as a principle of feudal custom—by common law every free man may have a court for his tenants (*de commune ley chescun frank home deit aver court de ses tenantz*).[47] And the manorial jurisdiction covers both free and unfree tenants. Freeholders and tenants in villeinage may meet in one manorial court, for as Sir Edward Coke explained:

---

[44] P & M, I, 609.

[45] P & M, I, 611.

[46] For details of local jurisdiction, see the excellent work of Helen M. Cam, *The Hundred and Hundred Rolls: An Outline of Local Government in Medieval England* (London, 1930).

[47] *Select Pleas in Manorial Courts*, I, xli, n. 2, quoting *Y.B.* 17 Edw. II, f. 538.

This court is of two natures. The first is by the common law, and is called a court baron, as some have said, for that it is the freeholders or freemans court (for barons in one sense signifie freemen), and of that court the freeholders being suitors be judges, and this may be kept from three weekes to three weekes. The second is a customary court, and that doth concern copiholders, and therein the lord or his steward is the judge. . . . And when the court baron is of this double nature, the court roll containeth as well matters appertaining to the customary court, as to the court baron.[48]

If anything, Coke may have drawn too sharp a distinction between a manorial court organized in one way for freeholders and in another way for those with copyhold or unfree tenures. Certainly the thirteenth-century court rolls of some manors do not show a distinction between a court baron and a customary court.[49] By the end of the thirteenth century, the manorial court is rapidly losing any business which might be called purely feudal, and the court baron—for freeholders—is merely an adjunct to jurisdiction over villeins.

In his role as judge of a customary court the lord, or his bailiff, is limited by the custom of the manor. Again and again, the suitors of the court declare that custom in detail, and the lord seems to accept without interference the declaratory legislation of his villeins, just as the king in Parliament accepts the declaratory statutes of the community of the realm.

---

[48] Sir Edward Coke, *First Part of the Institutes of the Lawes of England: or, Commentarie upon Littleton* (first published 1628, 19th ed. by Charles Butler, 1832), 58a.

[49] See cases published by Maitland, in *Select Pleas in Manorial Courts*, I, pp. 165–75, from the rolls of the abbot of Battle's manor court at Brightwaltham, Berkshire (1293–1296), where six freeholders lived and worked among the tenants of twenty-seven virgates (unfree tenements).

PART THREE
LEGAL INSTITUTIONS

Chapter 6

Courts of Angevin England to 1307

Every legal system must be served by courts which interpret and enforce its substantive rules. Laws do not interpret themselves, and the very existence of a body of substantive rules implies the existence of courts for the administration of those rules. Even when the rules controlling a society are only vague customs, judicial procedures are still necessary to make authoritative determinations that customs have been broken.

Beyond interpreting existing formal rules, courts promote the growth of a legal system by identifying, in the course of legal controversy, customs and rules of conduct which had not been previously expressed or recognized. Thus the judgments of courts are a source of law and contribute to the body of substantive rules. Certainly the courts of medieval England made significant contributions to the common law. An eminent modern historian, William S. Holdsworth, has called attention to "the lawyer-made law . . . to be found in reports of decided cases, in the plea rolls, and in books of authority."[1] English

---

[1] William S. Holdsworth, *Sources and Literature of English Law* (Oxford, 1925), p. 4.

courts of the twelfth and thirteenth centuries guided procedure so that the plaintiff with a serious grievance received a hearing which culminated in a judgment settling the matter. Procedure became complex even in the early common law, and it is not our purpose here to explain it in all of its detail. However, before moving on to an examination of the court system in Angevin England, it will be helpful to state the basic elements in any civil action.

First, the aggrieved person must take the initiative. He must launch the process which will bring his opponent into court. If Thomas has appropriated and begun to cultivate the land of Robert, then Robert must do more than grumble in order to recover the land. He must make a formal complaint to a court and assure the court that he will prosecute his complaint vigorously to secure repossession.

Second, the court must act through appropriate officers such as sheriffs and bailiffs to bring Thomas, the defendant, before the court to answer the charges of Robert, the plaintiff.

Next, either in the exchange of oral or written arguments or in pleadings, the plaintiff and the defendant must be encouraged to formulate precisely the issues between them. If the court acts properly as the umpire of this stage, the pleadings will result in questions of fact or of law which can be determined or decided by trial.

Then follows the trial of these points material to the case. If a jury is employed, it gives a verdict about the facts. Having secured the best light that can be thrown on the facts, the judge or judges apply the appropriate rules of law to the facts and reach a judgment deciding which of the litigants, Robert or Thomas, has the better right to the disputed land.

Finally, there must be the execution, or enforcement, of the court's judgment by an order from the court to an official such as a sheriff.

The purpose of the verbal, combative procedure so briefly outlined here is the settlement of a dispute which might explode in violence if it were not channeled through a court. The Anglo-Saxon "dooms" of the early seventh century reveal a clear intent to thwart acts of private vengeance and family feuds.[2] To quiet the possibility—one might even say the right—of private vengeance, the murderer owed to the family of the slain man a money payment determined by the slain man's social status. Wounding and injury must also be paid for. The law of medieval England was not much influenced by Christian doctrines of the duty of forgiveness and turning the other cheek. It assumed that a deliberate wrong would be resented, and in the Middle Ages, at least, it held to a doctrine of strict liability for intentional or unintentional injury. It assumed that the desire for vengeance was natural and proper. Primarily, then, the money payment of the Anglo-Saxon dooms was expected to quench vengeance and prevent a long chain of killings, woundings, and injuries.

THE EVOLUTION OF COURTS

The Norman Conquest of England did not destroy the Anglo-Saxon courts of the counties and hundreds. They persisted as local courts, and only in the thirteenth century did they begin to lose their importance as the principal courts of first instance, giving way to the expanding jurisdiction of the royal courts. The county court was durable; it still exists in the twentieth century. The local courts of county and hundred were rooted deep in the communities which they served. They were not royal creations so far as we know, and if the Norman and Angevin kings used them for purposes of administration and taxation and justice, the local courts, nevertheless, often retained their local customs in the face of royal orders and com-

---

[2] See Dooms of Aethelbert of Kent (601–604), in S & M, pp. 2–4. For Anglo-Saxon laws generally, see the definitive edition by F. Liebermann, *Gesetze der Angelsachsen*, with German translation (Halle, 1903).

mon law. An outstanding illustration of the vitality of local custom was the persistence into modern times of gavelkind, the system of land tenure in Kent, where even the Norman genius for simplifying Anglo-Saxon property arrangements failed to overthrow an older custom of equal inheritance among heirs.

Alongside the local courts of Anglo-Saxon communities the Normans introduced seignorial courts which dealt with customary relations between lord and vassal, vassal and vassal, and lord and villein. By a doctrine of feudalism each lord was entitled to hold a court for his own tenants, free and unfree. Thus arose baronial courts for the freeholders and customary courts for the villeins.

Also alongside the older county courts and hundred courts there appeared after the Norman Conquest an elaborate system of ecclesiastical courts. William I initiated this arrangement, which separated the bishop from the business of the county court and led to the creation of provincial and diocesan courts for the clergy. These ecclesiastical courts still exist in modern England, but their preoccupation with canon law puts them outside the scope of this study.[3]

In the Angevin period many cities, towns, and boroughs purchased charters, by which they usually secured the privilege of trial by fellow townsmen in their own town courts. These borough courts, along with fair courts (*piepoudre* courts) and the staple courts later in the fourteenth century, determined suits according to law merchant and their own various local customs, which flourished under grants of special privileges.[4]

In the course of the twelfth and thirteenth centuries there

---

[3] F. Makower, *Constitutional History and Constitution of the Church of England* (1895), devotes eighty pages to the ecclesiastical courts.

[4] On borough privileges, see A. Ballard, *British Borough Charters*, 1042–1216 (Cambridge, 1913), for analyses of some 300 charters and documents. See also Mary Bateson, *Borough Customs*, Selden Society, Vols. 18, 21 (1904, 1906).

appeared in England a number of royal courts. In later centuries some were to be labeled common-law courts, others equity courts, and still others prerogative courts. However, in the twelfth and thirteenth centuries such labels and distinctions are not strictly applicable. The early Angevin monarchs did not think in the language of Montesquieu and his eighteenth-century division of powers into legislative, executive, and judicial. Rather, these monarchs employed the same personnel to perform any necessary task of royal government in the most direct and efficient manner.

In his coronation oath the medieval king assumed a three-fold responsibility: 1) the protection of the Church, 2) the preservation of the peace, and 3) the administration of justice.[5] Preservation of the peace was both a duty and a right of the king. Preservation of the peace underlay the handling of pleas of the Crown (*placita coronae*), which can be divided into two classes: 1) proprietary matters affecting royal property and 2) breaches of the king's peace. The latter gave the king jurisdiction over a group of crimes such as treason, arson, murder, mayhem, rape, ambush, highway robbery, burglary, and theft. By breaking the king's peace the felon became the king's enemy and might lose "life or member" and his lands. If the felon escaped capture, he might be outlawed.

The doctrine of the king's peace and its maintenance gave the king a large field for the exercise of authority. His power was absolute in the administration of justice, and he was free to innovate in the procedures by which he would act to protect proprietary rights and preserve the peace. Thus, if he wished, he could delegate his authority and send commissioners into all of the older local courts to enforce his regalian rights, and he could create new courts for the hearing of royal pleas. Royal freedom to innovate in the field of administration accounts for

---

[5] S & M, p. 192, The coronation oath of Edward II (1308); *Statutes of the Realm*, I, 168.

the fact that first from the *Curia Regis* and later from the king's council there evolved about thirty different courts without benefit of what would now be called statutory authorization. Here discussion will deal only with the king's courts known as *Curia Regis*, Exchequer, Common Pleas, King's Bench, Justices-in-Eyre, and those specially commissioned courts known as Assize, *Nisi Prius*, Gaol (Jail) Delivery, and *Oyer* and *Terminer*.

CURIA REGIS

To assist him in the management of his own affairs the medieval English king, like any other great lord, maintained a household of ministers and servants. Among these were such officials as the chancellor, treasurer, steward, butler, chamberlain, marshal, and constable. This core of officials traveled constantly with the king as he moved about his domains, carrying with them, in the twelfth century at least, the records of government. The modern capital city, housing official bureaus with their elaborate files of records, papers, and correspondence, has no counterpart in twelfth-century Christian Europe. When Henry II moved his residence, the principal officials of government and the entire household moved with him on horseback, attending to royal administration in the course of the itinerary.

For the determination of large and important matters the king occasionally sought the assistance of his tenants-in-chief, who were summoned to meet with the king at a certain place. There the king had the right to take the counsel of anyone, but his tenants-in-chief, by the customary terms of the feudal contract, were under a particular obligation to give the king "aid and counsel" (*concilium*). Such a meeting, or event, was a session of the court of the king (*curia regis*). In fact, any court in the king's presence (*coram rege*) or in his name was a royal court. The character of the meeting which produced the Assize of Clarendon (1166) is reflected in the opening lines of an ordinance outlining the procedure to be followed by itinerant justices going out to all of the counties of England. Henry II ordained this procedure "by the counsel of all his barons for the preservation of peace and the enforcement of justice. . . ."[6] The jurisdiction of the *Curia Regis* was so wide as to defy precise description. With some certainty we can call it a court of first resort between tenants-in-chief of the king on any matter. In such cases the king or his justiciar would preside over a court composed of feudal lords, who would judge the dispute according to feudal customary law. The jurisdiction of the *Curia Regis* was unaffected by distinctions between civil and criminal actions. And the greatest men in the realm might be judged by the *Curia Regis*. It was at a royal council at Northampton that Henry II's justiciar, William fitzStephen, earl of Leicester, pronounced judgment against Thomas Becket, archbishop of Canterbury.

The plea rolls of the *Curia Regis* date from 1194 and are the predecessors of the *De Banco* and *Coram Rege* rolls subsequently kept by the courts of Common Pleas and King's Bench.[7]

In the evolution of the king's council a distinction is sometimes made between meetings of the small group of officials constantly attending the king and meetings of the great council (*magnum concilium*). The great council containing the royal tenants-in-chief met infrequently; but the small council, itinerant with the king, could meet at any time throughout the year, for it was always in the king's presence. It was before the small council, meeting as the *Curia Regis*, that Richard of Anesty in 1158 finally received an award in his case against Mabel de Francheville. He had spent about five years and £188 8s. 8d. on travel expenses trying to find the swiftly moving king, Henry II, to secure a hearing.

The jurisdiction of the small council was identical with that

---

[6] Assize of Clarendon (1166), S & M, pp. 76–77.

[7] S. B. Chrimes, *An Introduction to the Administrative History of Medieval England* (Oxford, 1952), p. 77, n. 2.; see also *Curia Regis Rolls*, Public Record Office, and Pipe Roll Society, XIV and XXIV; C. T. Flower, *Introduction to Curia Regis Rolls* (1199–1230), Selden Society, Vol. 62 (1944).

of the great council, and in some of its work it anticipated the functions of King's Bench. Important cases of great difficulty were reserved for it. When litigants could secure a hearing, the small council served them well, for it contained judges expert in the administration of the realm and learned in its law. But these officials were often preoccupied with the king's business, such as the meeting of the Exchequer, and at such times could not meet as a court determining private litigation.

EXCHEQUER

The fluid, flexible character of royal administration in the twelfth century brought together many of the same officers for various purposes. The marshal, the chamberlain, the chancellor, the justiciar, and the treasurer were all members of the small council; they also sat in a court for royal financial matters. These men with the help of clerks and accountants formed the upper Exchequer, contrasted in the *Dialogue of the Exchequer* with a "treasury of receipt" called the lower Exchequer.[8] Since the officials constituting the Exchequer were also members of the king's council, great or small, they were able to hear at the Exchequer pleas touching the royal finances and other pleas as well. They did not need to move to another building and sit as another court when hearing matters other than the king's.

With the specialization of bureaucratic functions and staff in the thirteenth century, the court of Exchequer, probably the first offshoot from the king's council, began to keep its own special roll as a tribunal in the reign of Henry III.

For certain cases the Exchequer was the most desirable of the medieval royal courts because its orders could not be ignored, even in the palatinates of Durham and Chester, where

---

[8] *S.C.*, pp. 199–241, gives extracts from the Latin text of the *Dialogus de Scaccario* written in 1177 by Richard fitzNigel, treasurer of the Exchequer. R. L. Poole, *The Exchequer in the Twelfth Century* (Oxford, 1912) is a guide to the work.

the ordinary writs did not run. Exchequer was originally a court of equity as well as a court of common law, and it could take cognizance of suits directly; that is, the plaintiff need not initiate his suit in Exchequer by securing an original writ from Chancery. But in the middle of the fourteenth century Exchequer gave up its equity jurisdiction at a time when Chancery was emerging as the court most active in the administration of equitable remedies. By 1357 Exchequer had become but one of several royal courts judging cases by common law.

COMMON PLEAS

Henry II experimented with various arrangements for the dispensation of royal justice. In 1178 he appointed five judges—two ecclesiastics and three laymen—to sit as a permanent court to hear all pleas warranted by the king's writ. The British scholar S. B. Chrimes has warned against assuming that this commission of five judges marks the foundation of the later court of Common Pleas.[9] Rather, the commission of 1178 simply provided litigants with some assurance of receiving a hearing from a panel of judges, which may, incidentally, have followed the king.

Magna Carta definitely mentions the court of Common Pleas in Chapter 17: "Common pleas shall not follow our court but shall be held in some definite place." That place came to be Westminster, westward along the Thames River a short distance from the city of London.

The judicial business of this court was not so markedly different from that of the royal council that it was necessary at the outset to provide Common Pleas with its own records. However, the court of Common Pleas was principally concerned with disputes between subject and subject; the king was usually not involved. By 1234 the process of specialization

---

[9] Chrimes, *Introduction to Administrative History*, p. 49.

in the central administration touched the court of Common Pleas and it began to keep its own records or rolls; not long afterward it acquired its own seal, which was affixed to writs, or orders issuing from "the Bench" or "the Common Bench," as this court was variously called.

Henry II and his successors in the Angevin line were well served by judges learned in the law. Ranulph Glanvill became justiciar in 1180. Among his contemporaries were Richard of Ilchester, John of Oxford, and Geoffrey Ridel. These men were members of the king's council, sat as justices in courts at Westminster and also went out into the counties as justices-in-eyre. Such a man as John of Lexington knew canon law and Roman law as well as English laws and customs. Martin of Pateshull, the master of Bracton, served as a judge of Common Pleas in 1217, and William of Raleigh, whose work Bracton admired, was a judge of Common Pleas in 1228 and for some years thereafter.[10]

JUSTICES-IN-EYRE: THE GENERAL EYRE

Henry II experimented with arrangements for a court to make royal justice available for litigants who sought out the king and his court. Henry also experimented with the device of sending out judges on circuit into the counties of England to hold the pleas of the Crown and all other pleas as well. Earlier in the century Henry I had commissioned judges from the central court to try royal pleas in the counties, but it remained for his grandson Henry II to systematize this practice and build it into an institution, the general eyre. What Henry II began his successors continued until 1341, by which time other means of

---

[10] For biographies of medieval justices see John Campbell, *Lives of the Chief Justices of England from the Norman Conquest till the Death of Lord Tenterden*, 3 vols. (1849–57), and E. Foss, *Judges of England, with Sketches of Their Lives and Notices Connected with the Courts at Westminster, 1066–1864*, 9 vols. (1848–64).

raising money and other officers for keeping the peace were ready to supplant the general eyre. Henry II's first general eyre to hear all pleas went out in 1168. In 1175 he ordered three circuits through the counties, and he intended that he himself should take one of them with his entire household and court. The next year, in line with the Assize of Northampton, eighteen justices traveled on six circuits. In 1179 twenty-one justices were commissioned to go out on four circuits.

The jurisdiction of the judges was clear. They had instructions about the questions which they were to put to juries from every hundred and every vill. These articles of the eyre, *capitula itineris*, grew increasingly specific, and ultimately in the fourteenth century there were about 140 of them—enough to thresh and winnow every county visited.[11] The articles of the eyre have been grouped in four categories: 1) felonies, 2) the proprietary rights of the king, 3) the assumption or misuse of franchises, 4) the misdoings of royal officials, sheriffs, bailiffs, foresters, coroners, and the like.[12] Not all of the information obtained by the inquests led to trial or punishment. On some matters it was enough merely to record what juries reported under oath. But the eyre was definitely judicial as well as administrative; in the thirteenth century litigation at Westminster was transferred back to the county when the eyre arrived there.

Itinerant justices were delegates of the king, and petitioners sometimes presented grievances directly to them in hope of securing an equitable remedy. Many persons, perhaps by reason of poverty, infirmity, or other good cause, could not go to Westminster to secure from Chancery the original writ which

---

[11] Helen M. Cam, *Studies in the Hundred Rolls: Some Aspects of Thirteenth-Century Administration*, Oxford Studies in Social and Legal History, Vol. VI, No. XI (Oxford, 1921), Appendix II, pp. 92–101, provides an analysis of the chronological development of the articles of the eyre from Roger of Hoveden's list of 1194 onward.

[12] P & M, II, 521.

would initiate a trial. But at the time of a general eyre they could state their complaints in the form of a bill, or *querela*, and hope that the itinerant justices would provide a redress of grievances. The example which follows is but one of many such cases.[13] A few lines of the original text precede W. C. Bolland's translation.

Fesrekyn's Complaint A.D. 1292

Cher sire joe vus cri merci issi cum vus estis mis en lu seinur le Roy pur dreit fere a poveris e a riches. Joe Johan Fesrekyn face pleint a deu e a vus Sire Justice ke Richard le Carpenter Clerk du bayli de Salopesburie ke le vaundist Richard me de teent vi mars le queuz Joe li bayla par escrit. . . .

Dear Sir, of you who are put in the place of our lord the King to do right to poor and to rich, I cry mercy. I, John Fesrekyn, make my complaint to God and to you, Sir Justice, of Richard, the carpenter that is clerk of the bailiff of Shrewsbury, that the said Richard detains from me six marks which I paid him upon receiving from him an undertaking in writing by which he bound himself to find me in board and lodging in return for the money he had from me; and he keeps not what was agreed between us, but as soon as he had gotten hold of the money he abandoned me and constrained me by my body and gave me a scrap of bread as though I had been but a pauper begging his bread for God's sake, and through him I all but died for hunger. And for all this I cry to you mercy, dear Sir, and pray, for God's sake, that you will see that I get my money back before you leave this town, or else I shall never have it back again, for I tell you that the rich folk all back each other up to keep the poor folk in this town from getting their rights. As soon, my Lord, as I get my money I shall go to the Holy Land, and there I will pray for the King of England and for you by your name, Sir John de Berewick; for I tell you that not a farthing have I to spend on a pleader. And so, for this, dear Sir, be gracious to me that I may get me my money back.[14]

---

[13] See H. G. Richardson and G. O. Sayles, *Select Cases of Procedure without Writ under Henry III*, Selden Society, Vol. 60 (1941), for extracts from the *Curia Regis Rolls* and the *Assize Rolls*.

[14] W. C. Bolland, *Year Book of the Eyre of Kent, 6 and 7, Edward II (1313–14)*, Selden

Although the arrival of the general eyre may have meant justice otherwise unobtainable for a few individuals such as John Fesrekyn, the sustained and frequent use of the eyre was not a popular practice. About the time of the Provisions of Oxford (1258) and immediately afterward there was popular resistance to eyres held in any one county more frequently than every seven years. In May of 1261 at Hertford the royal justices were opposed as they attempted to open their court. Certain barons alleged that they had not received the customary notice forty days in advance and they also questioned the propriety of an eyre coming so close on the heels of a previous eyre court. The justices asked the king, Henry III, for instructions, and his reply showed an awareness of the seven-year interval: "Since we learn for a certainty that six years have not yet elapsed since our justices last came into this county, we command you to supersede this eyre, and pass on to Northampton."[15]

Apparently from this opinion that the general eyre ought not to be hold more frequently than seven years in any one county there emerged the idea that the justices should be assigned to hear and determine the articles of the eyre every seven years. Yet, in fact, as Helen Cam has demonstrated, the eyres were never established to take place automatically at seven-year intervals.[16]

From the earliest days of the institution, the king sent out his most distinguished councilors and justices on the general eyre. This practice had the beneficial result of bringing the justices into direct contact with all the conditions of local government throughout the realm while it trained the people of the English countryside to an awareness of the procedures and the substance of the common law. The linkage between the central courts and the county courts, effectively maintained for

Society, Vol. 27 (1912), pp. xxiii–xxiv. From the endorsement on the bill, the editor concludes that Fesrekyn recovered a substantial amount of his money.

[15] Cam, *The Hundred Rolls*, p. 85.

[16] Ibid., p. 84 and Appendix III, pp. 103–13.

about one hundred and fifty years, helps to explain the success of early parliaments, which drew representatives from the shires to central meetings. It is not too much to say that the general eyres helped to create the sense of a community of the realm.

KING'S BENCH

In the course of the thirteenth century, by an almost imperceptible evolution, the court of King's Bench acquired its distinct character and its own records, the *Coram Rege* rolls, which begin in 1234.

The jurisdiction of this court was based on the royal right and duty to preserve the peace, and the cases tried before King's Bench were principally pleas of the Crown (*placita coronae*), appeals of felony, breaches of the peace, criminal cases and actions in *quo warranto*, or why a subject exercised a franchise, that is, a particular right or liberty. Also King's Bench had an appellate jurisdiction over appeals of error from the court of Common Pleas. During the thirteenth century King's Bench and Common Pleas exercised a concurrent jurisdiction over civil actions. Some of the judicial work of King's Bench may be explained by the fact that it was itinerant with the king and consequently was sometimes available in county courts to try cases involving the Petty Assizes, the possessory actions touching seisin of real property. Unlike the court of Common Pleas, the court of King's Bench was not stationary in the thirteenth century. Accompanying the perambulating royal household, the court of King's Bench had ready access to the king's council for the determination of particularly difficult cases. Likewise, the king had ready access to the court of King's Bench, where he might occasionally join the judges and participate in the operation of the court peculiarly his own.[17]

[17] For the jurisdiction of King's Bench, see G. O. Sayles, *Select Cases in the Court of King's Bench under Edward I*, Selden Society, Vol. 57 (1938), II, xxxiv–lxxiii.

Not until the opening of the nineteenth century were the law terms, the sessions of royal courts, firmly linked with the calendar and separated from such variable ecclesiastical holy days as Easter. The medieval courts met during four periods of the year, and the nineteenth-century reform in 1831 preserved the names of the four medieval terms while giving them fixed spans of time as follows: 1) Hilary, 11–31 January; 2) Easter, 15 April–8 May; 3) Trinity, 22 May–12 June; 4) Michaelmas, 2–25 November.[18] In the Middle Ages, the court of King's Bench varied somewhat from the law terms of the nineteenth century. G. O. Sayles, in the introduction to Volume II of his *Select Cases in the Court of King's Bench under Edward I* (1938), tabulated the sessions of the court and concluded that its terms were as follows:

1) Michaelmas, 6 October to 25 November.
2) Hilary, 20 January to the beginning of Lent.
3) Easter, from the second Sunday after Easter until a date about four weeks later.
4) Trinity, from the octave of Trinity to the quindene of St. John the Baptist, 8 July.

These dates roughly approximate the periods during which other royal courts were in session. Exceptions should be mentioned: during vacation time between terms, the curial justices were often on circuit in the counties serving as justices-in-eyre or with one of the several commissions such as the Commission of Assize.

Several famous judges sat on the court of King's Bench in the thirteenth century. Foremost among them, in the light of his later reputation, was Henry de Bratton, or Bracton, the author of the most widely read law treatise of his age, *De legibus et consuetudinibus Angliae*. Bracton was a justice-in-eyre (1245),

---

[18] For a detailed account of the "law terms," see *Handbook of Dates for Students of English History*, C. R. Cheney, ed. (London: The Royal Historical Society, 1955), pp. 65–69.

took county assizes (1248–57), and became a justice of King's Bench and a member of the group of legal advisers in the king's council. He died in 1268.

SPECIALLY COMMISSIONED COURTS

The king in medieval England accepted a general responsibility to maintain the laws of the realm and to render justice impartially to rich and poor alike. Edward II at his coronation was asked, *inter alia*, "Sire, will you, so far as in you lies, cause justice to be rendered rightly, impartially, and wisely, in compassion and in truth?" And Edward answered, "I will do so." The question and Edward's promise were in keeping with medieval political thought, which supported a doctrine of the sovereignty of law. The sovereignty, or supremacy, of law was recognized not only in England but throughout Latin Christendom during the Middle Ages. The German scholar Fritz Kern has observed, "Not only the law of the realm, but also rights of property were considered laws which the king could not curtail on his initiative alone."[19] A political theory supporting absolute monarchy did not emerge in the Middle Ages. The king's coronation oath gave him a heavy responsibility to respect and enforce the law. He must, as Edward II promised, "cause justice to be rendered rightly, impartially, and wisely, in compassion and in truth."

But the political thought of the Middle Ages imposed no restrictions on the monarch as he devised administrative procedures for the rendering of justice. In the field of administration the king was supreme; he had no peer. He was free to create courts, to appoint justices, and to issue orders touching

[19] Fritz Kern, *Kingship and Law in the Middle Ages*, trans. and Introd. by S. B. Chrimes (Oxford, 1939), p. 194; and C. H. McIlwain, *The Growth of Political Thought in the West* (New York, 1932), p. 195: "The king is under the law, and he must rule justly and 'for the common profit of all the realm.' If he fails to do this he is no king but a tyrant."

times and places and persons through which the laws would be enforced. He could do justice in his council, which was always near the king, or he could create new courts as the need arose. The creation of new courts never depleted his authority to invent other means of doing justice. Thus the reservoir of royal authority in administration remained undiminished by the growth of the Exchequer's jurisdiction or the jurisdictions of King's Bench and Common Pleas. If the general eyre was insufficient as an instrument for rendering justice, then the king could use men specially commissioned to hear and decide certain cases in certain places and at certain times not necessarily within the customary law terms.

Assize. Henry II developed several procedures for handling disputes about property rights. The protection of seisin, the protection of possession, was at the center of Henry II's legislation over a period of years between 1164 and 1179. Moreover, Henry II clearly wished to see the jury employed in the settlement of disputes about who had the better right to the enjoyment of seisin. Out of this royal concern developed the doctrine that no man need answer for his free tenement without a royal writ. This quickly came to mean that when a plaintiff challenged a possessor's right to hold a certain free tenure, the possessor could secure a royal order commanding the dispute to be tried before a royal court, which would consider evidence presented by a jury of neighbors in the county where the dispute arose.

The first expression of Henry's concern about disputed possession and his preference for trial by jury occurs in the Constitutions of Clarendon (1164). The Church courts claimed jurisdiction over all land that had been granted in frankalmoin tenure, or free alms. If one party in a case claimed the land was frankalmoin and another claimed it was lay fee, then, said Chapter 9 of the Constitutions, the matter should be settled by the verdict of a jury. Thus arose the Assize of Utrum.

In 1166 the Assize of Novel Disseisin was established. Here the intent was to supply a speedy remedy for the dispossessed freeholder: "The king himself will protect by royal writ and inquest of neighbors every seisin of a free tenement."[20] The principle underlying this remedy may have been derived from the *actio spolii* of the canon law. At any rate, it aimed at restoring to possession a person whose seisin was recently disturbed. On the ground that a person recently dispossessed is at a great disadvantage in protecting his interests, the man recently disseised was entitled to repossess his property. The jury would identify the man recently disseised. Then, if need be, another legal action could test the question of who had the better right to the disputed property.

Still another action was developed to protect possession; this was known as the Assize of Mort d'Ancestor and may have been the work of the Council of Northampton (1176). The purpose of this remedy was to protect the possession of an heir whose ancestor had died seized of the land in dispute. The jury, a body of neighbors sworn to tell the truth to a royal court, was asked to answer whether the dead man had possession at the time of his death and whether the claimant was his heir.

Henry II created one more possessory action, the Assize of Darrein Presentment (*ultima presentatione*). Here the matter in dispute was not a tract of land. Rather, it was advowson, the power of nominating a clergyman to fill a vacant office in a church. The power of nomination was treated like a property right, and the jury was asked to state under oath who presented or nominated the last parson of a church.

The possessory assizes were then: 1) Utrum, 2) Novel Disseisin, 3) Mort d'Ancestor, and 4) Darrein Presentment. All provided work for royal courts and used juries from the counties in which the disputes arose. Cases involving these questions of possession could be handled either by royal justices or

---

[20] P & M, I, 146.

by commissioners appointed to travel on circuits for the sole purpose of hearing only possessory causes. Magna Carta in Chapter 18 reflected the concern of the barons in 1215 that justices for the possessory assizes should be available frequently, and they asked for "two justices through each county four times a year" to sit with four knights of each county. This proved to be an excessive number of assize courts, and the frequency was quickly reduced to one a year.

By the Statute of Westminster II (1285) the jurisdiction of justices of assize was enlarged to include all actions touching real property.

Nisi Prius. English royal courts insisted on use of the jury as a means of determining questions of fact. However, for many jurors the journey to Westminster Hall was expensive, fatiguing, and a serious interruption in their affairs. Edward I sought to maintain the use of juries but to lighten the burden on the juror by means of a procedure set out in the Statute of Westminster II, Chapter 30 (1285). The plaintiff and the defendant in an action at common law before the court of Common Pleas at Westminster would be allowed to argue the case until the pleadings resulted in an issue. If matters of fact were involved, then the case could be continued in the county where the dispute arose and the jurors resided. Thus the jurors were spared the journey to London. An additional step provided that at the opening of litigation the sheriff should be ordered to have the litigants at Westminster on a certain date "unless earlier" (*nisi prius*) royal justices should arrive in that county. If the royal justices arrived in time, then the litigants as well as the jurors could avoid the costs of travel.

The jurisdiction of *Nisi Prius* commissioners covered any action which could be initiated before one of the common-law courts at Westminster. And the connection with Westminster was not severed by *Nisi Prius* commissions, for after the pleadings and the verdict of a jury, the commission did not give judgment. After trial the record was returned to Westminster, where judgment was pronounced in the court in which the case presumably originated.

The Statute of Westminster II ordered three commissions a year, but in practice they were reduced to two commissions annually in each county.

Gaol Delivery. In the Middle Ages, as in more modern times, inadequate prisons were frequently overcrowded with prisoners awaiting trial. If these prisoners were charged with breaking the king's peace by committing some great crime or felony, they could be tried only before a royal court with jurisdiction over pleas of the Crown. But the general eyres came infrequently to any one county, and justices of the King's Bench might not be available. Early in the thirteenth century the king began to appoint commissions to try prisoners, not so much to free the prisoners from a certain jail as to free (*deliverare*) the jail of its burden of prisoners. All of the prisoners would eventually receive trial.

Most of the cases handled by commissioners of Gaol Delivery involved high criminal justice. Charges of homicide were typical of the judicial business of this commission, which would be made up of three or four knights of the shire, prominent men of the locality. Their proceedings were recorded, and although not strictly assize rolls, they were, nevertheless, bound with the Assize Rolls.

Oyer and Terminer. The most specialized of all commissions in the reign of Edward I was that which appointed two or three royal justices and occasionally a great landholder to hear and determine (*oyer* and *terminer*) a single case—which might involve a felony or another crime such as rebellion or riot. The person charged with such a high crime might not be in prison and the commission would have jurisdiction over indictment as well as pleading, trial, judgment, and sentence.

Each commission kept a record of its work in regular common-law form. The records of all commissions of *Oyer* and *Terminer* were grouped under the name Assize Rolls.

The steady employment of juries of freeholders and the appointment of knights of the shire as commissioners to serve as justices show the Crown making excellent use of men prominent in their localities. These "lay judges"—to contrast them with the professional justices—represented the royal authority in their counties and, even more readily, represented their county courts at Westminster. After the decline of the general eyre they became essential to administration of royal justice in the late fourteenth and fifteenth centuries. Under the title "Justice of the Peace," many knights of the shire shouldered heavy administrative and judicial work for the Crown. But this later development in commissioned courts lies beyond the present discussion.

C h a p t e r   7
Chancery: Secretariat
and Writ-Shop

Chancery emerged as the principal secretariat of the English royal court long before the opening of the thirteenth century. Thereafter the chancellor and his staff steadily enlarged the scope of their services, and by the close of the fifteenth century the chancellor presided over his own court of equity, supplementing by his jurisdiction the more inflexible rules of common law.[1] The development of the independent equitable jurisdiction of the chancellor lies beyond the period under discussion here; even so, we should note that before 1307 the chancellor had responsibilities for the handling of petitions, from which it was not a long step to the role of judge in a court of equity. And Chancery is a division of the royal administrative machinery also inseparably linked with the procedures of the common law. From the Chancery of the twelfth and thirteenth centuries went out the original writs initiating litigation as well as the judicial writs guiding procedures in litigation. All actions touching freehold required a royal writ from Chancery to set the judicial process in motion.[2] The

---

[1] J.E.A. Jolliffe, *The Constitutional History of Medieval England*, 3rd ed. (London, 1954), pp. 466–68.

[2] Provisions of Westminster (1259), in S & M, p. 147.

requirement about freehold, which Henry II early compelled the realm to accept, did not hold in other matters; nevertheless, plaintiffs appeared at the Chancery to obtain royal justice by means of common-law writs, for which they willingly paid substantial fees. The chancellor and his staff, better than any other group of officials, knew the records of royal administration and procedures of the common law.

From the household post of king's chaplain, as personal secretary in charge of the king's chapel and in charge of royal charters, the chancellor moved up in the thirteenth century to become the principal figure in the royal council. Although his duties and his prominence increased, the ecclesiastical character of his office was never completely forgotten; not until the fourteenth century do we come on the appointment of a layman, Sir Robert Bouchier, to this high post. A chancellor who served the king loyally and well could look forward confidently to the reward of a bishopric.[3] In this instance, as in others, the resources of the Church were called into the aid of the civil administration.

The chancellor was a peer of the other great officers of state who were always at court daily consulting the king's will. Like the justiciar and the treasurer, the chancellor was in a position to affect the character of the administration. The barons of England recognized the chancellor's powerful role when they attempted on more than one occasion to secure control over the machinery of royal administration, from which they felt more and more excluded as the thirteenth century wore on. They considered making the chancellor's office elective; they also attempted to prevent the issuance of extraordinary or unusual writs by Chancery.[4]

---

[3] *Fleta*, Book II, Chapter 13, reflects a tradition. The chancellor's office "ought to be entrusted, along with the charge of the greater seal of the realm, to a wise and discreet man, such as a bishop or a clerk of great dignity." Trans. by H. G. Richardson and G. O. Sayles, Selden Society, Vol. 72 (1953), p. 123.

[4] Provisions of Oxford (1258), in S & M, pp. 144–45.

About the year 1200 the chancellor was assisted by a staff with mixed duties—to distinguish the sergeants of the king's chapel from the clerks of the Chancery would have been very difficult. The chancellor then had no salary or secular income as a payment for his civil duties other than the irregular profits from the use of the Great Seal. The private subject obtaining an original writ bearing the Great Seal was required to pay a fee for invoking royal authority, and for these fees the chancellor then made no account to the Exchequer.

Within a few years, however, the chancellor's office became more definite and his staff more specialized. About 1238 the chapel and Chancery personnel separated. Then, on the appointment of Nicholas of Ely as chancellor in 1260, the Exchequer began to pay him an annual salary grant of 400 marks, a practice later continued and confirmed by Edward I.

According to traditional political theory and practice, the appointment of the chancellor and other officials was one of the rights of the king—a royal prerogative which he might not give away or share with other persons. In the middle of the thirteenth century, this concept was challenged by the English baronage, who sensed that the royal administration had become increasingly bureaucratic and professional and that the barons no longer shared in the management of the affairs of the realm as their ancestors had at times when the king summoned a great council of his tenants-in-chief. They took the line of argument, to be used repeatedly after the thirteenth century, that the king should serve the good of the realm, that the king should be served by men guided by other than selfish interests, and that the barons should have a voice in appointing the principal officials. A representative group of barons should be constantly at the royal court to supervise the activity of the king's ministers. The baronial policy, if it had been translated into reality, would have been an incisive blow at medieval kingship.[5]

---

[5] See above, pp. 60–66, for a discussion of baronial efforts to share in administration.

A foreshadowing of the baronial effort at control of great offices may appear in the case of Ralph de Neville (1222–44), who insisted that his appointment as chancellor was a grant for life. This man took a very proprietary attitude toward his office, asserting that the Great Seal had come to him in 1226 by royal grant and the "common council of the realm." In 1231 he extracted a charter from Henry III giving him the office for life and the power, moreover, to transfer the keeping of the Great Seal to some assignee. Not satisfied with this, he secured a renewal and confirmation of the charter in 1235. Then, when his obvious uneasiness was fully justified by Henry's efforts to remove him from office in 1238, Ralph de Neville stubbornly refused to resign, insisting that his charters provided "that he was not to be deposed from his custody of the Seal unless so ordered by the consent and council of the entire realm."[6] It would be unwise to read into Ralph de Neville's language a sense on his part of the modern idea of ministerial responsibility. Rather, his case should be considered with that of other officials in a turbulent period when great men, such as the justiciar Hubert de Burgh, suddenly fell from the heights of power, and others, such as Peter des Roches, towered up in their places. Ralph de Neville clung pathetically to his office and tried to bolster his position by invoking the consent and council of the entire realm. In this hope he failed.[7]

The time was not far off, however, when a baronial faction would claim as a general principle what Ralph de Neville claimed as a personal right: namely, that the common council of the realm, not the king, should control the chancellor's office

---

[6] Matthew Paris, *Chronica Majora*, H. R. Luard, ed., Rolls Series, 7 vols. (London, 1872–84), III, 74: *"Ut non deponetur ab eius sigilli custodia nisi totius regni ordinante consensu et concilio."*

[7] Probably the office of chancellor was in abeyance between the fall of Ralph de Neville (1238) and his death (1244). See T. D. Hardy, *A Catalogue of Lord Chancellors, Keepers of the Seal, Masters of the Rolls, and Principal Officers of the High Court of Chancery from the Earliest Period* (London, 1843); and L. B. Dibben, "Chancellor and Keeper of the Seal in Henry III's Reign," *English Historical Review*, XXVII, 39–53.

as well as others. Repeatedly the barons requested that the chancellor's office should not be left vacant; it should be filled by a man who would perform his duties faithfully while guided by the common council of the realm (*per commune consilium regni*). In 1244 a joint committee of barons and prelates demanded the appointment of a chancellor, a justiciar, and a treasurer—men who were to be always with the king. Owing to the lack of a chancellor, the barons declared, the Great Seal was often set to writs that were contrary to justice.[8] Again in 1248 and in 1249 the barons attempted to obtain a chancellor who would act in line with baronial views. They complained that the functions of the Chancery were performed by men who consulted their own advantage instead of the good of the realm.[9] Again in the Provisions of Oxford (1258) the barons demanded an annual report from the chancellor, the treasurer, and the justiciar to a committee of twenty-four barons representing the common council of the realm.[10] In the Provisions of Oxford the barons voiced their anxiety about the proper issuing of writs. "Concerning the Chancellor: The same [has been decided] with regard to the Chancellor; so that he shall render account of his term at the end of the year, and that merely by the king's will he shall seal nothing out of course, but shall do so by the advice of the council that surrounds the king."[11]

By including the chancellor among the other great offices to be controlled, the barons underscored the intimate connection between Chancery and the administration of justice. Simon de Montfort and his followers fought hard for their position but lost the war; the program which they advocated died with Earl Simon at the battle of Evesham. The royal victory of Henry III and his son Edward permitted the king to exercise the royal prerogative in appointments and also in the field of

---

[8] Paris, *Chronica Majora*, IV, 362.

[9] Ibid., V, 5.

[10] *S.C.*, pp. 385–86; S & M, pp. 143–46.

[11] S & M, pp. 144–45.

administration, with the result that the common law continued to grow under royal rather than baronial direction.

Royal victories on the battlefield also confirmed what King Louis IX of France had stated in his award, the Mise of Amiens (1264), after the barons and Henry III had submitted their dispute to him as arbitrator.[12] Louis declared a theory of monarchy widely held throughout Europe in the thirteenth century when he decided that the king could freely promote, dismiss, and set aside his chief justiciar, chancellor, treasurer, and councilors and all other officials according to his own free will.[13]

The *Song of Lewes*, a Latin poem written about 1264, fairly stated both the royalist and the baronial arguments while favoring definitely the baronial side.

> Nor should the magnates of the realm heed whom he [the king] set over his own counties, or on whom he conferred the wardenship of castles, or whom he would have to show justice to his people. Further, he would have as chancellor and treasurer of his realm anyone soever at his own will, and counsellors of whatever nation, and various ministers at his own discretion, without the barons of England interfering in the king's acts. . . . They would disinherit the king. . . .[14]

In the long run the king kept control of the chancellor's appointment in the face of baronial demands. But the magnates of the realm continued to press the king to keep about him men learned in the law, as one can see in the *Articuli Super Cartas* of 1300.

> Moreover no common pleas shall henceforth be held in the exchequer, contrary to the form of the Great Charter. On the other hand the king wills that the chancery and the justices of his bench shall follow him; so that he may always have near him certain men

---

[12] See above, p. 64, for a discussion of the Mise of Amiens.
[13] *S.C.*, p. 396.
[14] *The Song of Lewes*, C. L. Kingsford, ed. (Oxford, 1890), quoted by B. Wilkinson, *Constitutional History of Medieval England* (London, 1958), III, 105.

expert in the law, who, whenever the need arises, will know how rightfully to dispatch all such business as may come before the court. Henceforth no writ touching the common law shall be issued under the small seal.[15]

The magnates never entirely abandoned the theory that law rules the dignity of the king, that the magnates, as well as the king, have a duty to protect the common good and to be concerned about the governance of the realm.

The contest over appointments had serious implications for the growth of the common law. In the thirteenth century the royal courts were the most progressive courts of England. The royal courts, while providing equitable remedies and expanding their jurisdictions, cooperated with the Chancery as it issued writs touching legal procedures. If the royal justices and the chancellor had been the tools of a baronial party representing solely the conservative interests of a feudal class, it is quite possible that the common-law forms of action would not have grown as rapidly, for as we have seen, the barons distrusted the inventiveness of the king's council and the Chancery in the creation of new writs; the barons attempted to confine Chancery to the issue of writs of course, i.e., the customary, the known, and the familiar remedies.

When new and unfamiliar cases were taken to the king, he acted with the advice of his council to provide a remedy. Even as new remedies were formulated in a steady flow of new writs, petitions and plaints continued to pour into the council. Some were presented to the treasurer in Exchequer, still others were presented to the chancellor, and by far the largest number were presented to the itinerant justices whose powers while on eyre represented those of the council.[16] If petitions reached the council, they were endorsed and disposed of; endorsements might read, "sue at common law"—"a writ on the sub-

---

[15] *Articuli Super Cartas* (1300), *Statutes of the Realm*, I, 138 f.; S & M, p. 175.

[16] On the matter of plaints, see H. G. Richardson and G. O. Sayles, *Select Cases of Procedure without Writ under Henry II*, Selden Society, Vol. 60 (1941).

ject shall be dispatched out of Chancery"—"the king will consider"—"a remedy will be provided," and so on.[17]

The chancellor, as a member of the council and chief of the writ-issuing bureau, knew both the pressure of petitions and the framing of new writs.[18] Thus the chancellor participated in the process by which the demands of a changing society were gradually translated into the concise formulas of the English royal writ. E. M. Morgan suggests that:

> The Chancellor's office better than any other must know what cases the ordinary courts would and could entertain. He more than any other official would be likely to have a sound judgment as to the proper remedy. And when the applications became too numerous for the king, or council, or Parliament to manage, he was the member of the official family best fitted to take them over and his office the best equipped to care for them.[19]

The career of Robert Burnell (d. 1292) shows the great chancellor of Edward I at the center of royal administration, involved in diplomacy, involved in legislation, busy with every aspect of Edward's strenuous early years as king. Burnell presided in the Parliament of May, 1275, which enacted the fifty-one sections of the Statute of Westminster I. Other significant statutes were framed within his term of office: Gloucester (1278), Mortmain (1279), and De Mercatoribus (1283). Before the Parliament of 1290 Burnell brought charges of corruption against certain judges.[20] He was active in the settlement of the disputed succession to the Scottish throne, which John Balliol and Robert Bruce both claimed by inheritance. A learned judge and statesman, Chancellor Burnell was easily, next to the king, the principal figure in the government of England "in touch

---

[17] *Rotuli Litterarum Clausarum in Turri Londinensi Asservati, 1204–27*, T. D. Hardy, ed., 2 vols. (London, 1833–44), Introduction, I, xxvi.

[18] F. M. Powicke, *The Thirteenth Century, 1216–1307* (Oxford, 1953), pp. 334–35.

[19] E. M. Morgan, *Introduction to the Study of Law* (Chicago and New York, 1926), p. 11.

[20] Powicke, *The Thirteenth Century* (Oxford, 1953), p. 335.

with all who wanted something done and were intimate enough with administrative processes to seek his advice or his authority."[21]

It is not possible to determine precisely when Chancery ceased to follow the king, but we can infer that London was becoming its home during the chancellorship of Burnell. In 1279, according to the *Annales Monastici* (II, 393), he left the king to hunt in the New Forest and returned from Winchester to London "as the fixed place where those who seek writs and pursue their rights might find the appropriate remedy."[22]

Realizing the chancellor's preeminence in the council and his intimate connection with all legal procedures, petitioners in the fourteenth century went directly "au Chancellor du Roi," begging a remedy; the usual form was a request in piteous phrases begging a remedy for the love of God and as a matter of grace and favor: "pur quei le did A.B. prie votre graciouse seignurie que vous ordinez remedie pour lonneur de dieu et en oevre de charitie."[23] Edward I tried to lessen the pressure of petitions on the council and to confine them to cases of great importance. The volume of petitions was apt to increase at a meeting of Parliament, and Edward endeavored to handle them systematically. "All the petitions shall be well examined immediately they have been received. Those which pertain to the Chancery shall be put in a separate bundle and those which pertain to the Exchequer in another bundle; and similarly let it be done with those which pertain to the justices."[24] The increasing business of the royal courts and of the council forced the delegation of some cases to the chancellor.[25] This

---

[21] Ibid.

[22] *Annales Monastici*, H. Luard, ed., Rolls Series, 5 vols. (London, 1864–69).

[23] J. F. Baldwin, *The King's Council in England during the Middle Ages* (Oxford, 1913), p. 250.

[24] William Stubbs, *The Constitutional History of England*, 3 vols. (Oxford, 1880), II, 286, n. 3, gives the ordinance in the Close Rolls, 21 Edw. I, m. 7.

[25] John Campbell, *Lives of the Lord Chancellors and Keepers of the Great Seal*, 8 vols. (London, 1869), I, 160, cites ten instances of petitions referred to Chancery for settlement in the reign of Edward I.

practice continued into the fourteenth century until the chancellor finally had his own court located in the upper end of Westminster Hall.[26]

The greater one's familiarity with the law of England, the more he will appreciate the long-range effects of the chancellor's acquiring an independent jurisdiction as judge of a court of equity. The English legal system has always shown a concern for what *ought* to be the results of a legal principle as well as a concern for the strict application of that principle. This distinction between *what is* and *what ought to be* may serve as a rough guide to the difference between common law and equity in the centuries after the fourteenth. Equity supplements the common law; its rules do not contradict the common law; rather, they aim at securing substantial justice when the strict rule of common law might work hardship.

The administration of equity did not begin with Chancery; the *Curia Regis* and the king's council were courts of equity long before Chancery began its judicial activity, and the king's council continued to act in this capacity after the Chancery court was clearly distinguished from the common-law courts. The equitable jurisdiction of the chancellor drained away none of the royal prerogative, none of the judicial power of the royal council; rather, the chancellor, after the fourteenth century, might be thought of as doing work which in an earlier time would have been handled by the council. He eventually carried into the court of Chancery the power to hear certain cases in much the same way as the itinerant justice carried into the county court the royal power to hear certain cases. In the county court itinerant justices dispensed justice as though in the presence of the king; persons seeking justice presented petitions, or plaints, to the justices-in-eyre in the thirteenth century in much the same fashion and in much the same words as persons later on in the fourteenth century presented

---

[26] T. D. Hardy, *Close Rolls*, I, xxvii; see also D. M. Kerly, *Historical Sketch of the Equitable Jurisdiction of the Court of Chancery* (Cambridge, 1890), pp. 1–92.

petitions to Chancery. Whether or not the jurisdiction of the justices-in-eyre or the jurisdiction of the chancellor should be described as a delegated jurisdiction, one point is clear—the justices-in-eyre and the chancellor acted as judges in equity when they heard plaints and petitions.

A discussion of Equity as a distinct body of procedures and legal principles can easily bog down in a swamp of definitions when it reaches backward into the Middle Ages. In theory, at least, all laws are equitable when they first come into use. With the passage of time laws become rigid and fixed in their application. Timid judges or unthinking officials fail to grasp the principle or the intent embodied in a rule. They hesitate to widen its application. The social order constantly changes, but the laws all too frequently lag behind. It then becomes necessary to close in some fashion the gap between social change and the legal system. In the thirteenth century the English king and his council, including his judges and great officers, were able to exercise the royal duty and right to develop new remedies for new wrongs. Thus new forms of action, new writs such as Trespass, and new royal courts such as Common Pleas and King's Bench were all "equitable" in the thirteenth century. The emergence of Chancery as a court of "equity" in the fourteenth century is worth noting, because its procedures ultimately led to a widening distinction between what were later called the common-law courts and the equity courts. But we should not look for the sixteenth- or seventeenth-century distinctions between common law and equity in the court system of the thirteenth century. In the thirteenth century every institution concerned with the administration of justice was equitable in the sense that it was free to provide substantial justice by enlarging the existing remedies. The Crown, working through the chancellor's office, seems to have been prompt to invent new remedies, and the baronage, resenting the activity, sought at times to curb it. Nevertheless, the chancellor's office was so central for the administration of justice that it continued its equitable functions, particularly in the handling of petitions. Since the chancellor, better than any other official, knew the existing law, he was in an excellent position to make judgments about what the law ought to be.

CHANCERY OFFICIALS

CHANCELLOR'S DEPUTY IN THE EXCHEQUER

In the epitome of Bracton, commonly designated as *Fleta*, we have in Book II, Chapter 13, "Of the Chancery," a full statement of the serious responsibilities of the chancellor's staff, who are to be "trustworthy and prudent clerks, who have sworn an oath to the king and have a wide experience in the laws and customs of England. It is their duty to hear and examine the petitions and plaints of petitioners and by means of royal writs to provide them with a remedy suitable to the nature of the wrongs they have revealed."[27]

One of the chancellor's staff was eventually lost to the Exchequer, which drew to its semiannual sessions at Easter and Michaelmas the principal figures of the small council permanently at court: the justiciar, chancellor, marshal, chamberlain, and constable. Among the clerks seated around the Exchequer table, with its large abacus for calculating the royal revenues, was the chancellor's clerk, who had the important function of verifying accounts presented and comparing Chancery and Exchequer records.[28] This man became the effective head of the Exchequer in the thirteenth century, chancellor of the Exchequer, guarding its seal and even then

[27] *Fleta*, Book II, 123.

[28] For a diagram of seating arrangements and personnel of the Exchequer sitting as a court for financial matters, see Charles Johnson, *The Course of the Exchequer by Richard son of Nigel* (London, 1950); a diagram, based on Johnson's work, appears in the text by Bryce Lyon, *A Constitutional and Legal History of Medieval England* (New York, 1961), p. 260.

performing functions not unlike those of his modern counterpart bearing the same title.

MASTER OF THE ROLLS

Chief of the Masters in Chancery was the Master of the Rolls or Keeper of the Rolls of Chancery, *custos rotulorum cancellariae domini regis.* The modern judicial Master of the Rolls, through a deputy Keeper, continues to bear at the Public Record Office the responsibilities of his medieval predecessors for the custody of the public records, now swollen to an incredible bulk and complexity. The Master of the Rolls acquired judicial powers as early as the reign of Edward I, when bills and petitions were presented to him for settlement.[29] Moreover, he had the power of appointment of a staff which grew from five or six clerks in the twelfth century to about twenty-four in the fourteenth century.

MASTERS IN CHANCERY

As the staff grew, it developed into grades, or forms, the upper grade consisting of twelve superior clerks *(de primo gradu)* or the Masters in Chancery *(magistri cancellarii).* Universally these men were ecclesiastics, trained in the use of Latin, and frequently they possessed a knowledge of canon and Roman civil law.

As assistants of the chancellor, it was part of the Masters' duty to hear and examine petitions and complaints and afford the petitioner a suitable remedy by a writ.[30] This was not a simple task, for if Chancery issued a writ which did not fit the facts alleged by the plaintiff, then the plaintiff would be defeated immediately when he appeared before a court. He could

[29] George Spence, *The Equitable Jurisdiction of the Court of Chancery*, 2 vols. (Philadelphia, 1846–50), I, 358.

[30] *Fleta*, Book II, Chapter 13.

not bring the action of Debt, say, when he should have brought Detinue, and the justices would tell him so. If a writ were improperly framed and did not state a sufficient cause of action, the judge might quash it in court. Or if the writ contradicted one of the provisions of Magna Carta, the plaintiff would have wasted time and money, for the judges would quash it on that ground. The Masters in Chancery were obliged, then, to know their law and to work in concert with the views of royal judges, especially when issuing original writs.

THE SIX CLERKS

The second form, or grade, of Chancery officials included a number of clerks; in the fully developed fourteenth-century staff there were twelve. Within this class probably belonged the Six Clerks, or Six other Clerks, who engrossed in "Chancery hand" under the supervision of the Masters in Chancery writs not strictly writs of course—that is, the exceptional and uncommon writs, which are important nevertheless for the growth of the common law because they might be altered from the exceptional to the common category.[31]

THE CURSITORS

At the bottom of the Chancery hierarchy stood the cursitors. In the fourteenth century they numbered twenty-four—all of them unmarried ecclesiastics. They were kept under close supervision, according to *Fleta:*

> There are . . . youthful and attendant clerks, to whom the Chancellor concedes by his grace that they shall make writs of course to expedite the business of the people. These shall, however, be under the warranty of the greater clerks, who shall take what they write at their own peril; and in each writ which they write there

---

[31] Spence, *Equitable Jurisdiction*, I, 238.

should be inscribed the name of the writer, who can warrant it if necessary to those who sue out the writ. . . .[32]

Like students in a college, the cursitors lived in an inn governed by a principal, and they were forbidden to lodge with superior officers, apprentices of the law, attorneys, or strangers. Appointed by either the chancellor or the Master of the Rolls, they were required, naturally enough, to master the Chancery hand employed in engrossing documents; and, like all other Chancery personnel, the cursitors would be required to know Latin, the language of the Chancery in the Middle Ages and for many centuries later. Except for a brief period during the seventeenth-century Commonwealth, Latin continued to be used in Chancery documents until 1733. The abolition of the writ system in the course of nineteenth-century reforms of legal procedure eliminated the cursitors. They disappeared into oblivion, leaving only their name on a street in London leading off Chancery Lane near the Public Record Office.

CHANCERY RECORDS

The subject of Chancery records touches the practical aspects of record-keeping and filing at an itinerant court. One of the problems facing a medieval clerk was the use of parchment for royal records. A thin sheet of carefully prepared sheepskin is tough and wear-resistant. Moreover, it can be finished to make an excellent writing surface which has the virtue of holding ink for centuries. But parchment buckles with every change in temperature and humidity. Under even the most favorable conditions a stack of parchment records would be difficult to file and keep in order, and a stack of loose parchment documents of uneven size would be completely unmanageable.

---

[32] *Fleta*, Book II, Chapter 13; as quoted by B. Wilkinson, *Constitutional History*, III, 132.

About 1200 the English Chancery developed a method of keeping together parchment records in certain categories. Undoubtedly the method also proved convenient for the transport of records on packhorses. Parchment membranes, approximately 12 by 24 inches, were covered with writing on both sides. When one membrane was filled, it was stitched with its head joined to the bottom of the preceding membrane. The stitching continued until about thirty membranes had been sewn together end-to-end, forming a roll. This long strip could be literally rolled up and tied in a compact bundle which would not be disarranged by jostling on a packhorse at a trot or gallop. The system had a certain flexibility of course: the entire roll need not be opened up to add new records to old files in the day-by-day business of royal government. But it is not difficult to imagine with what emotions the Chancery clerks must have received a request to search the records, especially if the matter had been enrolled several years previously.

The records were kept solely for use in royal administration, and the king was particularly interested in knowing who owed him money and how much. The king's officers did not then make records of legal cases for the benefit of the legal profession. Only such facts of a case as were of value to the royal administration were entered in the rolls: the decision in a real property case between private subjects, or one between Crown and subject, would be examples. But the reasoned opinion of the justices employed in arriving at the decision was not considered of value in the thirteenth century. The decision alone was recorded. Even after the beginning of reporting and the making of those unusual volumes known as *Year Books*, the modern doctrine of *stare decisis* could not develop because uniform reports of cases could not be widely distributed until the beginning of printing in the fifteenth century. When there were not printed records or reports, who could verify citations to previous decisions without first obtaining permission to consult the royal plea rolls?

PART FOUR
THE NATURE AND SOURCES
OF THE COMMON LAW

Chapter 8

Sources of English Law
in the Middle Ages

The brief working definition of the common law in the opening chapter of this study called it simply that body of rules prescribing social conduct which was justiciable in the royal courts of England.[1] A fuller statement may provide a better understanding of common law in the Middle Ages and in later centuries as well. S. B. Chrimes, a modern British historian, has remarked on the unfortunate confusion in British historical studies emerging from a deeply ingrained reluctance to make definitions.[2] Definitions are particularly helpful for the history of common law. Certain terms, such as "trial by jury" or "judicial precedents," appear in thirteenth-century materials and also in twentieth-century materials, but with very different meanings. Judicial precedents were known in the Middle Ages. Bracton, the author of the most authoritative treatise on medieval English law, referred to more than five hundred cases in his *De legibus et consuetudinibus Angliae*,[3] but his use of the

---

[1] See above, p. 5.

[2] S. B. Chrimes, Introduction to his translation of Fritz Kern, *Kingship and Law in the Middle Ages* (Oxford, 1956), p. xi.

[3] F. W. Maitland, *Constitutional History of England*, (London: Cambridge Univ. Press, 1908), p. 17.

judicial decisions of his predecessors was not the same as the sophisticated twentieth-century doctrine of *stare decisis*, requiring a hierarchy of courts, certain conventions in the reporting of cases, and the printed publication of reports. As for trial by jury, it too was affected by its long history. In the Middle Ages the jurors told under oath what they knew about the facts of a case, but in the twentieth century the jury weighs evidence presented to it about the facts of a case in order to reach a verdict. These two terms sufficiently point up the value of definitions to a study of an institution which is at least eight hundred years old. Definitions may indicate the proper sources of the common law, put them in a clearer light, and uncover elements which have given the English legal system its distinctive character.

WHAT THE COMMON LAW IS NOT

The common law is not a written code. It is unlike the civil law of Rome as set forth in Justinian's *Corpus Juris Civilis*, which for the Middle Ages in western Europe was the great example of written law. The principles of common law have always eluded complete embodiment in any code or collection of writings. Judicial decisions recorded on the plea rolls of common-law courts, declaratory statutes, and learned treatises on the common law may all express the principles of the common law, but these writings never comprise its totality. The modern continental jurist, trained in a system of written law, is disappointed by the precarious "certainty" of statutes in Great Britain, especially those of the Middle Ages. Professor Henri Lévy-Ullmann, a specialist in comparative law at the University of Paris, has pointed with dismay at the calm admissions of the eminent English legal historians, Sir W. S. Holdsworth and Percy H. Winfield, that "English law has never known an officially authentic collection of the Statutes. . . ."[4] Professor

---

[4] Henri Lévy-Ullmann, *The English Legal Tradition*, trans. M. Mitchell, rev. and ed. Frederic M. Goadby (London, 1935), p. 269; see also Percy H. Winfield, *The Chief*

Lévy-Ullmann concludes his own discussion of the growth of English statutes by saying that never at any period in the development of her legal tradition has England been "a country of written law."[5] Common-law principles can be expressed in various ways. The principle that no man ought to be illegally deprived of his liberty may be expressed in a judicial decision, in a parliamentary statute, or in a learned treatise on the writ of Habeas Corpus. Writings will merely reveal the principle. The principle can exist, without a writing, in the form of a generally accepted tradition.

Second, the common law is not the law of special groups or interests. Consequently, it is not to be identified with rules of canon law, particularly those which touch churchmen within the ecclesiastical hierarchy.

Third, the common law, properly so called, is not local custom. It is not ordinarily spoken of as the usage of a locality or territory such as the shire of Kent, the classic exemplum, which was permitted to enjoy until 1926 its own peculiar rules of inheritance by gavelkind.[6] Moreover, the common law is not to be identified with rules of law administered by baronial, manorial, or borough courts. Common-law rules are general rules; whatever "smacks of a specialty" is not common law.

Fourth, the common law is not the body of rules enforced in Chancery courts; that is, common law is not to be identified with what is now called Equity. The distinction between common law and Equity is technical and has special meaning for jurists, but it could not arise until the late fourteenth century, when Chancery began to exercise an independent jurisdiction. In the thirteenth century the modern distinction between law and Equity would have been incomprehensible, because the Chancery of the thirteenth century was simply the royal secretariat, and the chancellor was its head. In the thirteenth cen-

---

Sources of English Legal History (Cambridge, Mass., 1925), p. 83; W. S. Holdsworth, *Sources and Literature of English Law* (Oxford, 1925), p. 57.

[5] Lévy-Ullmann, p. 270.

[6] Gavelkind is discussed below at pp. 195–96.

tury the chancellor's staff issued writs, legal orders initiating legal action, but Chancery did not then try issues between litigants. The common law was growing rapidly, and if Bracton represents the thinking of royal judges, the courts were then prepared to apply new remedies as they were needed. As Bracton remarked, it pertains to the king to apply a competent remedy for the curbing of any wrong.[7] In the time of Bracton, the common law was equitable. So long as those who administered the common law were prepared to create and apply competent remedies, the common-law courts required no supplemental jurisdiction such as Chancery later supplied. The mysterious hardening of common-law procedures at the close of the thirteenth century, perhaps due to the lack of confident invention and initiative, forced the development of other means of rendering justice in new and difficult cases and ultimately created the division between common-law and Equity courts, which endured until the reorganization of English courts by the Judicature Acts of 1873 and 1875.

WHAT THE COMMON LAW IS

Negative statements have a value, but they fail here to suggest the full distinctive character of the common law; for that some positive elements are needed.

The common law is a body of general rules prescribing social conduct. It applies throughout the realm, save in those special jurisdictions where a recognized local custom or "liberty" is recognized by the royal courts. The residents of London, for example, kept alive for centuries their own body of peculiar law and custom, confirmed by William the Conqueror,[8] and they

---

[7] Bracton, fol. 414b.
[8] For the charter of William I to London, see S & M, p. 61.

were imbued with "an acute sense of the personality of their city."[9]

Second, the general rules of common law are enforced and applied by royal courts. To speak of royal courts raises, of course, the whole question of the relation of the Crown to the administration of justice in any English court, and by the end of the thirteenth century the treatise called *Fleta* indicated that the Crown asserted a general responsibility for the judicial work of every secular court in the land.[10] But the royal courts which are most intimately associated with the common law and which are, in fact, usually designated as common-law courts are seven: 1) General Eyres, 2) Common Pleas, 3) King's Bench, 4) Exchequer, 5) Commissions of Assize, 6) *Oyer* and *Terminer*, and 7) Gaol Delivery.[11] Indeed, one might safely shorten the list of common-law courts to three: Common Pleas, King's Bench, and Exchequer.[12]

Third, the common law develops its principles from the grounds of decision in actual legal controversies. We shall have more to say on this element when we take up the medieval use of judicial precedents.

Fourth, the common law is marked by its extensive use of the jury to provide the court with facts necessary for the decision of a case. In the twelfth century and later, the jurors were chosen for their knowledge of the facts of a case; presumably their unanimous collective statement, or verdict, would contain information available about the facts. It remained for the court to apply the proper rules of law to the facts as the jury had established them.

[9] Gwyn A. Williams, *Medieval London: From Commune to Capital* (Oxford Univ. Press, 1963), p. 26.

[10] *Fleta*, ed. with a trans. by H. G. Richardson and G. O. Sayles, Selden Society, Vol. 72 (1953), Book II, Chapters 2, 25, 34, 43, 52, 53.

[11] For excellent diagrams of the English system of courts past and present, see H. Potter, *Historical Introduction to English Law and Its Institutions*, 4th ed., by A.K.R. Kiralfy (London, 1958), pp. 644–47.

[12] Lévy-Ullmann, *The English Legal Tradition*, pp. 28–29.

Fifth, the common law is marked by a doctrine of the supremacy of law. Perhaps the ideal of the rule of law was more widely accepted in the medieval than in the modern world, but it still survives. The doctrine of the supremacy of law implies that all agencies of government must act upon established principles; even the highest bodies and officials are not permitted to act upon arbitrary will or caprice. The supremacy of law means that all the acts of government agencies are subject to examination in the courts, which are compelled in their turn to follow established procedures, "due process," and to reach decisions guided not by whim but by generally accepted principles and sound reason.

These five elements suggest a positive definition: the common law is a body of general rules prescribing social conduct, enforced by the ordinary royal courts, and characterized by the development of its own principles in actual legal controversies, by the procedure of trial by jury, and by the doctrine of the supremacy of law.

THE NATURE OF LEGAL CUSTOM

Treatise writers and historians of the common law have long given custom a prominent place among the sources of this body of general rules. More than half a century ago, Maitland noted a three-stage progression from customs originating in the "common wisdom and experience of society," through the stage of becoming "established customs," to the point at which they receive "judicial sanction in courts of last resort."[13] Sir Frederick Pollock, Maitland's contemporary and collaborator, also pointed to the prominence of custom in the common law by remarking that for six centuries everybody who had occasion to consider the matter believed that "the Common Law is a

---

[13] F. W. Maitland and F. C. Montagu, *Sketch of English Legal History*, ed. by J. F. Colby (New York, 1915), p. 213.

customary law. . . . To this day *coutume* is the nearest equivalent that learned Frenchmen can find for its English name."[14]

William Blackstone in the eighteenth century included within his *Commentaries on the Laws of England* a classic statement distinguishing between general and particular customs.

> This unwritten, or common law, is properly distinguishable into three kinds: 1) General customs; which are the universal rule of the whole kingdom, and form the common law, in its stricter and more usual signification. 2) Particular customs, which for the most part, affect only the inhabitants of particular districts. 3) Certain particular Laws; which, by custom, are adopted and used by some particular courts, of pretty general and extensive jurisdiction. . . . All these are doctrines that are not set down in any written statute or ordinance, but depend merely upon immemorial usage, that is, upon common law, for their support.[15]

Blackstone wrote at a time when the legislative activity of Parliament was swelling the statute books with one enactment after another. Consequently it is not surprising to see him distinguishing between written statute and immemorial usage. But in the medieval treatises of the twelfth and thirteenth centuries, before Parliament was firmly established as a lawmaking institution, the element of custom stands out as the principal source of law. In fact, the word "customs" appears prominently in the titles of books of authority. Glanvill in the late twelfth century asserted in the first treatise on English law that English rules, although unwritten, equaled the dignity of Roman *leges*. Glanvill also stated that the multiplicity of English laws and rights could not be reduced to writing in every instance.[16]

---

[14] F. Pollock, *First Book of Jurisprudence*, 6th ed. (London: Macmillan, 1929), p. 254.

[15] W. Blackstone, *Commentaries on the Laws of England,* 9th ed., 4 vols. (London, 1783), Introduction, Section 3; Vol. I, pp. 45–46.

[16] Ranulf Glanvill, *Tractatus de legibus et consuetudinibus regni Angliae*, ed.

In the middle of the thirteenth century Bracton described even more explicitly than Glanvill the place of custom in English law. Bracton bluntly maintained that "in England legal right is based on unwritten law which usage has approved. . . . For the English hold many things by customary law which they do not hold by *lex.*"[17]

SOCIAL PRACTICE AND LEGAL CUSTOM

Although many learned and profound jurists have named custom as a source of law, there have been serious differences among them as they searched for the origins of legal customs and the processes by which social practices have obtained recognition in courts of law. In the present, as in the past, the incidents of daily life are hedged about with customary rules of etiquette. The man who insists on wearing a hat during a Christian church service may deeply offend other members of the congregation, who are accustomed to removing their hats on entering the building. But a hat-wearing church member is not punishable in a court of law.

On the basis of certain tests of custom laid down in later centuries, one can conjecture why the common-law courts of medieval England accepted some customs and refused others. In the Middle Ages, as in the present, large areas of life were controlled by custom, but not all social customs became legal customs enforceable in law courts as part of the common law.

Early in the seventeenth century, the *Tanistry Case* (1608) produced a definition of custom as the English courts then saw it:

> A custom, in the intendment of law, is such a usage as hath obtained the force of a law, and is in truth a binding law to such

---

George Woodbine (New Haven, 1932). English trans. by John Beames and Introd. by J. H. Beale (Washington, D.C., 1900). See pp. xxxvii–xxxix.

[17] Henry de Bracton, *De legibus et consuetudinibus Angliae*, ed. and trans. Sir Travers Twiss, 6 vols., Rolls Series (1878–83), fol. 1a.

particular places, persons, and things which it concerns. . . . But it is a *ius non scriptum*, and made by the people only of such place where the custom is.[18]

Although the *Tanistry Case* became a leading case with a great deal of learning on custom clustered about it, its definition of custom was later amplified. Perhaps Blackstone is the best guide on the subject of legal custom because he gives specific illustrations, some of which reveal the medieval foundations of the common law.[19] He heads his list of general customs with examples from the law of Property—the law of inheritance; "the manner and form of acquiring and transferring property; the solemnities and obligation of contracts; the rules of expounding wills, deeds, and acts of Parliament; the respective remedies of civil injuries; the several species of temporal offences with the manner and degree of punishment." Blackstone also attributes to general custom the system of courts in his day, mentioning Chancery, King's Bench, Common Pleas, and Exchequer as the four superior courts of record—by custom. He continues with examples of general customs by returning to the law of inheritance—"the eldest son alone is heir to his ancestor; property may be acquired and transferred by writing; a deed is of no validity unless sealed and delivered; wills shall be construed more favourably and deeds more strictly; money lent upon bond is recoverable by action of debt; breaking the public peace is an offence and punishable by fine and imprisonment."[20]

18 Viner, Abr. VII, 164, citing *Tanistry Case* (1608) Dav. 31b. See C. K. Allen, *Law in the Making*, 6th ed. (1958), p. 67, n. 1. Tanistry is a species of tenure in Ireland. Under this immemorial usage, primogeniture gives way to inheritance by "the oldest and most worthy man" of the blood and surname of the deceased tenant. Although it was possible to determine who might be the oldest man *(senior)* with the proper relationship and name, the English courts would not accept responsibility for determining who was the "most worthy" *(dignissimus)*, and the custom was not accepted as applicable in common law.

19 See W. Blackstone, *Commentaries*, I, 68–71, for his discussion of general and particular customs.

20 Ibid., I, 45–46.

GENERAL AND PARTICULAR CUSTOMS

Blackstone in the eighteenth century makes the royal judges of the common-law courts the depositaries of the laws. Presumably their long experience and studies enable them to determine the validity of general customs known throughout the realm, and their decisions, consequently, are the most authoritative evidence about customs included in the common law. These decisions, having been recorded and preserved, are available for consultation in difficult cases. There were excellent reasons for attributing to the royal judges of the twelfth and thirteenth centuries a superior knowledge of the law of the land. Heavy judicial work at Westminster court terms and on itineraries, eyres, and commissions gave them a knowledge of the law matched, perhaps, only in the Chancery, where litigants from all parts of the realm sought the original writs which set judicial procedures in motion.

On all matters of general custom the royal judges assumed the power to recognize what was good custom. While listing qualities of good custom, Blackstone provided in his *Commentaries* a clear account of tests which customs should meet before they were admitted to have the force of law. Although Blackstone was an eighteenth-century justice of the court of Common Pleas, his analysis of customs agrees at several points with the handling of customs in specific medieval cases. Above all, he makes clear that not all customs are good customs and that the courts will permit litigants to rely on customs only when those customs meet certain criteria such as antiquity and continuity.[21]

Professor Theodore F. T. Plucknett reminds us that for Azo, the civilian jurist, ten or twenty years of usage was a "long custom," thirty years a "very long" custom, and forty years an "age-old" custom.[22] But in any period good custom is spoken of

---

[21] Ibid., I, 76.

[22] T.F.T. Plucknett, *Legislation of Edward I* (Oxford, 1949), pp. 6–7.

as "ancient." Whenever customs are recognized by a court and set down in writing, their antiquity may be mentioned. Illustrative here is the language of Magna Carta revealing the earlier existence of many customary services and payments which are assumed to be so well known and understood that they are given in the charter without explanation. Thus Chapter 2 refers to "the ancient custom of fiefs"; Chapter 13 states that "the city of London shall have all its ancient liberties and free customs"; Chapter 23 refers to "right and ancient custom," and this phrase recurs in Chapter 41. The common law drew heavily on the long-established customs of feudalism which regulated inheritance of land, transfer of title, leasing of land, wardship of tenures, and marriage of widows and daughters of marriageable age. The doctrine of escheat, or the reversion of land to the overlord on the failure of heirs, was also part of feudal custom. So far as we know, the varieties of free tenure and their obligations were all the result of custom. Indeed, the body of English customs, general and particular, which have obtained the force of law, is so large that no one would seriously endeavor to prepare an exhaustive collection.

Apart from general customs forming the common law in its stricter sense were certain particular customs possessing sufficient vitality, in Kent at least, to live into the twentieth century. The ancient Kentish customs gathered about a form of land tenure known as gavelkind deserve a brief notice. Tenants by gavelkind do not hold their lands by military or agricultural services; they pay money rents to their lords and they are freeholders.[23] By these customs, called the *lex Kantiae*, the common-law principle of primogeniture is set aside in favor of equal inheritance among all sons. The youngest son inherits his father's hearth.[24] Moreover, by gavelkind tenure lands are

---

[23] P & M, I, 186–88.

[24] Ibid., II, 271–73. Plucknett in his *Legislation of Edward I*, pp. 89–90, mentions another Kentish custom called gavelet, by which the "lord who could find no

devisable by will, do not escheat in case of attainder or felony, and can be aliened by the tenant at age fifteen.[25]

A preference for the youngest son was found also in the customs of inheritance used in certain towns where ultimogeniture acquired the name of borough-English. Gavelkind and borough-English are particular customs diverging from the general custom and common-law rule of primogeniture in the inheritance of real property.

Royal judges would accept the validity of local and particular customs so long as these conformed to certain criteria. Although royal judges never asserted a claim to superior knowledge of particular customs, they firmly insisted on testing particular customs when these were formally declared before them. This judicial caution was revealed in a case in the Eyre of Kent (1313). The inhabitants sought confirmation of their customs of gavelkind—some were inscribed on an "escrowet," and others were to be presented by the testimony of persons appearing before the court. But according to the *Year Book* account, Stanton, J. instructed the petitioner on how to proceed.

It is desirable that all of them [the customs] should be certainly set out; so take back your escrowet, and, after full consideration of the matter, insert therein the whole of your customs; and such of them as we find you have actually enjoyed and have also been allowed in Eyre, we will freely confirm to you now; for you may rest assured that you will be shorn of nothing to which you are entitled; and of that you need entertain no doubt.[26]

---

chattels to distrain could take the fee into his hand by judgment of his court, but without doing any work upon it. If the services were still in default after a year and a day he could apply to the county court, which would authorize him to hold the land to cultivate it; but the custom still allowed the tenant an illusory hope of redeeming the land by claiming nine times and paying nine times."

[25] H. A. Bigelow, *Introduction to the Law of Real Property* (St. Paul: West, 1919), p. 10.

[26] *Y.B.*, 6 & 7 Edw. II (1313–14), Selden Society, Vol. 27, p. 18, quoted by C. K. Allen, *Law in the Making*, 6th ed. (1958), p. 150, n. 1.

By the time of Blackstone the tests of both general and particular customs were clearly formulated. Good custom is: 1) *ancient*, no man can remember the beginning of it, 2) *continuous*, the rights claimed under it have never been abandoned or interrupted, 3) *peaceable*, supported by the common consent of those using the custom, 4) *reasonable*, in the light of "legal" reason, 5) *certain*, in the sense of being ascertainable, 6) *compulsory*, it is not left to the option of every man whether he will obey it or not, and 7) *consistent*, for one custom cannot contradict another custom without producing an absurdity.[27]

When a medieval court wished to make certain that a custom met the criteria for the establishment of good legal custom, how would it proceed? The jury provided one technique and we can observe it at work in manorial courts of the thirteenth century. The plea rolls show litigants relying on "the custom of the manor," which is declared in some instances by the full court and in others by jurors presumably chosen for their special knowledge of the local custom. The enrollment of the custom on the manorial plea rolls would tend to preserve it and make it available for the settlement of later disputes. The process of declaring customs in court is so important for the growing consciousness of customary law at all levels in the thirteenth century that we give several examples of the procedure.

At the manor of Weedon Beck (Northamptonshire) in 1275

the full court declares [*dicit plena curia*] that in case any woman shall have altogether quitted the lord's domain and shall marry a free man, she may return and recover whatever right and claim she has in any land; but if she shall be joined to a serf, then she cannot do this during the serf's lifetime, but after his death she may.[28]

---

[27] Blackstone, *Commentaries*, I, 53–54.
[28] *Select Pleas in Manorial Courts*, F. W. Maitland, ed., Selden Society, Vol. 2 (1888), pp. 24–25.

At Tooting (Surrey), a manor of the Abbey of Bec, in 1280–81

it is presented by unanimous verdict of the whole court that if anyone marries a woman who has right in any land according to the custom of the manor and is seised thereof by the will of the lord, and the said woman surrenders her right and her seisin into the hands of the lord and her husband receives that right and seisin from the hands of the lord, in such case the heirs of the woman are for ever barred from the said land and the said right remains to the husband and his heirs. Therefore let William Wood, whose case falls under this rule, hold his land in manner aforesaid. And for the making of this inquest William gives the lord 6 s. 8 d.[29]

At Ruislip (Middlesex) in 1290

Beneger Cobbler gives the lord 12 d. for a judgment whether in the present year he ought to have the hay of a certain meadow. . . . And the inquest says [*et inquisicio dicit quod*] that Beneger ought to have the said hay according to the custom of the manor.[30]

At Atherstone (Warwickshire) in 1291

twelve jurors of the court [who are listed by name] say upon their oath that the said Agnes did come into full court and did render into the lord's hands all right and claim which she in any wise might have in the said burgage, and therefore they say upon their oath that she has no right according to the custom of the manor of Atherstone to demand a third part of the said burgage. Therefore it is considered that the said Reginald do go without day and that the said Agnes be in mercy.[31]

At the manor of King's Ripton (Huntingdonshire) in 1295, in a case involving the claim of Joan, daughter of William of Alconbury, to eight acres of land

the jurors say upon their oath that the said Joan was of full age according to the usage of the manor [*secundum usum maneris*]

---

[29] Ibid., p. 29.
[30] Ibid., p. 38.
[31] Ibid., p. 41.

when she surrendered the said land, and the full age of a woman is thirteen years and a half and the full age for males is fourteen years and a half, and that the said Joan has no right in the said land but it is the proper escheat of the lord Abbot. Therefore it is considered that she take nothing by her writ, and be in mercy for her false plaint. She is pardoned on the ground of poverty.[32]

These examples of the declaration of the custom of manors suggest the process by which well-established custom received the sanction of the manorial court and expression in the written record, the manorial plea roll. Actually the process of declaring custom in the manor court was not unlike the process in courts serving larger communities—even the community of the realm. Thus the Constitutions of Clarendon (1164), representing the work of a royal council, contain in the preamble some revealing phrases—"this *record and recognition* of a certain portion of the customs and liberties and rights . . . which ought to be observed and held in the kingdom."[33] The "recognition" is made to settle disputes and dissensions concerning customs, and the persons summoned to Clarendon in the presence of the king are listed as archbishops, bishops, clergy, earls, barons, and magnates of the realm. Many bishops are individually named along with thirty-eight "of the nobler and more venerable men of the realm." Presumably the council assembled at Clarendon contained the men in all of England who were best informed about the customs of the realm on matters touching ecclesiastical and secular jurisdiction. Earlier disputes, dissensions, and challenges to customs here produced a declaration, a recognition, a verdict, and a written record by men who were not technically sworn jurors; yet their recognition was something like the jurors' verdict; the procedure at Clarendon was remarkably like an inquest in any court of the twelfth and thirteenth centuries. At Clarendon the recognition resulted in a record.

[32] Ibid., p. 121.
[33] S & M, pp. 73–74.

Litigation, a serious challenge, and the sense of administrative difficulties may all produce written evidence of custom in the Middle Ages. When customs are accepted by the royal judges and enforced in royal courts, they immediately become part of the common law. Court decisions and court records give customs a dignified formulation confirming their practice. The acceptance of certain customs in the royal courts means that they become part of the "laws and customs . . . approved by the consent of those who use them, and confirmed by the oath of kings."[34]

MEDIEVAL USE OF JUDICIAL PRECEDENTS

In the twelfth and thirteenth centuries the judges of the English royal courts commanded respect as legal experts exercising the king's right and duty to administer justice in all causes. And Bracton, the best known of these judges, was capable of formulating a doctrine of precedents in a treatise containing references to some five hundred cases in the plea rolls of royal courts. Bracton laid down the principle that "if any new and unwonted circumstances . . . shall arise, then if anything analogous has happened before, let the case be adjudged in like manner (*si tamen similia evenerint per simile iudicentur*), since it is a good opportunity for proceeding from like to like (*a similibus ad similia*). "[35] He then went on to express his belief that in new and difficult cases it was wiser to secure the advice of the Great Council than to arrive at a rash decision.

Bracton (d. 1268) was exceptional in his age, and other treatise writers did not—possibly they dared not—imitate his method of making references to decided cases. Bracton's use of the plea rolls was extraordinary. Other justices may not have

[34] Bracton, fol. 1b.
[35] Ibid.

been able to secure custody of royal plea rolls for the purpose of compiling anything comparable to Bracton's *Note Book,* which consisted of about two thousand cases selected to illustrate the law at its best.[36] The author of *Fleta,* writing about forty years after Bracton, refers to one case; Britton, who wrote an epitome of Bracton soon after 1290, refers to none; Littleton in his authoritative work on *Tenures* (ca. 1481?) refers to eleven cases.[37]

MEDIEVAL AND MODERN CITATION

Bracton's use of cases differs from the modern reference to cases. In the twentieth century the authority of the case decided in a higher court has a binding authority on a lower court. But Bracton and other medieval justices cite cases merely to illustrate or to explain the law. The citations are general at times and are in phrases to the effect that "We have often seen," or "It has been decided before this," or "It is held in our books."[38] Judges in the Middle Ages were compelled to aim at no higher standard than judicial consistency. Even though the *Year Books,* the earliest efforts at something like reporting, will occasionally mention a case by name, this does not mean that the case is expected to bind the decision of courts. In the first place, there had not developed the sophisticated practice

---

[36] *Bracton's Note Book: A Collection of Cases Decided in the King's Courts during the Reign of Henry III,* ed. F. W. Maitland, 3 vols. (1887). Bracton took his cases from the first twenty-four years of the reign of Henry III and from the records kept by three courts: the *De Banco* rolls, the *Coram Rege* rolls, and the eyres of Martin of Pateshull, a justice whose work Bracton much admired. Bracton also relied on the decisions of William of Raleigh (d. 1250). A native of Devonshire, and probably Bracton's master, he was a justice of the bench in 1228, itinerant justice in 1229, 1231, and 1232, and chief among the judges of the court until 1238, when he became bishop of Winchester.

[37] C. K. Allen, *Law in the Making,* 6th ed. (London: Oxford Univ. Press, 1958), p. 183.

[38] "*Homme ad souvent vu*"; "*Il ad este adjudge avant ceo*"; "*Il est tenu en nostre livres.*" See C. K. Allen, op. cit., p. 187, n. 4; and P. H. Winfield, *Chief Sources of English Legal History* (Cambridge, Mass., 1925), pp. 147–48, on Bracton's use of cases.

of reporting, which is now controlled by rules and conventions making it almost a science in itself. In the second place, until the invention of printing, it was impossible to secure absolute uniformity of materials. Manuscripts differed. "As against your book," remarked Fitzherbert, J. in the trial of a case, "I can produce four books where the contrary has been decided."[39] The *Year Books* often present only fragments of the case as it was argued in court. The printing of books from movable type was of little value to the legal profession in England until the close of the fifteenth century, and not until the sixteenth century could lawyers secure printed reports of cases.[40]

In the Middle Ages the courts were unquestionably guided by traditions and customs built up in the handling of case after case. But there was not the citation of cases in the modern fashion. Rather, citation took the form of professional memory and ultimately "the only authority cognizable by the court was the record of the case."[41] But this record, it must be remembered, might be buried under several hundred pounds of parchment rolls and consequently be very difficult to find; to "search the record" was a serious task which the court would not lightly assign to anyone.

We can observe the respect of the medieval courts for certain principles: like cases should be judged in like fashion; new cases should be judged with great care, for their decision will amount to law-making and will mould the common law. The *Year Books*, which were notes, probably show the respect of those who compiled them for the arguments and pleadings which led to specific decisions. Presumably what had once happened in the course of a trial might happen again.[42] From the foregoing, it should be clear that the medieval English

[39] See. T. Ellis Lewis, "The History of Judicial Precedent," *Law Quarterly Review*, Vol. 47, p. 411.

[40] In 1585 Tottell published Dyer's Reports covering the years 1513–82. Littleton's *Tenures* were first published about 1481.

[41] Allen, *Law in the Making*, p. 189.

[42] See the arguments advanced by Allen, *Law in the Making*, pp. 192–98, supporting the view that "the foundations of our case-law do most plainly exist in

common law grew along lines far removed from the instructions of the Byzantine emperor Justinian (d. A.D. 565), who ordered his judges to disregard completely the decisions of other courts:

> No judge or arbitrator is to deem himself bound by juristic opinions (*consultationes*) which he considers wrong: still less by the decisions of learned prefects or other judges. . . . Decisions should be based on laws, not on precedents. This rule holds good even if the opinions relied upon are those of the most exalted prefecture or the highest magistracy of any kind.[43]

It was not with the constitutions of Justinian before him that Bracton collected his two thousand cases from the plea rolls and advanced his own formula, from like to like (*a similibus ad similia*), by which he established a foundation for the development of a legal system by the course of trying case after case. English law of the twelfth and thirteenth centuries was judge-made law to a degree unknown in later periods. Probably the royal judges by their decisions in specific cases made greater contributions to the body of rules enforced in royal courts than any other body of men in England. It should be noted that in the eyes of a jurist trained in the written law (*lex scripta*) the decisions of medieval courts were merely adding to the body of *customary* rules in force in England, and it might be difficult, if not impossible, to draw a satisfactory distinction between medieval legal customs and medieval judicial decisions. Only a shadow line divides respect for consistency in judicial decision from respect for legal custom.

ENACTMENTS AND STATUTES

RELATION OF ENACTMENT TO COMMON LAW

Professor Lévy-Ullmann, a continental jurist obviously trained to revere the official written text, describes the period in En-

---

these medieval reports" (the *Year Books*). But see P. H. Winfield, *Chief Sources*, pp. 156–57.

[43] Allen, op. cit., pp. 168–69, quoting *Corpus Juris Civilis*, C. 7, 45, 13.

gland before the time of Edward I as one "bristling with ob-
scurities and enigmas" and "a confusion of incongruous and
disorderly elements." He does not hesitate to use the word
"barbarism."[44] Accordingly Lévy-Ullmann devotes only 63 of a
total of 370 pages to a discussion of statutes—and this in a
volume surveying the entire course of English legal development. "Common law and Statute law," he remarks, "are of an
identical nature."[45] This serious and considered opinion, startling perhaps to readers in the twentieth century, is arrived at
after consulting works by the most eminent British scholars in
the field of English jurisprudence. The French jurist is obviously shaken to discover that "English law has never known an
officially authentic collection of the statutes"[46] and that "when
within the time of memory [i.e., since A.D. 1189]—although the
record does not exist," statutes do not lose their value "if any
authentic memorials be found in books assisted by a general
received tradition concurring in the statement and approval of
the same facts."[47] "Authentic memorials" and "a general received tradition" are not adequate for the jurist trained in *lex
scripta;* he requires an official text.

Yet the English do have statutes and have been citing them
for centuries. Blackstone, in the Introduction to his *Commentaries,* provided a frequently quoted definition of English statutory law: "The written laws of the kingdom are statutes, acts,
or edicts, made by the king's majesty, by and with the advice
and consent of the lords spiritual and temporal, and commons
in parliament assembled."[48] In Blackstone's view, the English
leges scriptae are identified with acts of Parliament, and he

[44] Lévy-Ullmann, p. 15.
[45] Ibid., p. 235.
[46] W. S. Holdsworth, *Sources and Literature of English Law* (Oxford, 1925), p. 57;
see also P. Winfield, *Chief Sources of English Legal History* (Cambridge, Mass.,
1925), p. 83.
[47] Matthew Hale, *The History of the Common Law of England,* 6th ed. (London,
1820), p. 19.
[48] Blackstone, *Commentaries,* I, 58.

goes so far as to say that Magna Carta is the oldest statute extant and that it was confirmed in Parliament during the reign of Henry III.[49] Blackstone was not entirely correct about Magna Carta; certainly in 1225 there was no Parliament, as he knew it, composed of king, lords, and commons.

Because Blackstone wrote in the latter part of the eighteenth century he held views of the sovereignty of Parliament which would have amazed men of the thirteenth century. He asserted that "the legislature, being in truth the sovereign power, is always of equal, always of absolute authority: it acknowledges no superior upon earth."[50] And elsewhere, speaking of the powers of Parliament, Blackstone maintained the same opinion: "It can, in short, do everything that is not naturally impossible."[51] On the subject of judicial review of the acts of Parliament, Blackstone was quite plain: "to set the judicial power above that of the legislature . . . would be subversive of all government."[52] Accurate though it may have been for the eighteenth century, Blackstone's opinion about legislative sovereignty of Parliament cannot apply to enactments of the twelfth and thirteenth centuries. Legislative sovereignty is a modern invention; the legal historian must set aside many modern ideas while working back to the foundation years of the common law.

The separation of government into legislative, executive, and judicial functions cannot be observed in the English government of the Middle Ages. Certainly medieval judges were not reluctant to proclaim their participation in the making of statutes. In 1305 Hengham, C. J. broke in on the discourse of a barrister who attempted in the course of a trial to construe the Statute of Westminster II (1285). "Do not gloss the statute," Hengham ordered, "we know it better than you do, for we made

[49] Ibid.
[50] Ibid., I, 63.
[51] Ibid., I, 117.
[52] Ibid., I, 90.

it."[53] The king's expedience, rather than a division of powers, guided the medieval machinery of government. Direct, spontaneous action by the king and his council resulted in decisions and orders which were at once executive, legislative, judicial, and administrative. The medieval English government could be comparatively simple; it was not engaged in the manifold activities of twentieth-century governments. Population was comparatively small; the thirteenth-century English government ruled between two and a half and three million subjects, a number slightly greater than the population of Los Angeles in 1960 and decidedly smaller than that of the city of Chicago in the same year.[54] In the time of Edward I the functions of the Parliament, the law courts, and the king's council cannot be readily distinguished from one another. No one in thirteenth-century government hesitated to cross functional boundary lines. Parliament in the Middle Ages was unquestionably a court as well as an enacting body: judges made law in Parliament as well as in their own courts; the royal council freely considered any question touching the law or the administration of it.

The relation of enactment to the medieval law, and particularly the common law, has long been a subject of spirited controversy among professional jurists and legal historians. Should common law in the thirteenth century be treated as something distinct from statutes? If Magna Carta was a formal enactment by the competent authority of the time, should it also be included in the common law? Did early statutes merely affirm the existing law or did they make significant changes in the law? Could the king, by asserting royal prerogative, legislate for the realm or must he always obtain the consent of Parliament?[55] Numerous contests in England between advocates of

---

[53] Y.B., 33–35 Edw. I, ed. Horwood, Rolls Series (1866–79), V. 83: "Ne glosez pas le statut: nous le savons mieulz que vous, car nous les feimes."

[54] Figures from the census of 1960.

[55] For an excellent article on the relations between common law and statute, see McIlwain, "Magna Carta and the Common Law," Magna Carta Commemoration Essays, ed. H. E. Malden (1917), pp. 122–79.

the royal prerogative and supporters of the privileges and powers of Parliament have stimulated historical research to discover medieval precedents supporting either the royalist or the parliamentary position. As we have just noted, by the time Blackstone was writing his famous *Commentaries*, parliamentary sovereignty was no longer seriously questioned as a matter of practical politics.[56] But certain questions have remained to trouble historians and jurists. For example, in any compilation of the legislation of England what materials should be included? Surely modern scholars have no other course open to them than to accept the practice of the medieval royal courts. If these courts admitted a document as a formal enactment or if there is good evidence of a "general received tradition," then scholars, like lawyers, must regard the document as enacted law, for in matters of interpretation we are in no position to take higher ground than the superior courts of any period. This approach widens an examination of medieval legislation to include many documents without the title of statute.

NAMES GIVEN TO FORMAL ENACTMENTS

Medieval enactments display a rich diversity of names, which are designated in this section by italics. The *Constitutions* of Clarendon (1164) are also called, in the preamble, "this *record* or *recognition*." In the time of Henry II there are also *assizes:* The Assize of Clarendon (1166), the Assize of Arms (1181), the Assize of the Forest (1184). A king could legislate by *charter;* Magna Carta, "the first statute of the realm," is called "this our present charter" (*hac praesenti carta nostra*). Then in 1236 Henry III issued the *Provisions* of Merton, eventually called the *Statute* of Merton. Later in the reign is an enactment called the *Dictum* of Kenilworth (1266). Henry III had issued an *ordinance*

---

[56] In 1753 Blackstone began his lectures on law at Oxford University. The *Commentaries*, in four volumes, were first published successively in 1765, 1766, 1768, and 1769.

in 1253 for the keeping of the peace, and other documents carried this name. The Statute of Westminster I (1275), being in French, used the word *établissement* for enacted law. Ten years later, in 1285, Edward I issued an order to his judges, then on eyre, instructing them to act circumspectly in matters touching the clergy of Norwich. The order is in the form of a *writ* issued solely by the royal authority and without a hint of participation or deliberation by the clergy in the framing of it. For reasons that are unclear, the writ ultimately grew into the dignity of a statute and can be found in the printed *Statutes of the Realm*.[57] It is now cited as the Statute of *Circumspecte Agatis*, after the first two words of the body of the writ following the salutation clause.[58]

MODES OF LEGISLATION BEFORE 1307

The names of formal enactments suggest that changes in the laws were made in different ways.[59] First are those carried out with little formality and leaving scant record. Second are those carried out by means of administrative orders to judges or officials. Third are those carried out by "statutes"—which had certain characteristics: the statute was a text; it received wide publicity; it was a deliberate act; it had a date; it was studied by the legal profession in a special way. Professor Plucknett asserts that by the time of Edward I a statute had become "a very special sort of law . . . and manifestly different from the common law."[60] But having made a distinction between statute and common law in the time of Edward I, Professor Plucknett then goes on to qualify somewhat his distinction. He concludes that "we are compelled, however, by the nature of our material to bear constantly in mind the cardinal fact that our common

---

[57] *Statutes of the Realm*, I, 101.
[58] S.C., pp. 469–70 for the Latin text. Stubbs calls it a writ, not a statute.
[59] T.F.T. Plucknett, *Legislation of Edward I* (Oxford, 1949), pp. 10–20.
[60] Ibid., p. 14.

law is custom, and that the various modes of legal change in the reign of Edward I were conceived . . . as being changes within that mass of fluctuating customary law."[61]

Out of the variety of opinion about the nature of medieval enactment in England emerge three facts which may appear clearer when the legislation itself is more fully considered. First, certain changes in English law before 1307 were the deliberate acts of English kings who took the advice of their councilors and judges; in the time of Edward I, at least, the monarch also secured the consent of representatives in parliament about the substance, if not the exact wording, of the written text of statutes. Second, certain enactments were confirmatory; they recapitulated and restated existing law. Third, the formal enactment of statutes was a source of English law before 1307, but it was by no means the principal source of new law. Equally important for the growth of the law were custom, judicial precedents, and those royal administrative orders to judges and officials which led to the growth of the Register of Writs.

FORMS OF ACTION:
THE FRAMEWORK OF THE COMMON LAW

Many mysteries surround the development of forms of action and the writs associated with them. Probably the modern importance of statutory enactment explains the attention that legal historians have given to the statutes and other forms of enactment, such as assizes, provisions, ordinances, and proclamations. But if half the attention already given to early statutes had been directed to the evolution of the writ system, we should now be in a much better position to understand the basic principles and foundations of the English law. For every

[61] Ibid., p. 20.

piece of formal legislation resulting in a widely publicized text before 1307, there were at least a score of writs of course, ordinary writs which controlled the course of litigation. Glanvill and Bracton and those who wrote epitomes of Bracton did not write elaborate commentaries on formal enactments or statutes; they dealt, rather, with the writ system. The enormous popularity of Bracton's work in the late thirteenth century amply proves that persons in the legal profession—and others who were concerned to know the law of England—wished to study the operation and the force of royal writs. Statutes might, and occasionally did, modify procedure, but as a source of legal change before 1307, they contributed less to the foundation years of the common law than did the crisp, precise formulas that issued from the Chancery and from the royal courts, ordering about sheriffs and litigants and directing trial procedures. The existence of more than four hundred formulas in the Register of Writs before 1307 makes this catalog loom large next to the substance of legislative acts which has come down to us from the same period.

Maitland went so far as to say that "the system of Forms of Action or the Writ System is the most important characteristic of English medieval law, and it was not abolished until its piecemeal destruction in the nineteenth century."[62] Even in the twentieth century—and in the United States—a lawyer is expected to know the meaning of forms of action which go under such names as Covenant, Debt, Detinue, Replevin, Trespass, Assumpsit, Ejectment, and Case.

It is a very old principle of English law that the plaintiff must inform the defendant about the facts on which his grievance is grounded and the remedy which he seeks. Bereford, C. J. in 1310, referring to remarks of his contemporary, Sir Ralph Hengham, underscored this principle that all litigation must begin

---

[62] F. W. Maitland, *The Forms of Action at Common Law*, ed. A. H. Chaytor and W. J. Whittaker (Cambridge, 1954), p. 1.

with the proper writ. Bereford recalled that Isabel, Countess of Albemarle, was summoned to a parliament of Edward I to answer the king "touching what should be objected against her." The lady appeared in the court of Parliament, where she was "arraigned of divers articles." Through her sergeant she then asked for a judgment of the writ which had summoned her before Parliament; "the writ mentioned no certain article." Hengham, in the king's presence, opposed two justices who were ready to uphold the king's writ. "The law," he said, "wills that no one be taken by surprise in the King's Court. But, if you had your way, this lady would answer in court for what she has not been warned to answer by writ. Therefore she shall be warned by writ of the articles of which she is to answer, and this is the law of the land."[63]

Without the writ system the Angevin kings would have been powerless to administer justice: without writs of course the common law would have lacked a framework on which to grow. Each of the forms of action has its history: the problem, however, is to secure good evidence about the origins of writs of course. Some of them may have been formulated by royal judges, others by the royal council. To invent a new remedy is to make a new law.

REMEDIES OF THE LEASEHOLDER:
AN EXAMPLE OF LEGAL CHANGE

The relationship between writ and statute appears in any examination of the legal rights of early leaseholders. The action of Covenant, the Statute of Gloucester, and a variation on Trespass called Ejectment all touch leasehold and the remedies available to the lessee when he is disturbed in the possession of the lease.

For some years Covenant was the only action available for the

---

[63] *Y.B.*, 3 Edw. II, Selden Society, Year Book Series, Vol. 3, pp. 194, 196.

lessee, and it was useful only against the lessor who broke the agreement. Almost as soon as the common-law courts began to try actions of Covenant—about 1227—they established the rule that contracts of record, or other written sealed agreements which could be established as genuine, were the proper support for the action of Covenant. Understandably enough, the written document simplified procedure when the lessee endeavored to secure specific performance from the lessor and hold him to the details of a written, sealed agreement.

But it sometimes happened that a lessor reneged on his agreement and tried to eject the lessee by a collusive arrangement involving, perhaps, a sale to a third party. The buyer ejects the lessee. What is the lessee's remedy? The doctrine of seisin shut out leaseholders from the so-called possessory assizes such as Novel Disseisin. Leaseholders were never permitted by the courts to claim a real interest in land; they could have, said the courts, only a chattel interest in land. Consequently the leaseholder ejected by someone other than the lessor had no legal remedy before 1235. In this year William Raleigh, a royal justice, invented the writ *Quare ejecit infra terminum*.[64] Raleigh's action enabled the lessee to compel the buyer to appear in court to show why he deforced the lessee from certain lands which the lessor had demised to him for a term which had not yet expired.[65]

Bracton thought that *Quare ejecit infra terminum* could be brought against *all* ejectors and that the termor (leaseholder) should enjoy a possession of his term as secure as the seisin of any freeholder.[66] If Bracton's opinion had prevailed, the termor's position would have required no additional remedy. But other judges did not accept Bracton's view. In their eyes the

---

[64] P & M, II, 107–8, n. 2.

[65] Maitland, *Forms of Action*, p. 86, gives the text of this writ, quoting Fitzherbert, *Natura Brevium*, 198 b. See also W. S. Holdsworth, *History of English Law*, III, Appendix 1A, 14.

[66] Bracton, fol. 27 and fol. 220.

lease was merely a covenant, an agreement about the use of land for a definite term, and during the lease, for reasons judges never explained, seisin of the land remained in the lessor. Adhering strictly to these positions, English courts were unwilling to allow the termor any real property interest. The term was first called a quasi-chattel. By the time of Edward I the courts were saying boldly that it was nothing but a chattel.[67] Consequently, a leashold passed in wills to the executors along with other chattels, and there the matter stands to this day.

For all of its disadvantages the lease arrangement had certain attractive features, and despite legal difficulties in protecting it, the lease was a popular device. It avoided ecclesiastical prohibitions against usury while it enabled the debtor to raise a sum of money quickly. Let us suppose that a certain Richard, tenant of the manor of Trumpington, wishes to get together the sum of £200. Trumpington produces on the average only £20 per annum. Richard finds a wealthy merchant, Gregory, who gives him £200 in exchange for a lease of fifteen years. During the fifteen years, Gregory expects to recover approximately £300 from Trumpington, but no one can state precisely how much he will obtain. Richard owes nothing to Gregory. There is no "sum certain" to be repaid and consequently no debt; therefore, Gregory cannot be charged with usury even though he confidently expects to recover his principal of £200 and another £100 as well. So long as Gregory can enjoy peaceful possession of the leased manor of Trumpington, he will be content.

But suppose that in the year 1240 a certain Thomas, in collusion with Richard, disturbs Gregory's enjoyment of the lease of Trumpington—what can Gregory do? He cannot bring the action *Quare ejecit infra terminum*, because Thomas is not a buyer. Gregory cannot bring the assize of *Novel Disseisin*, because the courts say he has no seisin of a freehold. He cannot

---

[67] Y.B., 33–35 Edw. I, 165. "*la terme n'est que chattel.*"

expect Richard to act, because Richard is in collusion with Thomas and has no intention of recovering seisin himself. Gregory can only rely on Covenant and seek to force Richard to live up to his agreement. Even if Gregory wins his case, in 1240 he can hope only for damages; he cannot secure recovery of his term by litigation, and he may therefore lose a lot of money.

The Statute of Gloucester, Chapter 11 (1278), did nothing to correct this situation. It merely confirmed the operation of Raleigh's writ, *Quare ejecit infra terminum.* But a new remedy for the termor was soon to appear, an offshoot of Trespass. The writ called Ejectment gave the termor what he needed—an action against anyone who disturbed his possession of the term. Like other actions related to Trespass—assault and battery, false imprisonment, breaking "close," and trespass to chattels—*de ejectione firmae* had about it some of the swift process associated with a criminal action. The defendant was asked to show why "with force and arms" *(vis et armis)* he entered into land, demised for a term which is not yet passed, and ejected the plaintiff from his farm "and other enormous things did to the great damage" of the plaintiff and against the king's peace.[68]

In the writ of Ejectment there was mention of damages but no mention of recovery of the term. The courts seem to have hesitated about giving the termor more than damages if his lease was disturbed. Certainly by the close of the fifteenth century the courts were giving both damages and recovery of the lease to the ejected termor. By the fifteenth century men were saying that the termor was "possessed," while the freeholder had "seisin."

There was thus a progressive development from the action of Covenant to the writ *Quare ejecit infra terminum.* The latter was confirmed by the Statute of Gloucester without regard for the ideas of Bracton. Finally the writ of Ejectment, as handled

---

[68] See the form in Maitland, *Forms of Action,* p. 89.

by the courts, gave the termor both damages and recovery of the term. In this slow acquisition of remedies by the termor, procedural forms played a large role.

An appraisal of the sources of medieval English law will not disclose a single predominant source; custom, judicial precedent, and enactment all contributed to the English legal system. Presiding over the confluence of these sources stand the royal courts. Custom is tested by the courts; the traditions of judicial precedents are maintained by the courts; statutes are interpreted by the courts. Foremost among the medieval creators of the common law are the judges of the courts of Exchequer, Common Pleas, and King's Bench guiding litigation which was moved forward from beginning to end by writs from the Register.

C h a p t e r   9
Enactments of Edward I

The reputation of Edward I as law-maker has not suffered from lack of praise by historians of the nineteenth and twentieth centuries. Bishop William Stubbs, writing between 1858 and 1889, extravagantly admired Edward as a monarch and legislator whose enactments he regarded as "the basis of all subsequent legislation, anticipating and almost super-seding constructive legislation for two centuries."[1] Almost seventy years after Stubbs, T.F.T. Plucknett concluded that "a thorough commentary upon the statutes of Edward I would be in effect a history of the common law from the thirteenth century down to the close of the eighteenth."[2] Plucknett did not, like Stubbs, attribute to Edward I an almost prophetic view of future centuries and the institutions and laws which England would require. On the contrary, Plucknett has argued convincingly that Edward I aimed his legislation at the regulation of matters troubling the realm in the late thirteenth century. The extraordinary long-term results of Edwardian statutes were neither foreseen nor intended.[3] This fact, nevertheless, diminishes not one whit the subsequent

---

[1] William Stubbs, *Constitutional History of England,* 3 vols. (Oxford, 1880), II, 171.

[2] T.F.T. Plucknett, *Legislation of Edward I* (Oxford, 1949), p. 156.

[3] Ibid., pp. 104–5.

importance of Edwardian legislation, which touched almost every topic of English common law.

In this chapter discussion of thirteenth-century statutes will center on three themes. The first will show Edward acting to preserve the ancient customary rights of freeholders while also providing swift procedures for merchants and townsmen. The result was the Statute of Merchants (1285), which produced side effects not intended by those who drafted the statute.

The second topic will show Edward regulating gifts of land by the Statute of Westminster II, Chapter 1 (1285), sometimes called *De Donis Conditionalibus*. This enactment furnished the statutory foundation for conditional estates in land. *De Donis* reflects the efforts of English families to perpetuate family fortunes and to provide for daughters and younger sons in such a way that upon the failure of heirs, or other conditions set out in the gift, the land would revert to the original donor or his heirs.

The third and final topic will disclose great changes in feudalism, nowhere more plainly than in the law of real property. During the reign of Henry II the royal courts had been concerned to protect seisin of freehold. Feudalism was still very much alive; tenants by military service still contributed heavily to the defense of the realm; the fief was still the normal economic base for the support of a man-at-arms and his family. But by the reign of Edward I much had altered; the outward formalities of tenures failed to conceal the fact that men invested in land as a means of accumulating wealth. Although feudal forms of tenure persisted, tenures were bought and sold freely in an active market. If this traffic in land were not regulated, it would quickly spawn long chains of tenure and deprive great barons and magnates of the incidents of feudal tenures. By statute, Edward provided for the substitution of the buyer for the seller in any transfer of lands and prohibited further subinfeudation of land. Thus the Statute of *Quia Emptores* regulated the selling and buying of land with the intention of preserving to the barons—and the Crown—the wealth obtainable from wardships, marriages, and escheats.

REGULATION OF CREDITORS AND DEBTORS

STATUTE OF ACTON BURNELL (1283)

In 1283 Edward assembled a great council at Shrewsbury in the west of England to try David, brother of Llewelyn of Wales, for breaking his oath of fealty. Edward employed the assembly both as a court and also as a legislative body to regulate the business affairs of merchants, some of whom were represented among the persons summoned by special writ to Shrewsbury: eleven earls, ninety-nine barons, and nineteen others, including councilors, judges, and constables.[4]

Completely unrelated to the trial of David was legislation on procedures to enable creditors to collect their debts more easily. Robert Burnell, Edward's chancellor and bishop of Bath, had a residence at Acton Burnell, which gave its name to the new regulations. The interests of foreign merchants—always important for Edward's schemes—were not overlooked in these rules, which we are about to summarize.[5]

Before the time of Edward I, creditors in medieval England could take certain precautions to assure recovery of their loans. First, the creditor needed good evidence of the existence of a debt, something in writing, a sealed document setting forth the exact amount of money to be repaid and the time of repayment. Second, the creditor might secure the enrollment of the debt on a royal record and thus assure that the existence of the debt would never be questioned. No one was permitted to question the validity of royal records. The enrollment of matters touching creditors and debtors began much earlier than the time of

---

[4] Stubbs, *Const. Hist.*, II, 126.

[5] See the analysis of Edward's commercial regulation in Plucknett, *Legislation of Edward I*, pp. 136–61.

Edward I. It was a conspicuous practice in the communities of Jews in England, whose moneylending activities had been supervised by the Crown since the days of Richard I. Also, when the term of years and the gage of land were employed by creditors as a means of recovering principal and interest and when inadequate possessory remedies were available, foreign merchants had occasionally secured the enrollment of a "protection," as a matter of royal grace. For example, in 1227 when his debtor, Robert Passelewe, was in disfavor, a certain Gregory le Palmer, merchant of Sen' (Sens?), and his assignees secured two documents and their enrollment on the Patent Rolls.[6] The first was a royal protection in the enjoyment of the lands of Robert Passelewe. The second apparently represents the sale of Gregory's interest to two English subjects, Alexander of Dorset and Walter of Stavele. Whatever this transaction may have been called, the transfer of a mortgagee's interest or the assignment of a lease, the creditors' interests were protected by the Crown and the debtor's lands were being used as a means of recovering money lent.

The enrollment of the affairs of Gregory and Alexander and Walter were precautions at a date when lessees had no remedy save the action of Covenant.[7] The writ of Ejectment lay several years in the future. It is clear that by means of sealed documents and formally drafted bonds, creditors had learned before Edward's legislation how to remove all doubt about the existence of a debt. There had been the *occasional* enrollment of debts owed to Christians,[8] but Jewish practices after 1240 had *always* meant the preparation of a chirograph, the foot of

---

[6] Patent Rolls, 11 Hen. III (1227), m. 4. "We command you that you maintain, protect, and defend Gregorio le Palmer, merchant of Sens' and his own servants, in the lands and rents of Robert Passelewe, which he has from the same Robert as a means of acquieting the debt which the same Robert owes him."

[7] See discussion of this action, above, pp. 211–212.

[8] P & M, II, 202. In Michaelmas term 1278 the single firm of the Ricciardi of Lucca appeared as creditors in eleven recognizances to the total amount of £1,399/ 1s./9d., according to R. J. Whitwell, "Italian Bankers and the English Crown," *Transactions of the Royal Historical Society*, N.S., xviii, p. 205.

which was deposited in a chest where it would be open to the scrutiny of royal officers. Beyond the preparation of certain evidence of indebtedness, the creditor needed a procedure which would obviate delays if the debtor failed to repay on the appointed day. The creditor needed a procedure which would enable him quickly to recover his debt from the assets of the defaulting debtor.

The Statute of Acton Burnell addressed itself to the matter of procedure open to creditors and in the preamble frankly confessed a desire to assist foreign merchants who had previously refrained from coming into the realm.[9] By this statute the merchant who

> will be sure of his Debt shall cause his debtor to come before the mayor of London or of York or of Bristol and before the mayor and a clerk which the King shall appoint . . . to acknowledge the date and day of payment and the Recognisance shall be entered into a Roll with the Hand of the said Clerk, which shall be known. Moreover the clerk shall make with his own hand a Bill Obligatory, whereupon the seal of the debtor shall be put, with the King's seal, that shall be provided for the same purpose. . . . And if the Debtor doth not pay at the day to him limited, the creditor may come before the said mayor and clerk with his bill obligatory. . . . [And] if the day of payment is expired, the mayor shall incontinent cause the moveables of the Debtor to be sold as far as the Debt doth amount by the [ap]praising of honest men. . . . And if the mayor can find no Buyer, he shall cause the moveables to be delivered to the creditor at a reasonable price [to the amount of the Debt].[10]

The debtor could not complain about the price obtained by the forced sale of his goods, for he had an opportunity to sell them himself before the day for repayment of the debt. If the debtor had no movables, no chattels, on which the debt could be levied, then he was imprisoned wherever he was found until he had made an agreement (with the creditor) or his friends for

---

[9] *Statutes of the Realm* [1225–1713], 9 vols. in 10 (London, 1810–1822), I, 53–54.
[10] Ibid.

him. Furthermore, the Statute of Acton Burnell provided that the creditor might move against the pledges or mainpernors of the debtor in the same manner as against the debtor himself, but only after the debtor's movable goods had been exhausted.

The Statute of Acton Burnell did not apply to Jews. It did not abate the ancient writ of Debt. And it did not prevent the chancellor, barons of the Exchequer, or the justices of either bench from taking recognizances "according to the law, usage, and manner heretofore used."

STATUTE OF MERCHANTS (1285)

In the Statute Rolls the parchment membrane carrying the enrollment of Acton Burnell has on the back of it the Statute of Merchants, which supplements and goes far beyond the procedures enacted two years earlier. This close physical association in the parchment rolls was probably not a purely clerical decision, for later forms of the recognizance mention "the penalty and punishment provided in the statute of the lord king at Acton Burnell and Westminster for merchants. . . ."[11] The two enactments went together in the thirteenth century, but the Statute of Merchants strengthened the earlier enactment. Clearly the Statute of Acton Burnell had not been easily administered. Changes and additions in procedure are noteworthy, for they resulted in an entirely new set of remedies available for the creditor who moved against the lands as well as the chattels of the debtor. The Statute of Merchants differed from Acton Burnell in the following principal points.[12]

1. The recognizance of a debt is to be made on *two* rolls, one to remain with the mayor, the other with the clerks.
2. If the debtor defaults he is to be imprisoned at his own

---

[11] Holdsworth, *History of English Law*, III, Appendix V.
[12] For the Statute of Merchants, see *Stat. Realm*, I, 98–100.

costs until he can raise the debt out of the sale of movables and his lands.

3. If the debtor does not come to an agreement with the creditor within a specified period (approximately three months), all of his lands and goods are to be delivered to the creditor to hold until the debt is satisfied. Meanwhile the debtor lives on bread and water in prison at the creditor's expense.

4. Next—and this reflects a remarkable change in the feudal concept of seisin—"the merchant [creditor] shall have such Seisin in the lands delivered unto him or his Assignee, that he may maintain the writ of Novel Disseisin . . . and Redisseisin also, as of freehold to hold to him and his assigns until the debt be paid." But the debtor has not lost all power over lands in his creditor's possession; while the merchant creditor holds the debtor's lands, the debtor may still sell them, provided he compensates the creditor for any improvements. The statutory grant of seisin to the creditor or his assignee, without destroying the seisin of the debtor, is an almost incredible manipulation of the mysteries of seisin.

But this is not all. By the Statute of Merchants the creditor is to secure all the lands of the debtor that were in the latter's hands the day the recognizance was made, "in whose hands soever that they come after. . . ." And on the day of the recognizance the debtor is to be informed of the penalties of default so that he will be unable to say that they are penalties he was not bound to.

The Statute of Merchants created a new estate in land, "tenure by Statute Merchant," and the procedure of making the recognizance came to be called the execution of a "statute merchant," or more simply a "statute."[13]

---

[13] Holdsworth, *History of English Law*, III, Appendix V, gives an example of the form of a recognizance or statute merchant.

How was the Statute of Merchants employed? The answers make interesting reading. The recognizance became a means of securing the specific performance of a promise completely unrelated to the creditor–debtor relationship. The historian Alice Beardwood has recently shown in her painstaking study of the trial of Walter Langton (1307–1312) how after 1295 the king's powerful treasurer and chief minister could abuse the procedures of the statute merchant for his own personal advantage.[14] A statute merchant was so often employed as a sanction that it is impossible to treat a thirteenth-century recognizance as conclusive evidence of a debt. For example, Langton secured three recognizances as security that minors would respect his rights in matters of their marriages. The predatory bishop Langton also used the statute merchant as security for the transfer of land. Miss Beardwood's account of the case of Peter Chaunceaux must stand for more than a score of such cases in Langton's unscrupulous career.

On 23 February, 1305, Peter Chaunceaux, his wife, Nicola, and his son, Robert, bound themselves to Langton in £200 and on the following day made an indenture providing for the cancellation of the statute merchant if Peter, by the feast of St. Peter next following, by fine in Common Pleas warranted his right to Castle Ashby. In January, 1305, Oliver la Zouche, who had held the manor earlier and had transferred it in 1297 to Chanceaux and others had made a statute to Langton in the sum of £2000. This was probably part of the same transaction. Thomas Wale also had rights in the manor and was found to be bound by a statute, undated here, in the amount of 100 marks. At [Langton's] trial, he [Thomas] said this should not be levied, because when Langton was acquiring Castle Ashby, he had Wale's lands taken into the king's hands for over a year, until Wale, who apparently had been uncooperative, was so terrified by threats that he agreed to remit whatever rights he had

14 Alice Beardwood, *The Trial of Walter Langton, Bishop of Lichfield, 1307–1312*, Transactions of the American Philosophical Society, N.S. Vol. 54, Part 3 (Philadelphia, 1964). See esp. p. 28.

in the manor and for security made the statute merchant. Langton had made a letter of acquittance and given it to his clerk, Thomas Adderbury, to hold until the agreement was fulfilled. Wale claimed he was able to prove this was done but seems not to have received the acquittance because Adderbury's executors were ordered to produce it. The case is unfinished.[15]

The Statute of Merchants produced as many problems as it solved. It plainly shows the difficulties of dealing with new commercial property interests while trying to retain older feudal property interests. The recognizance procedure of the Statute of Merchants was at first available to everyone in England and Ireland. But in itself the trial of Walter Langton may have produced a limitation of the scope of the statute, confining it to transactions between merchants.

When Langton's trial was in progress, a royal ordinance bluntly stated the limitation.

Many persons, other than known merchants, do feel themselves aggrieved and fined by the Statute of Merchants made at Acton Burnell; we do ordain that henceforth that statute shall not hold except between merchants and merchants, and of merchandizes made between them . . . and that to no one shall other lands be delivered to hold in the name of frank tenement by virtue of the said statute, except the burgages of merchants and their moveable chattels and that is to be understood between merchants and merchants, known merchants.[16]

The ordinance went on to limit the towns in which recognizances could be made. All of them were established commercial centers: Newcastle-on-Tyne, York, Nottingham, Exeter, Bristol, Southampton, Lincoln, Northampton, Canterbury, Shrewsbury, and Norwich.

In the twelfth century, and especially in the reign of Henry II, royal courts protected with solicitous care the tenant of a freehold. Whether or not this concern stemmed from a desire

---

[15] Ibid., pp. 29–30.
[16] *Rotuli Parliamentorum*, 6 vols. (London, 1767), I, 285; see also Plucknett, *Legislation of Edw. I*, p. 147.

to protect the normal source of income for the families of the feudal class, the evidence points to a judicial willingness to use the procedures of the jury in the action known as the writ of Right and also in what were known as the possessory assizes. The writ of Right tested which of two claimants had the better right to seisin of a freehold. It was a solemn and dignified action, which stood at the forefront in most Registers of Writs. The possessory assizes did not pretend to determine better right or title. The actions of Novel Disseisin, Mort d'Ancestor, and Darrein Presentment were summary remedies designed to protect possession-of-freehold estates and to preserve the peace. Generation after generation of English royal judges continued to display a preoccupation with the protection of seisin of freehold tenures, to such an extent, in fact, that the term of years was entirely excluded from the benefits of the possessory assizes and ended up in the English legal system as a chattel interest in land, or "chattel real." It is, therefore, a revolutionary change in legal thinking which gives, toward the close of the thirteenth century, the benefits of Novel Disseisin to the property interest of a judgment creditor. Once more we see in Edward's legislation an example of new commercial interests mingling with older and somewhat incompatible feudal ideas. The Statute of Westminster II, Chapter 18 (1285), opens up yet another course of action for a plaintiff seeking to recover a debt or damages awarded. He has a choice: he may elect to sue a writ to the sheriff ordering either 1) that he cause (the amount of the debt) to be made (*fieri facias*) out of the lands and goods, or 2) that "the sheriff deliver to him all the chattels of the debtor (except cattle and draft animals) and one-half of his land according to a reasonable price or extent [i.e., appraisal] until the debt shall have been levied. And if he be put out from the tenement, he shall recover by a writ of Novel Disseisin, and after that by a writ of Redisseisin if need be."[17] Here again Edward's legislation resulted in a new tenure: the creditor who chose to

---

[17] Westminster II, Chapter 18 (1285); *Stat. Realm*, I, 82.

take half of the debtor's lands was known as a tenant by *elegit* (he has chosen). The tenant by *elegit* had only a chattel interest in land, but his possession was as well protected as though he enjoyed seisin of a freehold. Tenure by *elegit* was not always the most desirable course of action for creditors. On the contrary, it probably indicated that the chattels of the debtor were insufficient to pay the debt and that a personal action against the debtor would be fruitless.

The procedure set forth in the Statute of Westminster II, Chapter 18, resembles somewhat the one outlined earlier in the *Statutum de Judeismo* (Statutes of the Jewry),[18] with only a slight difference: "If the chattels be not sufficient [to pay the debt], the lands shall be extended by the same oath . . . saving always to the Christian the moiety of his land and chattels for his maintenance as aforesaid and the chief mansion."[19] The similarity between the Statutes of the Jewry and the Statute of Westminster II led Maitland to remark that "the well-known writ of *elegit* . . . may be a lasting monument of the Hebrew money lender."[20]

In summary, the legislation of Edward I on the relations of debtors and creditors accomplished several things: 1) the provision of enrollment or recognizance of a debt created a record which could not be successfully challenged at a later date by the procedure of compurgation;[21] 2) the presentation of the bill obligatory bearing the debtor's seal and the king's seal could result in immediate execution out of the debtor's chattels if these were sufficient; 3) if the debtor's chattels were insufficient, then the creditor could take the debtor's lands to satisfy the debt while the debtor remained in prison; 4) enactment also created a less rigorous course which, at the cred-

[18] *Stat. Realm*, I, 221–22, classified among statutes of uncertain date. Cecil Roth, *History of the Jews in England*, 2nd ed. (Oxford, 1949), p. 70, places it in 1275.

[19] Ibid.

[20] P & M, I, 475.

[21] See above, pp. 219–220.

itor's option, allowed the debtor to go free but gave half his lands and chattels to the creditor until the debt could be extinguished; 5) these procedures created two new tenures: a) tenure by statute merchant and b) tenure by *elegit*. Both property interests came to be called "chattels real." Both property interests could be protected by remedies such as Novel Disseisin, formerly available only to freeholders.

There were similarities between the situation of the termor and the situation of the tenant by statute merchant or by *elegit*. The granting of adequate protection of chattels real in time of Edward I may represent the changes in legal thought produced by the long and successful struggle of leaseholders to secure undisturbed enjoyment of their leases.[22] When the termor had been given the action of Ejectment against all who disturbed him, it was not a long step for the courts and Parliament to do as much for tenants by statute merchant and *elegit*.

REGULATION OF ESTATES IN LAND

STATUTE OF WESTMINSTER II: *DE DONIS* (1285)

The year 1285, the *annus mirabilis* for Edward I, was one of exceptional legislative activity, resulting in no less than six great statutes. The Statute of Westminster II alone contained fifty chapters on a variety of matters. Interesting and important as other chapters may be, attention here centers on the opening chapter of Westminster II, concerning conditional gifts. This is often cited as *De Donis Conditionalibus*, or more simply *De Donis*. Its importance stems from its early appearance in the statutory regulation of interests or estates in land subject to the fulfillment of certain conditions expressed in the original gift or grant. The concept of various estates in land demands some

---

[22] See above, pp. 211–215.

explanation, and we begin by distinguishing free estates from unfree on much the same grounds used to distinguish free tenures from unfree tenures.[23]

Free tenures are important because they were employed both in the Middle Ages and afterward as the continuing, inheritable economic bases for the support of English families through several generations. Most of the estates in land beyond fee simple are the result of gifts or grants of freehold property to provide for younger sons or for daughters. Men in the Middle Ages, much more than in the twentieth century, thought in dynastic patterns encompassing the welfare and status of future generations. Estates other than the free estates did not lend themselves to long-range family arrangements about property.

Fee Simple. If we think of the various legal powers that an individual has over property and liken each power to a rod or stick, the largest bundle of such rods which one person can accumulate would be a fee-simple estate. It is the most extensive and the deepest property interest that the law protects. Among powers over property is the power to alienate it, that is, to transfer it to other hands by sale or gift. Consequently the fee-simple estate is alienable. Property may also be passed on to an heir: the fee-simple estate is inheritable. On the rules of inheritance feudal custom was clear and detailed: it favored primogeniture, a system hard on younger sons and daughters. Exercising the power to alienate their lands, men of property tried to provide for younger sons and daughters by giving them estates which their own children could inherit. The formula came to be in the thirteenth century a grant "to X and this heirs." However, a grant to X and his heirs did not always result in the descent of the land to the heirs of X. For reasons unknown, the royal courts of the thirteenth century began to attach a technical meaning to the phrase "and his heirs." It

---

[23] See above, pp. 114–116; see also Bigelow, *Real Property* (St. Paul, Minn., 1919), p. 19.

could be argued—perhaps it was argued—that not until the death of X could his heirs be determined, therefore the whole estate is in X. However, the royal courts decided that X had a fee simple and X could alienate a fee simple. "And his heirs" —these magical words of art described or connoted or delimited the estate of fee simple. And if a man had the highest estate then possible in land, he could sell it or alienate it. Thus arose the paradox that a grant of land "to X and his heirs" might result in "the heirs" not obtaining any part of it.

Conditional Fees and Fees Tail. Another formula resulted in estates bearing the label "fees conditional." We see at work here a determination on the part of men of property to mark out and control in some way the line of descent which their property will take in the future. But equally strong forces favored free alienation of land and thus defeated the intentions of donors who sought to keep property in the family or to control it, if not in perpetuity, then for three generations at least. Again the courts frustrated the intentions of donors; a grant "to X and the heirs of his body" was interpreted by the courts to mean that upon the birth of an heir a condition had been fulfilled which gave X a fee simple in the grant. Anyone having a fee simple could sell it or otherwise dispose of it.

Gifts in Free Marriage. When a daughter married, it was common practice among freeholders of sufficient wealth to give the bride an estate which, when added to her husband's property, would assure a sufficient economic foundation for the new family. This was a gift in marriage (*maritagium*). If the daughter's estate was not responsible for the payment of services, was "free" of services, it was a gift "in free marriage"—the phrase appears in the opening lines of *De Donis*.[24] The donor's intent was to provide for the newly wedded couple and es-

---

[24] On the *maritagium, liber maritagium,* and other matters of medieval family arrangements touching land, T.F.T. Plucknett has a lucid chapter in his *Legislation of Edward I* (1949), pp. 110–35.

pecially for the children of the marriage. If no children were born to the couple, the gift reverted on the daughter's death to the grantor or his heirs. Such a reversion was reasonable, since the gift was intended to benefit "the heirs of the body" of the wife and husband. The donees, consequently, should not alienate the gift. They did not have a fee simple, did not do feudal homage to the grantor or his heirs, and were not able to compel the donor to warrant their title. As a matter of custom the grantor of a free marriage assumed the burden of all feudal services during the lifetimes of the original donees, their son, and their grandson. But when the great-grandson entered the estate as the third heir and did homage, he took over the feudal services on the assumption that the younger branch of the family was by this time established sufficiently to carry the burden. The estate of the third heir was like a fee simple, and as we have already noted, a fee simple could be sold or otherwise alienated. The gift in marriage was not expected to be a gift perpetually limited by the original conditions. Eventually it became a fee simple, and the property could be alienated.

The artificial reasoning of the courts about such phrases as "to his heirs" and "to the heirs of the body" was not permitted in the time of Edward I to defeat arrangements for younger sons and daughters. For almost two hundred years the Statute of *De Monis* made possible, within the institutions of feudalism, some effective distribution of property providing for families other than that of the eldest son.[25] The language of *De Donis* is clear enough and reads as follows:

First concerning lands that many times are given upon condition, that is, to wit, where any giveth his land to any man and his wife with such condition expressed that if the same man and his

---

[25] Eventually, about 1472, the courts approved a method of breaking through the restrictions of entailed estates by means of legal fictions and the old form of action known as a common recovery. See *Taltarum's Case*, Y.B., 12 Edw. IV, 19 (1472).

wife die without heir of their bodies between them begotten, the land so given shall revert to the giver or his heir; in case also where one giveth lands in free marriage, which gift hath a condition annexed, though it be not expressed in the deed of gift, which is this, that if the husband and wife die without heirs of their bodies begotten, the land so given shall revert to the giver or his heir; in case also where one giveth land to another and the heirs of his body issuing, it seemed very hard and yet seemeth to the givers and their heirs, that their will be expressed in the gift was not heretofore nor yet observed. In all the cases aforesaid after issue begotten and born between them, to whom the lands were given under such condition, heretofore such feoffees had power to aliene [sic] the land so given, and to disinherit their issue of the land, contrary to the minds of the givers, and contrary to the form expressed in the gift: and further, when the issue of such feoffee is failing, the land so given ought to return to the giver or his heir by form of gift expressed in the deed, though the issue, if any were, had died; yet by the deed and feoffment to them to whom land was so given upon condition, the donors have heretofore been barred of their reversion of the same tenements which was directly repugnant to the form of the gift: wherefore our lord the king, perceiving how necessary and expedient it should be to provide remedy in the aforesaid cases, hath ordained, that the will of the giver according to the form in the deed of gift manifestly expressed shall be from henceforth observed so that they to whom the land was given under such condition shall have no power to aliene [sic] the land so given, but that it shall remain unto the issue of them to whom it was given after their death, or shall revert unto the giver or his heirs if issue fail either by reason that there is no issue at all, or if any issue be, it fail by death, the heir of such issue failing. Neither shall the second husband of any such woman from henceforth have anything in the land so given upon condition after the death of his wife, by the law of England, nor the issue of the second husband and wife shall succeed to the inheritance, but immediately after the death of the husband and wife, to whom the land was so given, it shall come to their issue or return unto the giver or his heir as before is said. . . . And it is to wit that this statute shall hold place touching alienation of land contrary to the form of gift hereafter to be made, and shall not extend to gifts made before. . . .[26]

In line with the statute the royal courts allowed donors to give lands upon a variety of conditions which limited the estates of the donees and guided the reversion of the lands upon failure of the designated line of heirs. The limitations carved out an estate known as the fee tail, which has a long history in English land law. The fee tail, or entailed estate, was so called from the French verb *tailler*, meaning "to cut"; hence the English fee tail is the French *fee taillé* (Lat. *feodum talliatum*). This estate was not a fee simple but one which had been cut down by the limitations of the donor, who directed how it should descend or revert or not revert.

Enactment of *De Donis* opened the door to the successful creation of highly specialized estates designed by the donor, who might go beyond a general grant "to A and the heirs of his body" and be more specific. The donor might create an estate tail to A and the male heirs of his body, or to A and the female heirs of his body, or to A and the heirs of his body by a particular wife. So long as the line indicated continues to produce heirs, the property will devolve that way. If the line runs out, the property then passes to the next person designated in the grant creating the fee tail. This designated person is known as the remainderman. If there is no remainderman, the property reverts to the original donor or his heirs.

Although developments in medieval family property interests mitigated hardships imposed by primogeniture on younger sons and daughters, serious difficulties were created by entailed estates. For example, the person who leased entailed land might find himself suddenly ousted by the death of the lessor, for the property would then pass into the hands of tenants who could claim that they had a title superior to the leaseholder's interest. For this and other reasons the courts at

---

[26] 13 Edw. I, Statute of Westminster II, *De Donis Conditionalibus* (1285).

the close of the fifteenth century allowed the evasion of entail arrangements. But these later developments, involving the fictions of the common recovery and the use of the fine to transfer title to land, lie beyond the scope of this study. Here we merely note that the interval between *De Donis* (1285) and *Taltarum's Case* (1472) was long enough to permit many experiments in the creation of entailed estates and the growth of a great body of legal learning on the subject of fees, remainders, and reversions. Finally, we should note that in the thirteenth century, and again in the fifteenth century, the common-law courts favored alienation of property and acted in ways to permit the barring of entailed estates in spite of the Statute of *De Donis.*

Discussion here has not included several other interests in land which were at the foundations of the law of Property and were also linked with the family. We have bypassed an examination of wardship and of the rights of a widower to hold, as "tenant by the curtesy of England," all his wife's lands during the term of his own life. We have bypassed the law of Dower, which assured a widow the enjoyment of one-third of her husband's lands. We have concentrated, rather, on inheritance, because inheritance was of such fundamental importance to men of the Middle Ages. Among the uncertainties of life, rules of inheritance provided for continuity of the family.

The earliest chapters of the 1215 version of Magna Carta reveal this concern. Chapter 2 touches on the relief that an heir will pay; Chapter 3 deals with the heir who is under age; Chapters 4 and 5 protect the heir against the abuses of wardship; Chapter 6 regulates marriages of heirs; Chapter 10 shields the heir who is under age against erosion of his estate by payment of usury on loans; Chapter 11 protects the widow and children against the sale of all of the inheritance to satisfy a debt. Further on, Magna Carta comes back to a concern for the family; Chapter 26 assures to the widow and children "their reasonable portions" of the chattels of a deceased free man;

Chapter 27 directs the distribution of the chattels of the man who dies intestate. These portions of Magna Carta are sufficient to point up the intimate connection between the medieval law of Property and the central position of the family in medieval society.

Feudal customs, manorial customs, the customs of Kent, and the customs of boroughs all reflect in various ways the desire of medieval men to protect the status of the family and to insure as best they could the continuity of the family by providing for it an adequate economic base. Common-law courts were responsive to this widespread concern to secure the devolution of property. Insofar as possible, inheritance was to be indefeasible. But the courts were also responsive to other pressures. If men should be free to buy and sell chattels, then it might be argued that men should also be free to buy and sell land. There were limits beyond which the courts would not protect family property from the effects of alienation. There was a tension between two desirable objectives: the protection of arrangements for family property on the one hand, and freedom of alienation on the other. The statutes *De Donis* and *Quia Emptores* show Parliament designing a course for the courts to follow. That parliamentary statutes of Edward I did not entirely resolve the tension between permanence of arrangements for the devolution of family property and the freedom of alienation is no cause for surprise. Here, as in many other matters, it long remained for the common-law courts to effect compromises which would not destroy either the possibility of the entailed estate or the possibility of alienation.

REGULATION OF PURCHASE
AND SALE OF FREE TENURES

STATUTE OF WESTMINSTER III: *QUIA EMPTORES* (1290)

By the Statute of Westminster III, Chapters 1, 2, 3, Edward I regulated the buying and selling of free tenures. Here is another enactment reflecting, like the Statute of Merchants, the difficulties of maintaining ancient customary feudal concepts of property in the face of new commercial attitudes toward land. The statute is clearly a compromise. It freely permits the complete alienation or sale of a tenure; then, to protect feudal property interests, the statute prohibits subinfeudation, or the addition of new links in the existing chain of tenure. The possibilities of a chain of tenure being shortened by escheats and forfeitures were not imaginary: the effect of this statute was to work any given tenure toward the top of the hierarchy of tenures. This process, operating over a long period, would tend ultimately to bring all tenants into the same relationship with the Crown. However, Edward I and the barons of his reign could not have planned a policy for the centuries. They were concerned with immediate results and wished to collect escheats, marriages, and wardships.

At the end of the thirteenth century the close personal relationships of lord and vassal had given way to more commercial monetary interests. The partitioning of fiefs and the subinfeudation of tenements had made the whole system of land tenure less personal. Lords had to accept new tenants, and old tenants had to "attorn" themselves to new lords. The doctrine of dependent tenure still remained, but the great men of the realm were now more concerned to enjoy the financial incidents of free tenure than to collect the ancient knight service.

Because it is useful to read the Statute of *Quia Emptores* literally, it is here quoted in full. The reference to Mortmain[27] in Chapter 3 is plainly a reference to the Statute for Religious Men (*Statutum de Viris Religiosis*), 7 Edw. I (1279), enacted eleven years earlier.

Quia Emptores   18 Edw. I, Chapters 1, 2, 3 (1290)

Forasmuch as puchasers of lands and tenements of the fees of great men and other lords have many times heretofore entered into their fees, to the prejudice of the lords, to whom the free-

---

[27] See the discussion of Mortmain above, pp. 74–76.

holder of such great men have sold their lands and tenements to be holden in fee of their feoffors and not of the chief lords of the fees, whereby the same lords have many times lost their escheats, marriages, and wardships of lands and tenements belonging to their fees, which thing seems very hard and extreme unto those lords and other great men, and moreover in this case manifest disinheritance, our lord the king in his Parliament at Westminster after Easter the eighteenth year of his reign, that is to wit in the quinzine of St. John Baptist, at the instance of the great men of the realm granted, provided and ordained, that from henceforth it should be lawful to every free man to sell at his own pleasure his lands and tenements or part of them, so that the feoffee shall hold the same lands or tenements of the chief lord of the same fee, by such service and customs as his feoffor held before.

c. 2   And if he sell any part of such lands or tenements to any, the feoffee shall immediately hold it of the chief lord and shall be forthwith charged with the services for so much as pertaineth or ought to pertain to the said chief lord, for the same parcel, according to the quantity of the land or tenement so sold; and so in this case the same part of the service shall remain to the lord, to be taken by the hands of the feoffee, for the which he ought to be attendant and answerable to the same chief lord according to the quantity of the land or tenement sold for the parcel of the service so due.

c. 3   And it is to be understood that by the said sales or purchase of lands or tenements, or any parcel of them, such lands or tenements shall in no wise come into mortmain, either in part or in whole, neither by policy ne craft, contrary to the form of the statute made thereon of late. And it is to wit that this statute extendeth but only to lands holden in fee simple, and that it extendeth to the time coming. And it shall begin to take effect at the feast of St. Andrew the Apostle next coming.[28]

The principle behind *Quia Emptores* was not entirely new. The 1217 issue of Magna Carta, Chapter 39, had restricted alienation by saying that "no free man from henceforth shall

---

[28] See the text and discussion by Bigelow, *Real Property*, p. 12.

give or sell any more of his land but so that of the residue of the lands the lord of the fee may have the services due to him which belong to the fee." *Quia Emptores* declares the principle more elaborately and at the same time limits its application to lands held in fee simple, implying the existence of other estates or property interests.

CONCLUSION
THE MEDIEVAL LEGACY

Chapter 10
From Medieval Law
to Modern Law

THE VITALITY OF THE COMMON LAW

Among the nations of western Europe the English alone have managed to bring essential elements of their medieval customary legal system into the modern world. This extraordinary achievement should not be taken for granted, because the common law has had powerful critics and opponents along the way. It has survived, moreover, through several periods of political crisis which seriously disturbed the balance between three elements fundamental in the English constitution—the prerogative of the Crown, the privileges of Parliament, and the individual liberties of personal security, personal liberty, and private property. At times practitioners of absolutism, both royal and popular, threatened to sweep aside the substance of common-law rules. At other times civil wars interrupted the operation of common-law courts. The history of English law and politics is much more than a slow broadening down from precedent to precedent. England has known periods of terrible violence and disorder. More than once the common-law system has been in peril of its life. Its continuity through almost eight centuries is unique in the history of European legal systems.

It is easier to identify critical periods of English history than to account for the means by which the English people repeatedly restored conditions permitting their common law to continue its life and growth. No simple explanation will fit all the complex facts of restoration of equilibrium in English politics. Here it is enough to notice first a few critical periods through which the common law survived and then to offer tentative reasons for its continued vitality.

As a body of general rules the common law might have disappeared in the fifteenth century, when the House of Lancaster and York contested the succession to the English throne in the War of the Roses. Thirty years of dynastic quarrels seriously weakened the central government's powers of law enforcement, permitting the evils of maintenance and champerty to flourish. During the War of the Roses, men of wealth and influence terrorized juries, bribed witnesses, intimidated judges, and controlled sheriffs, while intervening in litigation not their own. The weak could not secure justice. In this century a new feudalism might have disintegrated the common law but for the restoration of good order after 1485, when Henry VII became the first of a line of Tudor monarchs.

A different sort of threat to the common law appeared in the sixteenth century. In many parts of Europe monarchs encouraged a "reception" of Roman law at the expense of medieval customary systems. On the Continent—in France, Holland, and Germany—the results of the reception of Roman law have tended to be permanent; the continental jurist in the twentieth century studies Roman law to grasp the jurisprudence underlying modern codes. And in the British Isles, the law of Scotland now contains so much borrowing from Roman law that there, too, the road to legal practice leads through study of the corpus of Roman civil law compiled at Justinian's direction. But a reception of Roman law never occurred in England. Henry VIII and his descendants favored Roman law, but they were satisfied to manipulate the medieval constitution and to realize their political purposes without disturbing traditional legal institutions and laws. Although Tudor monarchs exercised royal prerogative with stunning force, they did not fail to use parliamentary procedures or to continue the common-law courts.

The Tudor dynasty was more concerned with realities of power than with political theories. But after the death of Queen Elizabeth I in 1603, England was governed by Stuart kings who openly pressed for acceptance of theories of divine-right monarchy. This soon created political issues. And Puritans, Presbyterians, and other religious groups added the heat of their differences to an already complicated contest between Crown and Parliament. Throughout much of the seventeenth century both royalist and parliamentary factions had enough strength to prevent each other from winning permanent victories. Their conflict, however, put common law in great peril, for government by unrestrained divine right might have produced subservient judges sitting in prerogative courts responsive to the king's will in all cases. Without confident reliance on established rules and procedures, judges might have been reduced to interpreting royal ordinances and proclamations at royal direction. Doctrines of the supremacy of law and of judicial precedents cannot thrive in the presence of a divine-right monarch claiming to be supreme lawgiver as well as supreme administrator. Once more the common law escaped. The revolution of 1688 and the flight of King James II assured control of the government to the parliamentary faction and the continuance of common law and its courts.

Emergence of the legislative sovereignty of Parliament in the eighteenth century created the possibility of drastic change in the legal system by means of statute. And, in fact, since the eighteenth century many profound changes have been effected by statute. The legislative sovereignty of Parliament loomed awesome in the mind of Blackstone as he wrote his famous *Commentaries on the Laws of England* in the latter part of the eighteenth century. Blackstone was a justice of the court of Common Pleas as well as first Vinerian professor of English law in Oxford University. He could be expected to show keen interest in problems touching the judicial interpretation of statutes. For Blackstone the competence of Parliament was so great that he knew "of no power in the ordinary forms of the constitution that is vested with authority to control it." However unreasonable a statute might be, Blackstone saw no means of avoiding it; certainly no judge was at liberty to reject a statute, for, in Blackstone's opinion, setting the judicial above the legislative authority would be subversive of all government.[1] Legislative sovereignty of Parliament, combined with demands for drastic reform in the legal system, produced a flood of reforming statutes throughout the nineteenth century. The common-law writ system was abolished piecemeal, and common-law courts were reorganized between 1830 and 1880, most notably by the Judicature Act of 1873. This act and still other wide-ranging legislation merged the courts of Common Pleas, Queen's Bench, and Exchequer in the Queen's Bench Division and Commercial Court. Three medieval common-law courts survived the reorganization: courts of Assize, *Oyer* and *Terminer*, and Gaol Delivery. Reforms in the nineteenth century might have gone further, of course; they might have created a legal system consisting entirely of statutory enactments produced and changed by constant legislative activity.

But as it has worked out, the legislative sovereignty of Parliament has destroyed neither the common-law doctrine of *stare decisis* nor the common-law doctrine of established legal principles. Reorganization of the judicature system simplified the group of competing common-law courts and clarified procedures of appeal. The essential elements of common law remain

---

[1] William Blackstone, *Commentaries*, Introduction, Section III.

unchanged. Modern doctrines of *stare decisis* now amplify and go far beyond medieval doctrines about the use of precedents. At the same time, of course, modern doctrines recognize the wisdom of adapting law to new conditions. In 1833, an eminent English judge, Baron Parke, neatly stated the modern theory of case law in a dictum:

> Our Common Law system consists in the applying to new combi-nations of circumstances those rules of law which we derive from legal principles and judicial precedents; and for the sake of at-taining uniformity, consistency, and certainty, we must apply those rules, where they are not plainly unreasonable and incon-venient, to all cases which arise; and we are not at liberty to reject them, and to abandon all analogy to them, in those to which they have not yet been judicially applied, because we think that the rules are not as convenient and reasonable as we ourselves could have devised. It appears to me to be of great importance to keep this principle of decision steadily in view, not merely for the determination of the particular case, but for the interests of law as a science.[2]

The common-law system survived enormous social and po-litical changes along the road between the medieval and the modern world. Possibly the balance between Crown, Parlia-ment, and individual rights of the subject has been maintained over the centuries because so many Englishmen, common lawyers, country squires, and city merchants have been drawn into the operation of a legal system which has borne directly on the incidents of daily life. In their minds, title to property and enjoyment of personal liberty have been intimately associated with the perpetuation of the common law.

Of the several forces which have operated to preserve its essential character, two should be mentioned in any dis-cussion of the vitality of common law. First, the early maturity of the common law made it a system of technical complexity

---

[2] *Per* Parke J., *Mirehouse* v. *Rennell*, I C1 & F., 527, 546.

before the end of the thirteenth century. Thereafter laymen could not hope to conduct their own litigation successfully without professional help from pleaders and attorneys. The appearance of a legal profession was soon followed by the appearance of Inns of Court.[3] What they were precisely in their medieval beginnings is mere conjecture. They may have been hostels, clubs, and chambers as well as schools of legal education. Certain it is that before the end of the Middle Ages England had a legal profession in close touch with legal education in the Inns of Court, all located near the common-law courts at Westminster. Judges were chosen from the ranks of the legal profession. Judges, pleaders, attorneys, and students formed a professional community with an interest in perpetuating a legal system which they had mastered during training in the Inns of Court. There they had learned to think in patterns set forth in formulas of the common-law writs. Students at the Inns of Court heard lectures, disputed in moot courts, and argued cases put at the dinner table. This system of legal education, always in touch with actual legal controversies at Westminster, was beautifully suited to transmit common-law traditions from the medieval to the modern period. Medieval Inns of Court were private corporations and their histories were not all fortunate; many have disappeared. In the twentieth century four Inns of Court remain: Gray's Inn, Inner Temple, Lincoln's Inn, and Middle Temple.

A second notable factor working for the perpetuation of common law was, again, related to the early maturity of the system. Medieval common law was principally land law. Rules of land law, first enforced in the reign of Henry II, were later elaborated, especially in the time of Edward I, who provided for the alienation of freehold and for the creation of long-term

---

[3] Sir Cecil Carr has written an excellent short account of the Inns of Court together with a detailed examination of Clement's Inn during the eighteenth century; see the Introduction to his edition of the *Pension Book of Clement's Inn*, Selden Society, Vol. 73 (1960), pp. xvi–lxvii.

family property arrangements by means of conditional gifts. Land was the principal source of wealth in the Middle Ages and so continued until the commercial and industrial revolutions created alternative sources of personal property, which in their turn fell under common-law rules. Thus for several centuries every family fortune in England has been protected and regulated by intricate rules of common law. At any period between the twelfth and the twentieth centuries, a complete overthrow of common-law rules and the courts administering them would have affected every property owner.[4] Thanks to the rise of Parliament in the Middle Ages and to the medieval evolution of the House of Commons, English property owners thereafter had a channel for the expression of alarm and opposition to sudden, revolutionary changes in the law of Property. Economic interests with a voice in politics have also worked to perpetuate common law.

THE CONTINUING GROWTH
OF COMMON LAW

The survival of the common law has depended in large part on the ability of its practitioners to adapt the legal system to new conditions—and adaptation has meant growth. Bold judges have created precedents adding new rules to meet new social and economic circumstances. This is not the place to outline the multitude of social and economic developments between the Middle Ages and the present. But here a glance at some events of the eighteenth century will illustrate the process of continuing growth of common law.

In this century occurred a revolution in agricultural techniques producing crop yields unknown to medieval culti-

---

[4] Theodore F. T. Plucknett, *Concise History of the Common Law*, 5th ed. (Boston, 1956), p. 44.

vators. Innovators enclosed blocks of land, removing them from open fields; they added legumes and root crops to old rotation schemes; new horse-drawn implements replaced hand hoeing; selective breeding improved cattle, sheep, horses, and swine, all of which benefited from a new abundance of forage. Also in the eighteenth century English sea power protected a volume of commerce with the Orient and with America, yielding profits unknown to medieval merchants. Inventors designed steam engines to pump water from coal mines and to supply power for machinery in factories, where English workers turned out an incredible flow of goods for a world market. These changes in agriculture, commerce, and manufacturing all demanded the organization of capital in new patterns. As new technology created wealth largely in the form of personal property, feudal land law obviously required additions. Parliamentary legislation could do much to supply needed regulation, but common lawyers also made significant contributions. Again we limit the account to one illustration of common-law growth in the eighteenth century and choose for this purpose the judicial work of Lord Mansfield, Chief Justice of the court of King's Bench from 1756 to 1788.

During the Middle Ages the royal courts had treated English merchants as a special community with its own customs. They permitted merchants to regulate their own affairs by their own rules—the law merchant. It was the achievement of Mansfield to incorporate the law merchant into the common law and to fashion what had been a body of special customary law into general rules within a larger system. Mansfield was a man of broad learning whose wit and power of phrase made him effective in politics, first in the House of Commons and later in the House of Lords. In politics as well as in law, he showed a grasp of realities. He took a deep interest in English commerce. When a case before him touched commercial law, he saw to it that reputable merchants of the city of London formed the jury. Thus he secured in his court the participation of jurors who presumably understood every detail of material evidence. Outside court, on social occasions, he cultivated the acquaintance of merchants to acquire for himself a precise knowledge of their ways of doing business. By his decisions in many important cases, Mansfield adapted and reworked the law bearing on such large topics as commercial transactions, shipping, and insurance. It should be remembered that Mansfield was doing his judicial work during the years when Blackstone was proclaiming with great force the legislative sovereignty of Parliament. In the eighteenth century, as in the Middle Ages, case law continued to thrive alongside statutory enactment without being completely overshadowed. This concurrent activity of the legislature and the courts continues into the present.

EXPANSION OF THE COMMON LAW

The expansion of western European civilization since the late sixteenth century has scattered to all parts of the world elements of English common law and Roman law, the two principal legal systems known to Europeans. English colonists on the Atlantic seaboard introduced common law to the American continent, while French and Spanish colonial activity brought in laws originally derived from Roman law. The pattern of territorial expansion of the United States meant the predominance of English common-law traditions, but notably in Louisiana and also in territory acquired from Spain legal elements peculiarly Roman in origin still exist. In general, however, the common law has been taken to English-speaking countries along with the language. In the British Commonwealth nations, as in the United States, the common law is at the foundation of the legal systems.

English colonists in America brought with them the only law they knew, the law of England as it stood in the seventeenth and eighteenth centuries. When the colonies broke away from

England in the course of the American Revolution, they framed arguments about their rights taken straight from Blackstone's *Commentaries*, the classical statement of the common law. For decades American lawyers read Blackstone as their preparation for legal practice. Chancellor Kent of New York, famous for his own *Commentaries on American Law* (4 vols., 1826–1830), remarked that he "owed his reputation to the fact that when studying law . . . he had but one book, Blackstone's *Commentaries*, but that one book he mastered."[5] Chancellor Kent's opportunities for legal research at the library of Columbia College and other law libraries in New York were far superior to those of most American lawyers in the early nineteenth century. For lawyers on the frontier Blackstone was both legal education and law library. The enormous popularity of Blackstone in the most formative period of American national institutions may go far to explain why American law kept close to English law.

In technical journals one may find detailed discussion of differences between American and English law. For the layman, at least, areas of agreement are much more obvious than areas of disagreement, but there may be value in noting here some of the differences most commonly referred to. From the outset in America there has been neither trial by battle nor trial by ordeal. In America witnesses were not denied to a person accused of a felony. Special pleading ceased in America. Ancient feudal tenures were not transplanted from England to the American wilderness, although the Carolina proprietors seriously considered making the attempt and asked John Locke to draft a scheme. In America married women have had more independence from their husbands in control over property. Imprisonment for debt gradually disappeared in America. The English rule of unanimity in juries for civil cases has given way in some states to statutes prescribing acceptance of a majority.

---

[5] Quoted in Daniel Boorstin, *The Mysterious Science of the Law* (Boston, 1958), p. 3.

In America the multiplication of reports has widened the field of citation of precedents much more than in England. Courts are more numerous in America; each of the states has its own body of precedents and the federal courts also have their own precedents. Since the formation of the American Bar Association in 1878, there has been pressure by that organization to secure uniform state legislation and also to secure codes or digests which would simplify the law on certain large topics. This is a development for which English lawyers have occasionally provided models. For example, the American Negotiable Instruments Act, drafted in 1896 and promoted by the American Bar Association, is an adaptation of the English Bills of Exchange Act, which became law in 1882.[6]

Similarities between English and American law are innumerable, largely for historical reasons. The fact that the common law crossed the Atlantic in the seventeenth and eighteenth centuries accounts for such a kinship between the two countries that it is quite correct to speak today of an Anglo-American common-law system.

THE LEGACY OF THE MIDDLE AGES

The legacy of medieval law to modern law in England and in America must be stated in general rather than specific remarks, although there are some notable examples of the citation of medieval English cases and treatises by American judges, among whom Oliver Wendell Holmes, Jr., would take a prominent place.[7] However, it is more important to note here the persistence and force in the modern world of some ideas

---

[6] See Britton, *Bills and Notes*, 2nd ed. (1961), pp. 9–15, for the background of English and American legislation on negotiable instruments.

[7] See *Commonwealth* v. *Rubin*, 165 Massachusetts Reports, 453, in which Holmes traces a rule of common-law liability back into the *Year Books*; and *Commonwealth* v. *Cleary*, 172 Massachusetts Reports, 175, in which Holmes refers to Glanvill and *Fleta* as authority.

which men of the Middle Ages incorporated in the common law of England.

Foremost among these is the idea of the supremacy of law, a concept also expressed in such phrases as "the rule of law" and "due process." This idea implies that there are limits to the power of ruling, that all government agencies and the law courts themselves must operate according to known rules and procedures. The rule of law was difficult to apply against medieval kings with absolutist policies and no regard for established customs. The rule of law is now difficult to apply in the face of modern ideas of sovereignty which admit no limitation on the power of ruling. But whatever the difficulties, the preservation of the rules of law, or due process, may be the only means of preserving the enjoyment of private rights and personal freedoms. What is required in the twentieth century is a much wider understanding of legal rights, how they have been gained, how they may be lost. For programs promising social justice and economic justice are certain to be unfulfilled unless the programs can be translated into legal rights protected by courts free to apply known rules. Many lawyers understand this; many laymen do not.

It is not easy to see how the rule of law will survive in the midst of revolutionary changes in population density, in technical complexity of communications systems, in commercial transportation, in banking, and, above all, in the production of atomic energy. The complexity of modern society has created problems beyond the capacity of legislators to regulate effectively by statute or of courts to solve by case law—so the argument runs for the creation of a self-directing bureaucracy. If problems are complex, turn them over to experts, specialists in the management of public transportation, communications, commerce, banking, and atomic energy. By means of a legislative act, commission experts with authority to control conditions within a certain field. This is the modern solution. But a government agency must accomplish its mission by ordering people to act or not to act. The commission must issue directives with the force of laws. The directives, however, are difficult to find and they are frequently changed. It is not always possible to discover precisely what the agency has ordered. Moreover, the agency may be the judge and interpreter of its own administrative orders. Problems of the government of complex industrial societies present serious threats to the continuance of the common-law system. The doctrine of the supremacy of law now confronts competition with a doctrine of government regulation by administrative orders. In the twentieth century many European nations have shown how easily "statism" can replace the rule of law. It is a peculiar quality of the Anglo-American legal system that it still retains respect for due process and for courts administering known rules.

A second idea inherited from the Middle Ages touches the work of courts in the legal system and the doctrine of judicial precedents. The dignity of medieval royal courts was impressive. As repositories of the legal tradition, royal judges in the Middle Ages exercised their right to control all matters of procedure—from judging the initial grounds of a legal action to the enforcement of a decision on it. When judges in medieval England failed to maintain the high standards of learning and disinterested action expected of them, English feudal barons, churchmen, and merchants insisted on reform. This appears in the Dictum of Kenilworth, Chapter 2, again in the Ordinances of 1311, Chapter 14, and in other places where public opinion demands justices learned in the law of the realm. In the Middle Ages common-law court decisions were recorded, and on special occasions the record was consulted, but for several centuries the common law lived more in the minds of its judges and practitioners than in plea rolls and reports. The law of the Middle Ages was largely judge-made, and whenever it was changed by deliberate action of the king's council or by Parliament, judges participated in the change. It is an essential feature of the common-law system that its principles are derived from decisions in actual cases in which, of course, judges play the principal part.

A third important legacy of the medieval law to the modern law is the writ system. This statement may seem absurd in light of the fact that nineteenth-century legislation abolished the writ system in England. But English lawyers could afford the luxury of throwing away the old forms of action only after the principles within those forms had become embedded in the law. After men have learned what constitutes a debt recoverable in the courts, the writ of Debt is unnecessary. And so with many other grounds of legal action, or causes of action, defined in the medieval writ system. Modern courts now recognize that a leaseholder is entitled to enjoy the full term of the lease and to recover both the lease and damages if he is ejected from the leased property. But the leaseholder's remedies were not taken for granted in the Middle Ages. They were acquired slowly in the form of actions associated with writs. The full catalog of writs known as the Register of Writs was the framework of the common law. When, in the present, a lawyer decides that his client has a good cause of action which the courts will recognize, he is drawing, more often than he may realize, on the medieval definition of that cause of action in one of the many formal writs.

The rule of law, the development of law by means of judicial precedents, the use of the jury to determine the material facts of a case, and the definition of numerous causes of action—these form the principal and valuable legacy of the medieval law to the modern law.

A Glossary for Laymen

The intention here is to provide short statements about some terms which appear in the text. Many items are words of art with elaborate technical meaning for lawyers, who will consult law dictionaries for full definitions.

action: a legal suit to secure the enforcement of one's rights in a court of law.

advowson: patronage of a church living; the legal right to present a candidate for installation in a vacant ecclesiastical office.

alienation: the transfer of property from one person to another.

assize: a session of a court or the decree or enactment made by it.

burgage tenure: a freehold, usually within a town or borough; the holder customarily pays a money rent in lieu of all services, military or other.

canon law: a body of rules administered by courts of the Church.

champerty: a procedure by which a person having no legal concern in a suit promises aid or influence to one party in return for a share of the matter in the suit, if successful; usually linked with maintenance (q.v.).

chattels: movable goods, personal property.

chattels real: interests in land less than freehold.

defendant: a person required to answer in an action.

dictum: a judicial opinion on a point other than the precise issue in a case before the court; sometimes *obiter dictum*, an opinion stated by the way.

equity: the body of rules administered in a court of equity or Chancery, supplementing the common law.

estate: the nature and extent of one's interest in land.

estate tail: an interest in land; can descend to bodily heirs only.

eyre: a journey in a prescribed circuit; used in connection with "justices-in-eyre," who held courts in various counties.

fealty: the fidelity of a feudal vassal to his lord; a promise under oath to be loyal.

fee simple: an estate of inheritance in land without limitation to any class of heirs or restrictions on alienation; the most extensive interest in property recognized by the common law.

felony: a serious crime such as murder, arson, rape, highway robbery: the convicted felon forfeits lands and goods and is sentenced to lose "life or member."

feoffment: a gift and grant of land by which the recipient acquires a freehold.

fief: property producing income; a grant by a lord to a vassal to secure the services of the vassal.

frankalmoin: an ecclesiastical tenure by which a monastery or other ecclesiastical corporation holds property under the obligation of saying prayers for the souls of the donor and his family.

freehold: an estate for life or more; a property interest larger than a lease for a period of years; an inheritable estate.

homage: a ceremony by which a man acknowledges himself to be the vassal of a lord; an act showing respect and deference, usually a preliminary step in the procedure by which a lord grants a fief to a vassal.

jury: in the Middle Ages, a body of men, presumed to know the facts of a case, summoned by a public officer to give upon oath a true answer (verdict) to some question.

leasehold: a tenure by a lease; an agreement that the tenant may enjoy possession for a specified period of time; sometimes called a term of years. The leaseholder may be designated as lessee, or termor.

maintenance: unlawful intervening or meddling in an action before a court to assist either party by money, or other means, to carry the case to a successful conclusion, possibly to share in the advantage of winning the case; usually linked with champerty (q.v.).

misdemeanor: a minor offense.

mortmain: literally "dead hand," applied to property held by ecclesiastical corporations.

obligation: a legal bond by which a person is bound to give or do something; failure to fulfill the obligation is sufficient ground for an action.

plaintiff: an aggrieved person who initiates an action in court.

precedent: a judicial decision or procedure, serving as a guide for the future settlement of similar cases.

recognition: a declaration by jurors in medieval cases, commonly answering a question about which of two claimants has the better title, or right, in land.

recognizance: an obligation recorded before a court, or an officer authorized to keep such records, with a condition to do some act required by law which is specified within the record.

remedy: a legal procedure used to enforce a right or to redress an injury.

rule of law: a principle of the law; a ground of decision, recognized by the courts; a guiding principle in the determination of new cases.

seignorial jurisdiction: the right of a lord of a manor to hold a court for the tenants of the manor.

seisin: the possession of land enjoyed by a person who is "seated" on the land, who is in a position to take what the land produces. Seisin of a freehold is occupation by one other than a tenant in villeinage, a tenant-at-will, a tenant for a term of years, or a guardian.

sergeanty: a tenure in the Middle Ages; a freehold in return for which the tenant renders specified services or their monetary equivalent.

socage tenure: the humblest of medieval freehold tenures; the tenant is commonly a free man, an agricultural worker, who owes to his lord money rent or clearly specified agricultural services such as ploughing or harvesting.

statute: a formal enactment of the highest dignity; it may be declaratory or interpretive of the law; it may also represent a deliberate change in the law.

tenant-in-chief: a "tenant-in-capite," one who holds land by a direct grant from the Crown; one who is a vassal of the king.

tenement: a tenure; an interest in land which may be either "free" or "unfree" according to the services which the tenant is obliged to render in return for it.

tenure: a general term for all interests in land; an act or right of holding; a right in land dependent upon a grant from a superior.

termor: a lessee, enjoying the possession of land for a specified period or term, while the lessor retains title.

trespass: a wrong done, an unlawful act against the person, the goods, or the land of another.

vassal: one who has placed himself under the protection of another as his lord and has vowed homage and fealty; a feudal tenant holding from a lord; one who is personally free, owing honorable services in return for a fief.

vill: a township; part of a territorial unit called a hundred, which is, in turn, a part of a county.

villein: in England, the holder of a villein tenement for which he usually owes agricultural services to his lord. The villein's rights in his tenement are customary and not enforceable against his lord by medieval common law. Personally free against all men but his lord, the villein nevertheless does not fully enjoy the rights of a free man. He is a tenant at the will of the lord; he cannot serve on a jury dealing with the rights of a free man; he cannot take ecclesiastical orders without emancipation; he cannot make a will; if he leaves his duties on the lord's manor, the lord can use all necessary force to bring him back to perform them.

writ: a royal order to a definite person; a mandate commanding something to be done, usually by the sheriff of the county wherein an injury is committed or is supposed to be, requiring him to command the wrongdoer or party accused, either to do justice to the complainant or else to appear in court and answer the accusation against him.

writ of course: a writ issued at the request of a complainant who desires to initiate an action for one of the ordinary or well-known causes such as the repayment of a debt or the enforcement of a written agreement. A writ not of course is issued to a complainant requesting an exceptional or extraordinary remedy which may be granted as a matter of royal favor, although it is not generally available.

Index

This book was set in ITC Zapf Book, a typeface designed for the International Typeface Corporation by one of the world's foremost typeface designers, Hermann Zapf. The creator of Optima, Palatino, Melior, Aldus, and many other acclaimed typefaces, Hermann Zapf spent more than two years developing ITC Zapf Book as a family of four different weights of type with matching italics. The elegant letterforms are an artful blend of Walbaum, Melior, and Bodoni, distinguished by many subtle refinements. Hermann Zapf was born in 1918 in Nuremberg, Germany. Designer of more than forty typefaces, his first typeface design was marketed in 1940; ten years later, the first of the famous Palatino type family was introduced. All of his typefaces are characterized by exquisite design, quiet distinction, and innovation without eccentricity. Zapf's primary concern is never with single letters, but with their fusion with each other in a working text. To Zapf, "Type is the tie or ligature between author and reader."

Printed on paper that is acid-free and meets the requirements of the American National Standard for Permanence of Paper for Printed Library Materials, Z39.84, 1984. ⊗

Book design by Hermann Strohbach, New York, New York
Editorial service by Harkavy Publishing Service,
New York, New York
Typography by Typoservice Corporation, Indianapolis, Indiana
Printed and bound by Worzalla Publishing Company,
Stevens Point, Wisconsin